THE LANGUAGE OF MUSIC

The
Language of Music

DERYCK COOKE

Trumpet

Molto sostenuto
e maestoso

pp — *f* > *pp*

OXFORD UNIVERSITY PRESS
OXFORD   LONDON   NEW YORK

Oxford University Press, Walton Street, Oxford OX2 6DP

OXFORD LONDON GLASGOW
NEW YORK TORONTO MELBOURNE WELLINGTON
KUALA LUMPUR SINGAPORE JAKARTA HONG KONG TOKYO
DELHI BOMBAY CALCUTTA MADRAS KARACHI
IBADAN NAIROBI DAR ES SALAAM CAPE TOWN

© *Oxford University Press 1959*

Hardback edition ISBN 0 19 311905 6
Paperback edition ISBN 0 19 284004 5

First published 1959
Reprinted 1960, 1964, 1974, 1978

Printed in Great Britain by
Fletcher & Son Ltd, Norwich

TO JACQUELINE

CONTENTS

ACKNOWLEDGEMENTS

Acknowledgements are due to the following for permission to quote extracts from the works indicated:

Boosey & Hawkes Ltd.: Béla Bartók's *Cantata Profana* (U.S.A. only), Benjamin Britten's *Albert Herring, Peter Grimes, The Rape of Lucretia, The Turn of the Screw, Sonnets of John Donne,* and *Sonnets of Michelangelo*; Frederick Delius's *Sea Drift* and *Songs of Farewell*; Dmitri Shostakovich's *Fifth Symphony*; and Igor Stravinsky's *Oedipus Rex, Orpheus, Symphony of Psalms,* and *The Rake's Progress.* Breitkopf & Härtel: F. Busoni's *Doktor Faust.* Campbell, Connelly & Co. Ltd.: Irving King's *Show me the way to go home.* Chappell & Co. Ltd.: George Gershwin's *Porgy and Bess* (My man's gone now) and *The man I love,* and Jay Gorney's *Brother can you spare a dime.* J. & W. Chester Ltd.: Igor Stravinsky's *The Soldier's Tale.* Durand & Cie., Editeurs-propriétaires, Paris: C. Saint-Saëns's *Danse Macabre.* Durand & Cie., Paris (United Music Publishers, London): Claude Debussy's *Le martyre de Saint-Sébastien, Pelléas et Mélisande, Pour ce que plaisance est morte,* and *Recueillement.* Editions Jean Jobert, Paris (United Music Publishers, London): Claude Debussy's *En sourdine* and *Il pleure dans mon coeur.* Handy Brothers Music Co. Inc., New York (Francis,Day & Hunter Ltd.): W. C. Handy's *St. Louis Blues.* Hinrichsen Edition Ltd.: Gustav Mahler's *Fifth Symphony;* and Richard Strauss's *Don Juan, Don Quixote,* and *Till Eulenspiegel.* Irving Berlin Ltd.: Irving Berlin's *Cheek to Cheek* and *Let's face the music and dance.* Kassner Associated Publishers Ltd.: Friedman and De Knight's *Rock around the Clock.* Keith Prowse Music Publishing Co. Ltd.: Lew Brown's *Beer Barrel Polka.* Novello & Co. Ltd.: Edward Elgar's *Dream of Gerontius.* G. Ricordi & Co. Ltd.: Arrigo Boito's *Mefistofele* and G. Puccini's *La Bohème.* Schott & Co. Ltd.: Gustav Mahler's *Song of the Earth.* Southern Music Publishing Co. Ltd.: Davies and Mitchell's *You are my sunshine.* Universal Edition (London) Ltd.: Béla Bartók's *Cantata Profana* (except U.S.A.), and Gustav Mahler's *Symphonies No. 1, 2, 8, and 9.* Josef Weinberger Ltd.: Gustav Mahler's *Lieder eines fahrenden Gesellen.*

PREFACE

The impulse to produce this book arose out of the following considerations.

When we try to assess the achievement of a great literary artist, one of the chief ways in which we approach his work is to examine it as a report on human experience. We feel that, in his art, he has said something significant in relation to life as it is lived; and that what he has said—whether we call this a 'criticism of life' or a *Weltanschauung* or something else—is as important as the purely formal aspect of his writing. Or rather, these two main aspects of his art—'content' and 'form'—are realized to be ultimately inseparable: what he has said is inextricably bound up with how he has said it; and how he has said it clearly cannot be considered separately from what he has said.

The same is unfortunately not felt to be true of the artist who makes his contribution to human culture, not in the language of speech, but in that of music. Music is widely regarded nowadays, not as a language at all, but as a 'pure', inexpressive art, like architecture; and even those who do feel it to be some kind of language regard it as an imprecise one, incapable of conveying anything so tangible as an experience of life or an attitude towards it. Thus Albert Roussel spoke of 'the musician . . . alone in the world with his more or less unintelligible language'. And Aaron Copland has expressed a similar opinion, in a slightly less radical way: '*Is there a meaning to music?*—My answer to that would be "Yes". *Can you state in so many words what the meaning is?*—My answer to that would be "No". Therein lies the difficulty'.

Hence, at the present time, attempts to elucidate the 'content' of music are felt to be misguided, to say the least; the writer on musical matters is expected to ignore or only hint at what the composer had to say, and to concentrate entirely on how he said it. Or, to put it in the contemporary way, he is expected to concentrate entirely on the 'form', which is not regarded as 'saying' anything at all. Thus the two inseparable aspects of an expressive art are separated, and one is utterly neglected—much to the detriment of our understanding of the other. Instead of responding to music as what it is—the expression of man's deepest self—we tend to regard it more and more as a purely decorative art; and by analysing the great works of musical expression purely as pieces of decoration, we misapprehend their true nature, purpose, and value. By regarding form as an end in itself, instead of as a means of expression, we make evaluations of composers' achievements which are largely irrelevant and worthless.

But there is another, more serious consequence of our attitude: one whole side of our culture is impoverished, since we deny ourselves the possibility of enlarging our understanding of human experience by a specifically musical view of it. After all, if man is ever to fulfil the mission he undertook at the very start —when he first began to philosophize, as a Greek, and evolved the slogan 'Know thyself'—he will have to understand his unconscious self; and the most articulate language of the unconscious is music. But we musicians, instead of trying to understand this language, preach the virtues of refusing to consider it a language at all; when we should be attempting, as literary critics do, to expound and interpret the great masterpieces of our art for the benefit of humanity at large, we concern ourselves more and more with parochial affairs—technical analyses and musicological *minutiae*—and pride ourselves on our detached, de-humanized approach.

This used not to be so. Some years ago it was regarded as the normal procedure to evaluate composers—notably Mozart, Beethoven, and Brahms—according to what they expressed. But unfortunately this approach was too vague and unscientific: the interpretation soon strayed far away from the actual stuff of the music to become a kind of private transcendental self-intoxication with words. And it was no doubt the wild and baseless conclusions of some of the writers of those days that led the aestheticians of our own time to lay an embargo on the interpretation of musical works. Better ignore the whole vexatious question, they must have felt, than wallow in such a morass of subjectivity. What Goethe, Baudelaire, and Kafka said may be valuable data for the final understanding of humanity; what Beethoven, Berlioz, and Mahler said is certainly not—simply because there is no way of agreeing as to exactly what they did say.

But perhaps we have given up the problem a little too easily. Perhaps, since music is the expression of emotion, and we so strongly distrust emotion nowadays, we have not been eager to come to grips with the problem at all. There is no reason why it should not prove capable of solution, as other problems are. If we cannot at present tell for certain what anything said in the language of music really means—if we continually argue about the 'emotional content' of this or that composition—we should not therefore despair of ever finding an objective basis to work on. It may be that we have just not yet found a way of understanding this language, and that much of our interpretation of it is simply misinterpretation. We too easily assume that our own private interpretations are fixed and immutable; we should remember that any one of us, at any time, may completely misinterpret the 'content' of a piece, and yet still enjoy his experience of it, even though it is based on a misapprehension. When this happens to the musically uninitiated, we smile, but it can just as easily happen to the musically sophisticated, for we none of us really understand the language. It may well be that if X declares that a certain piece is gay, and Y maintains that it is melancholy, then one or other, or even both, have failed to understand what the composer has said. If only we could come to understand the language better, we might well find ourselves agreeing more and more as to what any given piece expresses.

This book is an attempt to bring music back from the intellectual-aesthetic limbo in which it is now lost, and to reclaim it for humanity at large, by beginning the task of actually deciphering its language. It attempts to show that the conception of music as a language capable of expressing certain very definite things is not a romantic aberration, but has been the common unconscious assumption of composers for the past five-and-a-half centuries at least. It attempts to isolate the various means of expression available to the composer—the various procedures in the dimensions of pitch, time, and volume—and to discover what emotional effects these procedures can produce; but more

specifically, it tries to pinpoint the inherent emotional characters of the various notes of the major, minor, and chromatic
scales, and of certain basic melodic patterns which have been
used persistently throughout our musical history. It also investi-
gates the problem of musical communication, through the
various stages from the composer's unconscious to that of the
listener; and it offers detailed interpretations of two non-
programmatic symphonies—Mozart's Fortieth and Vaughan
Williams's Sixth—as specimen examples of how it may perhaps
be possible to come to some objective understanding of the
'emotional content' of 'pure' music.

It is hoped that this book will serve as a broad preliminary
survey of the ground, and perhaps also as a foundation on which
eventually to build a more comprehensive classification of most
of the terms of musical language; and that it will thereby make
it ultimately possible to understand and assess a composer's
work as a report on human experience, just as we do that of a
literary artist. It is not imagined, let me hasten to add, that
such assessments will take the form of philosophical discus-
sions of conceptual arguments, since music cannot express concepts; nor that they will be 'digests' of the 'meanings' of various
works, for the same reason; rather, since music can only express
feelings, it is thought that they will probably be in the nature of
interpretations of emotional attitudes, somewhat akin to the
type of analysis perfected by Wilson Knight for the elucidation
of the 'content' of literary works—an examination of the 'images'
used, and an interpretation of their emotional and psychological
connotations.

The investigation of musical language is confined to Europe,
since if music is an international language within a given con-
tinent, it is certainly not an inter-continental language. It has
also been confined almost entirely to art-music (including
modern popular music): although the roots of musical language
must certainly lie in folk-music, this approach has been completely rejected, for the simple reason that it is impossible to
verify the original emotional impulse of a folk-tune. Even in
those many cases where a text has come down in conjunction
with the tune, it is impossible to be sure that it is the original
text; people are at any time only too capable of taking, say, a
gay old tune and writing some melancholy new words for it.

The investigation is further confined to tonal music, in a key, in the widest sense of the word, whethe Dufay in 1440, Byrd in 1611, Mozart in 1782, (in 1953. It does not in any way attempt to deal wit new musical language which has arisen out of the tonality by some composers during the last half-(this new language clearly bears little or no relation to the long-established one based on the tonal system.

Nevertheless, if the findings of this book are accepted, a certain widely-held view on the new non-tonal language would now seem, on the face of it, to amount to a logically inescapable conclusion, which can be briefly stated as follows. Since the new language is unrelievedly chromatic by nature, it must be restricted to expressing what chromaticism always was restricted to expressing—what indeed we feel even the very earliest chromaticism of the sixteenth-century Italians still to this day expresses—emotions of the most painful type (though a wide variety of expression can naturally be achieved by presenting these emotions in diverse ways—gently, fiercely, satirically, grotesquely, even jestingly). It may be objected that since this new music makes no use of tonal centres, its persistent chromaticism has not the same expressive connotations as that of tonal music; but expressive connotations it must have, and how else can they be interpreted except in relation to the (much-expanded) tonal system, which ultimately derives its expressive qualities from acoustical facts? Thus, from the purely negative point of view, the fact that the new music shuns the basic acoustical consonances of the octave, fifth, fourth, and triad, suggests that it does not express the simple fundamental sense of being at one with nature and life. This may by no means be the case, of course; it could be that we are just misapprehending the new language, as we have often tended to misapprehend the old. But the burden of proof that it is *not* the case should now be fairly and squarely on the shoulders of non-tonal composers and theorists. If this state of affairs calls forth a clear and convincing outline of the *expressive* aims of the new language, with an account of some of the terms of its vocabulary and some of its forms of expression, to offset ever so slightly the present welter of aridly technical, not to say purely mathematical exegesis, no one will be more pleased than the present writer, who whole-heartedly

Preface

.mires such of this music as he has found expressive of emotion.

I am greatly indebted to Mr. Denis Stevens for placing his vast knowledge of the earlier periods of musical history at my disposal, in the matter of the correct notation and approximate dating of the many musical examples taken from those periods; also to members of the Oxford University Press, for invaluable constructive criticism, which has most fruitfully affected the final shaping of the work. Many thanks also to Miss Virginia Harding and Miss Ruth Lachmann, for their so gladly-given secretarial assistance.

Finally, I would like to place on record my deep gratitude to one who is no longer able to receive it: to the late Dr. Eric Wellisch, whose faith in the projected work and encouragement of its author, as well as the example of his own personal courage, renewed and strengthened the original impulse at a critical stage during the long wait between conception and completion.

1 June 1958   D. C.

1

WHAT KIND OF AN ART IS MUSIC?

Although all the arts are essentially autonomous, owing to the different materials and techniques which they employ, there is clearly a kind of bond between them. We speak of the 'architecture' of a symphony, and call architecture, in its turn, 'frozen music'. Again, we say that certain writing has a 'sculptural' quality, and sometimes describe a piece of sculpture as 'a poem in stone'.

Admittedly, much of the phraseology which traffics between the arts is purely *metaphorical*, being concerned only with the *effect* of a work of art. Thus, in calling a statue 'a poem in stone', we merely indicate that its effect on us is of that impalpable kind we normally receive from poetry; we do not make an objective statement about the sculptor's intention or technical procedure. Such a metaphor, while useful for descriptive purposes, cannot help us to gain a deeper understanding of the nature of art.

On the other hand, comparison between one art and another *can* help towards this end, when the comparison is not *metaphorical*, but *analogical*, being concerned with the artist's *intention* and *technical procedure*. Thus, when we speak of the 'architecture' of a fugue, we are making an objective statement that its composer has constructed it by methods analogous to those of the architect—that he has grouped masses of non-representational material (tone instead of stone) into significant form, governed by the principles of proportion, balance, and symmetry; and this throws some light on a particular type of music. In using such analogies, of course, we must keep in mind the differences inherent in the use of different materials.

Analogies of this kind are continually being made between music and the other arts. Besides speaking of the 'architecture' of a piece of music, we use the term 'tone-painting', and we say that composers who are preoccupied with expressing character, mood, and feeling, have a leaning towards the 'literary'. And there is no doubt that music can be analogically related to each of these three arts: to architecture, in its quasi-mathematical construction; to painting, in its representation of physical objects; and to literature, in its use of a language to express emotion.

In various periods of musical history, composers have concentrated on one of these three aspects to the partial exclusion of the others. Medieval music was largely architectural in conception: the romantics were much concerned with the literary, the impressionists with the pictorial; modern music has swung back again to the architectural. Yet all three aspects have persisted in all periods: tone-painting and emotionally expressive music date right back to plainsong; and some of the romantics, notably Bruckner and Reger, were nothing if not tonal architects. In a work like Beethoven's Pastoral Symphony, we find all three aspects in a single composition: inspired by a 'literary' idea (the expression of moods and feelings arising out of contact with the countryside), the work is full of tone-painting, and has a perfectly satisfactory 'architectural' design. And in a movement like 'Sind Blitze, sind Donner in Wolken verschwunden?' (Have lightnings and thunders vanished behind the clouds?) in Bach's St. Matthew Passion, the three aspects are actually fused: the whole chorus is at once a piece of musical architecture (imitative polyphony), a tone-painting (of a gathering storm), and a piece of emotional expression (a smouldering and erupting of anger).

Let us now relate music analogically to architecture, painting, and literature, in more detail, and see if this can help us to establish the true nature of music as an art.

We may turn first to the analogy with painting, since this would seem to be the least essential, existing only in the case of a limited number of works, and passages of works. It exists where the composer imitates physical objects in terms of sound, addressed to the ear, as the painter does in terms of light, addressed to the eye. (We need not concern ourselves with painting which does not represent objects, but abstract patterns, since this is rather a case of painting's analogical relationship to music).

There are three ways in which music can represent physical objects. First, by *direct imitation* of something which emits a sound of definite pitch, such as a cuckoo, a shepherd's pipe, or a hunting horn. Here the parallel with painting is almost exact: the painter can represent the visual but not the aural aspect of the object, the composer the aural but not the visual. (In the case of a cuckoo, the composer may even be said to have the advantage, since to anyone but a naturalist it is a purely aural phenomenon!)

The second way is by *approximate imitation* of something which emits a sound of indefinite pitch, such as a thunderstorm, a rippling brook, or rustling branches. Here the composer's representation is inevitably less faithful than the painter's: a painting of a storm strikes the eye as a more or less exact reproduction of the appearance of a storm, but a musical representation of a storm strikes the ear as only an approximate reproduction of the sound of a storm. The definite sounds of music are different from the indefinite sounds of nature: rolls on the timpani do not sound exactly like thunder, nor chromatic scales on the violins exactly like the wind. Nevertheless, even here, the composer has a certain compensatory advantage: he can reproduce the sensation of physical movement which the painter can only suggest.

The third way in which music can represent physical objects is by the *suggestion* or *symbolization* of a purely visual thing, such as lightning, clouds or mountains, using sounds which have an effect on the ear similar to that which the appearance of the object has on the eye. Here music at once approaches closest to painting, and recedes farthest from it. In its attempt to stimulate the visual faculty, it seeks to usurp the very function of painting; but in so far as it lacks the power of direct communication—being unable to represent the object so that it can be immediately identified without recourse to an explanatory title—it is less analogous with painting than when it confines itself to the imitation of aural phenomena. Knowing, as we do, that the first of Debussy's Three Nocturnes is entitled *Nuages*, we are persuaded into interpreting the shifting patterns of sound in terms of the visual imagination—shifting patterns of light, such as we experience from the movement of clouds. But if Debussy had not given the Nocturne its title, we should have been uncertain what the composer intended to represent, if anything at all.

(The fact that, in such cases, a title is necessary to set the imagination working, is often taken as proof of the illegitimacy of this kind of musical tone-painting. But it is not always realized that even some poems are not fully intelligible without their titles. Take this one by Tennyson:

> *He clasps the crag with crooked hands;*
> *Close to the sun in lonely lands,*
> *Ring'd with the azure world, he stands.*
>
> *The wrinkled sea beneath him crawls;*
> *He watches from his mountain walls,*
> *And like a thunderbolt he falls.*

One wonders whether, if Tennyson had merely called this poem 'Lines', readers would have realized exactly what it was supposed to be describing. Once the actual title is known, of course, there is nothing ambiguous about the poem at all.)

Frequently, music's three methods of tone-painting are fused, or superimposed on one another, in a single composition. In Beethoven's Pastoral Symphony, for example, the direct imitation of bird-calls (cuckoo and quail) interrupt the approximate imitation of a murmuring brook, while the third bird-call (nightingale) is also approximate; the thunder in the storm movement is approximately imitated, the lightning and rain are suggested, and these are followed by the direct imitation of a shepherd's pipe.

So far, our attention has been strictly confined to the element of imitation; but this, of course, is neither the composer's nor the painter's sole intention. The imitation is only a framework on which each type of artist, using the materials of his own art, superimposes his *vision* of the imitated object, or his *subjective experience* of it. Beethoven's comment on his Pastoral Symphony is apposite here: 'more feeling than tone-painting'.

Now the painter is always free to impose his subjective experience on the basic framework of imitation, by the very nature of his art: the object imitated will still be immediately recogniz-

able even after considerable modification in the interests of subjectivity.[1] But the composer can only impose his subjective
experience on his imitation when he is free to choose his own
notes to embody the general pattern necessitated by the imitation. Therefore, the power to reproduce sounds from the external world in their exact form is the least valuable part of
music's tone-painting equipment, since the composer cannot
choose his own notes, but only accept those emitted by the
object imitated. Direct imitation is most acceptable when the
composer uses it as a single element in a larger whole, weaving
it into a web of notes already chosen by him to embody an
approximate imitation or a suggestion of that whole. Thus, the
cuckoo-calls in Delius's *On Hearing the First Cuckoo in Spring* take
their rightful place as a significant detail in the composer's
suggestion of the atmosphere of a spring day; and that suggestion already embodies the composer's own subjective experience
of spring.

Indirect imitation is more valuable in that it allows the composer considerable latitude to choose exactly what notes he shall
use to body forth the general pattern required for the imitation;
and by his choice he is able to convey his subjective experience
of the object imitated. In most of the songs in Schubert's *Die
schöne Müllerin*, for example, the accompaniment indirectly imitates the flowing motion of a brook by regular patterns of
quavers or semiquavers; but by embodying the generalized
pattern in a different series of notes in each case, Schubert is able
to convey the emotional experiences of his young miller (joy,
apprehension, jealous fury, etc.) through a subjective vision of
the brook. (*Die schöne Müllerin*, in fact, like so much of Schubert's
vocal music, works on the principle defined by Ruskin as 'the
pathetic fallacy'—the projection by the artist of his own moods
into some natural object.)[2]

Suggestion or symbolization of visual phenomena is equally
valuable, since it depends wholly on the actual notes used, which
must vividly convey the composer's subjective experience of the
phenomenon represented, or we shall not recognize it, even
when supplied with a title. Thus, Debussy's symbolization of

---

[1] We are concerned here with painting as it has been known for centuries, not
with the revolutionary art of the last fifty years or so.
[2] *Modern Painters*, Vol. 3, Chap. 12.

clouds, in *Nuages*, is achieved by shifting patterns of sound; but shifting patterns may be used to symbolize many things: it is the actual notes in which Debussy chose to embody these patterns that convey his subjective vision of clouds.

To sum up: tone-painting is a legitimate, if subsidiary function of music. Its value increases the more it is used as a vehicle for the composer's subjective experience of the object represented; and it is by means of the actual notes chosen by the composer that the experience is conveyed. Here the analogy with painting ends, since there is obviously no connection between the technical organization of notes and that of paint.[1] The composer's way of conveying his subjective experience is a different one from the painter's; it resides in the 'literary' aspect of music—its use of a tonal language to express moods and feelings—which will be discussed in the section concerned with the analogy between music and literature.

First, however, it should be said that any piece of tone-painting is of negligible value unless it is integrated into some kind of musical structure; and this brings us to our next section, an examination of the analogy between music and architecture.

The final realization of any work of art is achieved through structure, or form; hence each of the arts can be analogically related to architecture, which is itself the visible embodiment of pure form. The power of large-scale organization which made possible the poetry of Dante, the painting of Michelangelo, and the music of Bach, is obviously analogous to the monumental constructive genius needed in architecture; and it was clearly employed in each of the three cases to produce structures which would satisfy the desire of the aesthetic sense for formal harmony, in the way that architectural forms do.

In the case of music, the analogy would seem to be particularly close, in that, as has been mentioned, both composer and architect group masses of non-representational material (pure sound in time, and stone in space) into significant form, governed by the principles of proportion, balance, and symmetry. At first, our analogy looks to be a simple and conclusive

[1] Comparisons such as those of piano-writing with black-and-white drawing, of orchestration with colour, and of a certain type of impressionist orchestration with the *pointilliste* technique in painting, are clearly metaphorical, and cannot bring us a deeper understanding of the nature of music.

one: music is the audible, as architecture is the visible, embodiment of pure form. Stravinsky adheres to this view of the matter: 'One could not better define the sensation produced by music than by saying that it is identical with that evoked by the contemplation of the interplay of architectural forms'.[1]

But let us look into the analogy a little more closely. How far can we apply it? To all music, or only to certain kinds of music? It is easy to justify the common application of it to some of the greatest music ever written—the contrapuntal masterpieces of the old polyphonic composers, down to and including Bach. In these, the themes are sometimes scarcely more emotionally expressive than bricks or blocks of stone (e.g. those of Bach's 'great' organ fugues in A minor and G minor), and are used simply as raw material capable of being built up into large-scale sound-constructions by means of interwoven lines, various sections being balanced one against another in size, until their combined mass makes possible a final climax, setting a seal on the whole like a tower or a dome. Moreover, the interwoven lines actually 'support' one another in a quasi-mathematical system of stresses and strains. The old polyphonic composers might truly be regarded as tonal architects, in that, when they wanted to write, say, invertible counterpoint at the twelfth, they had to work according to the following table if the result was to be satisfactory:

1	=	12	7	=	6
2	=	11	8	=	5
3	=	10	9	=	4
4	=	9	10	=	3
5	=	8	11	=	2
6	=	7	12	=	1

What is more, the experience provided by this kind of music is definitely akin to that provided by architecture—the enjoyment of the beauty of pure form. What attracts us is not so much the thematic material as the satisfying way in which it is woven together; not so much, say, the fugue-subject, as the masterly working-out of it in *stretto*, to produce a sonorous climax.

The analogy holds good, of course, for all music that is

[1] *Chronicle of My Life*, translated from the French, p. 93.

primarily contrapuntal: for the non-expressive fugal music of
later periods (lesser, both in amount and calibre), and for that
limited amount of modern music in which non-expressive
material is organized contrapuntally by means of quasi-
mathematical 'laws' similar to those which governed the old-
style polyphony (much *avant-garde* serial music, and the music
of Hindemith, for example). In all these cases, the raw material
is nothing, the intellectual construction everything, and the impact on the listener almost entirely a formal and aesthetic one.
But once we step outside the limited world of polyphony, in
which the intellect predominates, the analogy becomes vague
and unprofitable, for two reasons. Firstly, the difference in the
materials comes to the fore: the musical material of non-polyphonic music is not inexpressive like that of architecture, but is
charged with human feeling. Secondly, in the manipulation of
such material, purely intellectual techniques are replaced by
methods in which the intellect is to some extent at the service of
the feelings.

If a theme of the type used in polyphonic music acts very
much like a brick or a block of stone (as something of no importance in itself, only useful as raw material to be built into a
structure), the thematic material of other types of music—opera,
song, symphony—*is* important in itself, being emotionally expressive, as is the material of painting and literature. The experience derived from a piece of polyphony, like that derived
from a piece of architecture, consists mainly of a perception
and admiration of its form; but in most cases, the experience
derived from a piece of non-polyphonic music, like that derived
from a painting or a literary work, is only partly referable to an
appreciation of its form: much of it derives from our emotional
response to its actual material. A typical contrapuntal point or
fugue-subject has no real significance until it takes its place in
the construction as a whole; but a theme in a sonata, like a hand
in a painting or a line in a poem, is already of absorbing
emotional interest in itself, even if its full significance is only
appreciated when its integration into the overall form is understood. Indeed, in music, as to a greater degree in literature, a
work can be outstanding in spite of being cast into a most
unsatisfying form: we listen to works like *Boris Godunov* and
Delius's Violin Concerto, as we read books like *Tristram Shandy*

and *Moby Dick*, not for their formal beauty, but for the fascination of their material.

Actually, in many cases, the thematic material of polyphony is itself expressive, even highly expressive: a few examples are the opening Kyrie of Bach's B minor Mass, several of Purcell's string fantasias, 'For with His Stripes' in *Messiah*, Mozart's C minor Fugue for two pianos and the Quam Olim Abrahae in his Requiem Mass. Indeed, musical material (as it is hoped to show in this book) is by its very nature expressive; though of course its expressiveness can sometimes be extremely slight. Nevertheless, broadly speaking, the architectural analogy holds good for all polyphony, whether expressive or inexpressive, in that the construction is primarily intellectual and the impact primarily formal; and it breaks down outside polyphony because the construction is guided by feeling and the impact is to a considerable extent emotional.

Outside polyphony, in fact, it dwindles to the mere truism that a piece of music, no less than a piece of architecture, must have some kind of shape. Turning away from Bach's polyphony to another type of work by him, the St. Matthew Passion for example, we shall be hard put to it to discover any analogy with architectural construction at all. What small amount of polyphony it does contain is mostly 'free', and all of it is dramatic in conception—a portrayal of the hubbub of a crowd of people; and for the most part the work consists of operatic-type recitative, highly emotional arias of the melody-and-accompaniment kind, and traditional chorales in which the primitive emotions of folk-music are intensified by Bach's extraordinary command of deeply expressive harmony. Again, when we turn to the symphony (classical or romantic) we might just as well (more profitably, in fact) compare its structure to that of a drama, a succession of contrasted events in time following one another by a chain of cause and effect;[1] and an opera, of course, just *is* a sung drama. A work like Debussy's *L'après-midi d'un faune* is constructed (if so tough a word may be used) more like the poem to which it was intended to form a prelude—as a succession of changing moods melting in and out of one another according to the logic of emotion; and a song just *is* a sung poem.

[1] Bruckner alone of the symphonists found an 'architectural' way of composing his symphonies—balancing masses of melodic harmony one against another; but this is an isolated phenomenon which need not concern us here.

Clearly then, we cannot press the architectural analogy too far (as many are intent on doing at the present juncture of musical history). It has really just as limited an application as the analogy with painting: only a certain type of music, to a certain degree, can legitimately be regarded as pure, quasi-mathematical form. Other music has a different kind of form, and has a wider significance than is imparted to us by its form alone, being expressive of the composer's subjective experience.

So we may say that, except within very closely defined limits, music is neither a representative art, like painting, nor a purely formal art, like architecture. What kind of an art is it, then?

In some way or other, we feel, it conveys to us the subjective experience of composers. But in what way? It is easy to see how the thing is done in painting (by direct but subjective representation of physical objects) and in literature (by direct but subjective description of physical objects, thoughts, characters, and emotions); but how can it be done in music, which can only represent a few physical objects, vaguely suggest a few others, and make no explicit description of anything at all? To try and answer this question, we must turn to a consideration of the analogy between music and literature, and an investigation of the problem of music as language.

But first, a fairly lengthy digression will be necessary, in order to try and settle a vexed point. So far, this book has been persistently begging the question whether music does in fact express composers' subjective experience—a question which everyone once assumed instinctively had an affirmative answer, but which is assumed equally instinctively by many modern musicians to have been answered once and for all in the negative. If we are to establish the right to make any analogy at all between music and literature, the question will have to be reopened, and some reasons sought to support an affirmative answer. Not that we can hope to find any clinching proof; what proof can there be in these matters? In an age which doubts every one of the old intuitive assumptions, there can be no definite answers—not even the new confident negative ones (a fact which may well serve as encouragement at the start). What we may hope to do is to show that there is as much to be said on this side as on that; that the question is still open, whatever the fashionable opinion may be, and that one person's conviction is as good as another's.

It is not the intention here to investigate every theory of music considered as expression; theorists are notoriously limited by abstractions. I propose to deal with the matter in a more concrete way, setting forth the current case against the view of music as expression, in the words of two of our most outstanding present-day composers; and adducing several arguments on the other side— the views of other composers, the view of a poet, the experience of listeners in general, and the practice of composers in general.

First, the negative view, in the words of Stravinsky: 'I consider that music is, by its very nature, powerless to *express* anything at all, whether a feeling, an attitude of mind, a psychological mood, a phenomenon of nature, etc. . . . if, as is nearly always the case, music appears to express something, this is only an illusion, and not a reality'.[1] Obviously, everything depends on what Stravinsky means by 'express': if he means 'express explicitly, as words can', his remark is a truism; if he means 'convey to the listener in any way whatsoever', he is merely offering an expression of opinion, without adducing any proof.

Composers' theories tend to be based on their own artistic needs, and it is evident that Stravinsky, bent as he has been on removing music as far as possible from the romantic aesthetic, would naturally formulate a theory of this kind. It is an extremist theory, the product of an intensely individual composer's mind; but it has been widely accepted, as coming from such an eminent source, and its effect on contemporary aesthetic thought has been most harmful. Aaron Copland, himself a disciple of Stravinsky, and a composer who cannot by the wildest stretch of the imagination be called a romantic, has justly described Stravinsky's attitude in this matter as 'intransigent', saying that 'it may be due to the fact that so many people have tried to read different meanings into so many pieces'. He also adds the following: 'Heaven knows it is difficult enough to say what it is that a piece of music means, to say it finally so that

---

[1] Stravinsky, *Chronicle of My Life*, translated from the French, pp. 91–2.

everyone is satisfied with your explanation. But that should not lead one to the other extreme of denying to music the right to be expressive.'[1]

It is worth noting that, until Stravinsky came out with his flat statement to the contrary, everyone naturally assumed that music was expressive. Let us call in another, earlier composer, not an out-and-out romantic of the Wagnerian type, but one firmly grounded in the classical tradition.

Mendelssohn once wrote: 'People usually complain that music is so ambiguous; that it is so doubtful what they ought to think when they hear it; whereas everyone understands words. With me it is entirely the converse. And not only with regard to an entire speech, but also with individual words; these, too, seem to me to be so ambiguous, so vague, and so easily misunderstood in comparison with genuine music, which fills the soul with a thousand things better than words. The thoughts which are expressed to me by a piece of music which I love are not too indefinite to be put into words, but on the contrary too definite. And so I find, in every attempt to express such thoughts, that something is right, but at the same time something is unsatisfying in all of them. . . .'[2]

Now when Mendelssohn comes to give examples of *thoughts* (*Gedanken*) which music gives rise to, we find he is using the word in the generalized sense of 'mental activities', and in fact means *feelings*, rather; since he specifically mentions resignation, melancholy, and the praise of God. And those who have found music expressive of anything at all (the majority of mankind) have found it expressive of emotions. Let us here call in another witness, not even a semi-romantic composer this time, but one of the clearest-minded of classical poets.

Dryden, in his 'Song for St. Cecilia's Day', showed that he regarded music as emotionally expressive:

> *The soft complaining flute*
> *In dying notes discovers*
> *The woes of hopeless lovers,*
> *Whose dirge is whisper'd by the warbling lute.*

---

[1] Aaron Copland, *What to Listen For in Music*, Chap. 2.
[2] Mendelssohn, Letter to Marc André Souchay; Berlin, 5 October 1842.

> *Sharp violins proclaim*
> *Their jealous pangs and desperation,*
> *Fury, frantic indignation,*
> *Depths of pains, and height of passion*
> *For the fair disdainful dame.*

No doubt in Dryden's mind at all! As he said earlier in the same poem: 'What passion cannot Music raise and quell?' And emotional reaction to music has been the experience of listeners everywhere. One has only to read descriptions of musical compositions in programmes or musical biographies, whether in English or any other language, to find the writers limping in their more pedestrian way after Dryden: confident themes, agonizing chords, wistful melodies, ferocious rhythms, jubilant climaxes. . . .

And the composers: what did they themselves think they were doing? Neither Stravinsky nor Mendelssohn tells us, but one of the most classical of all composers has done. Listen to Mozart: 'Now, as for Belmonte's aria in A major—'O wie ängstlich, O wie feurig'—do you know how it is expressed (*ausgedrückt*)?—even the throbbing of his loving heart is indicated (*angezeigt*)—the two violins in octaves. . . . One sees the trembling—the wavering—one sees how his swelling breast heaves—this is expressed (*exprimirt*) by a *crescendo*—one hears the whispering and the sighing—which is expressed (*ausgedrückt*) by the first violins, muted, and a flute in unison'.[1] Nothing could be more definite than that.

Again, here is Schubert, writing home about the reception of his 'Ave Maria' at a private concert: 'They also wondered greatly at my piety, which I have expressed (*ausgedrückt*) in a Hymn to the Holy Virgin, and which, it appears, grips every soul and turns it to devotion. I think this is due to the fact that I never force devotion in myself and never compose hymns or prayers of that kind, unless I am overcome by it unawares; but then it is usually the right and true devotion'.[2]

In any case, it is undeniable (as Chapters 2 and 3 attempt to demonstrate) that composers have consciously or unconsciously

---

[1] Mozart, letter to his father, Vienna, 26 September 1781, concerning *The Seraglio*.
[2] Schubert, letter to his father and stepmother, Steyer, 25 (28?) July 1825.

used music as a language, from at least 1400 onwards—a language never formulated in a dictionary, because by its very nature it is incapable of such treatment. A few examples may suffice here. A phrase of two notes (the minor sixth of the scale falling to the fifth) is to be found expressing anguish in music by Josquin (*Déploration*); Morley ('Ah, break, alas!'); Bach (Crucifixus in the B minor Mass); Mozart (*Don Giovanni*—Donna Anna's grief at her father's death); Schubert (*The Erl King*—'my father, my father'); Mussorgsky (*Boris Godunov*—the Simpleton's Lament); Verdi (the end of *La Traviata*); Wagner (the so-called Servitude motive in *The Ring*); Schoenberg (*A Survivor from Warsaw*—'you had been separated from your children'); Stravinsky (*The Rake's Progress*—'In a foolish dream'); Britten (Donne Sonnet 'Oh might these sighs and tears'); and in innumerable other places in the music of these and practically all other composers.[1] Another example is a phrase of 1–3–5–6–5 in the major scale (sometimes with passing notes), used to express a simple, innocent, blessed joy: found in countless plainsong themes and Christmas carols; in Wilbye ('As fair as morn'); Handel (*Messiah*—Pastoral Symphony); Humperdinck (Children's Prayer in *Hansel and Gretel*); Busoni (Easter Hymn in *Doktor Faustus*); Vaughan Williams ('So shalt thou enter in' and 'Holy, holy, holy' in *The Pilgrim's Progress*); and in many other places.[2]

Again, we may note how the tragic subjects of the St. Matthew Passion and *Die Winterreise* forced on Bach and Schubert a heavy (almost too heavy) preponderance of minor keys; while the brighter subjects of the Easter Oratorio and most of *Die schöne Müllerin* turned them inevitably towards the major. Did anyone ever set the Resurrexit of the Mass to slow, soft, minor music? Or the Crucifixus to quick, loud, major strains? Try singing the word 'Crucifixus' to the music of Handel's Hallelujah Chorus, or the word 'Hallelujah' to the music of the Crucifixus in Bach's B minor Mass! Stravinsky himself has complied with the common practice in these matters. In the *Symphony of Psalms*, the first two movements (settings of sombre prayer-psalms) are in E minor and C minor respectively, while the last (a setting of a praise-psalm) moves between E flat major and C major. And his *Oedipus Rex* is mainly in minor keys, his *Rake's Progress*

[1] See Exs. 48, 50, and 62.   [2] See Ex. 64.

mainly in major ones. Within the orbit of tonality, composers have always been bound by certain expressive laws of the medium, laws which are analogous to those of language.[1]

So we must admit that composers have set out to express emotion, and that listeners have felt it to be present in their music. But we must still consider Stravinsky's opinion that 'if, as is nearly always the case, music appears to express something, this is only an illusion, and not a reality'.

This point of view has been set forth in greater detail by Hindemith in his book *A Composer's World*. His theory is that music does have an emotive effect on the listener, but the apparent emotions are not those of the composer, nor do they arouse the real emotions of the listener; in Stravinsky's words 'this is only an illusion'. Hindemith says: 'Music cannot express the composer's feelings. Let us suppose a composer is writing an extremely funereal piece, which may require three months of intensive work. Is he, during this three-months period, thinking of nothing but funerals? Or can he, in those hours that are not devoted to his work because of his desire to eat and sleep, put his grief on ice, so to speak, and be gay until the moment when he resumes his sombre activity? If he really expressed his feelings accurately during the time of composing and writing, we would be presented with a horrible motley of expressions, among which the grievous part would necessarily occupy but a small space.'[2] Later, he continues; 'If the composer himself thinks he is expressing his own feelings, we have to accuse him of lack of observation. Here is what he really does: he knows by experience that certain patterns of tone-setting correspond with certain emotional reactions on the listener's part. Writing these patterns frequently and finding his observations confirmed, in anticipating the listener's reaction he believes himself to be in the same mental situation.'[3]

The naïveté and illogicality of this analysis, coming from a composer of Hindemith's mental stature, is truly regrettable. But we have to remember again that composers write out of their own experience; and we know that Hindemith is, and sees himself as, a superior kind of craftsman, not an 'inspired genius'—

[1] The ambiguities of the major-minor opposition (as shown, for example, by the Dead March in *Saul* being in the *major*) are dealt with in Chapter 2.

[2] Hindemith, *A Composer's World*, pp. 35–6.

[3] Ibid., p. 36.

that, in fact, he rather derisively denies the existence of inspiration: 'Melodies can, in our time, be constructed rationally. We do not need to believe in benign fairies, bestowing angelic tunes upon their favourites.'[1] Being this kind of a composer, he is unable, despite his intellectual insight into musical construction and his laudable concern for music's moral values, to understand the deep unconscious urges that gave birth to music of the deeply emotive kind—viz., most of the music written between 1400 and the present day.

There seems to be in Hindemith's analysis an almost wilful refusal to understand that an artist has two separate selves: the everyday, conscious self, which is a prey to many passing trivial emotions, and a deep, unconscious, creative self, which is always there to return to, 'inspiration' permitting, and which is apt to intrude itself intermittently, as 'inspiration', during his everyday life. If Hindemith has no personal experience of this, surely he has heard of the fits of 'absent-mindedness' that some great artists have been subject to, when this occurred? Surely he must have some conception of the way in which this unconscious creative self persists beneath the distractions of everyday life, concentrated on its all-important realities?[2] When we state that a composer, writing a lengthy piece over a long period, expresses his emotions in it, we really ought not to have to explain that we mean his deep, permanent, significant emotions, not the superficial fleeting ones called forth by trivial pleasures and disappointments.

There is only one way to make clear the superficiality of Hindemith's 'realistic' analysis, and that is to take a concrete example. Let us consider the *Eroica* Symphony, as it came to Beethoven. We know that Beethoven was intoxicated by the libertarian ideals of the French Revolution, and that, at first regarding Napoleon as the hero who would liberate mankind, he conceived the idea of composing a symphony in his honour.

---

[1] Ibid., p. 97.

[2] 'So much in writing depends on the superficiality of one's days. One may be preoccupied with shopping and income-tax returns, but the stream of the unconscious continues to flow undisturbed, solving problems, planning ahead: one sits down sterile and dispirited at the desk, and suddenly the words come as though from the air . . . the work has been done while one slept or shopped or talked with friends.' (Graham Greene, speaking through the character of Maurice Bendrix, the narrator in *The End of the Affair*, Chap. 2.)

Now how would this state of mind function in Beethoven? The heroic, libertarian ideal was (as were 'nature', the 'immortal beloved' and 'fate') the subject of one of his most intense emotions, which was liable to flare up at the slightest provocation (as we know from several anecdotes). And we know that he conceived the symphony to express this burning, persistent emotion, apparently having a vision of the work as a whole, and no doubt being possessed with certain musical themes for various parts of it. Now how did these themes originate? Let us take the Funeral March, since Hindemith's example is 'an extremely funereal piece'.

One of the emotions aroused in Beethoven by the heroic, libertarian ideal was, as we know, a deep grief for the unhappy fate that awaited many and many a liberator—that of annihilation. Wherefore he must have felt the compulsion to express this feeling in his symphony, in the natural place: the slow movement would be a Funeral March. Now, the laws of the language of tonality demanded a slow march-tempo, the minor key (relative minor, obviously, C minor, which was the 'tragic' key of Beethoven's great predecessor, Mozart), and a mournful theme. To imagine that these necessities were formulated, one by one, by Beethoven's conscious mind, is ridiculous; they must have crystallized, unconsciously, into the main C minor theme, built around the classical tragic formula of the minor triad.[1] Beethoven's unconscious mind thus embodied his own personal emotion concerning the death of a hero in the time-honoured terms of musical language—but in his own personal way: gradually it stamped on the raw material— the C minor triad— the impress of his own individual emotion so strongly that the resultant theme was 'original' and 'characteristic', and not to be confused with the slow C minor world of Mozart's *Masonic Funeral Music* or Wagner's *Siegfried's Funeral March*, both in the same tradition. (I say 'gradually' since the theme had to be hacked into shape, as was so often the case with Beethoven: the conscious craftsman had to take over, working towards the ideal form of expression envisaged by the creative unconscious.)

Let us compare, for a moment, a similar case in literature: Tennyson, writing his *Ode on the Death of the Duke of Wellington*. The same intense personal emotion (not in any way affected

[1] See Ex. 80.

by the fact that, as Poet Laureate, he was obliged to write the Ode, since one has to admit that Tennyson's heart and soul were obviously in the project, whatever one's personal reaction to the subject of the poem); and the same inevitable recourse to certain basic elements of language with time-honoured associations:

> *Bury* the *Great* Duke
> With an *empire's lamentation,*
> Let us *bury* the *Great* Duke
> To the noise of the *mourning* of a *mighty nation.*

There is the same heavy stress in the rhythm, the same obsessive repetition, the same unmistakably individual use of well-worn language (italicized here), and no doubt there was the same craftsman's struggle to hew the first inspiration into the dimly-apprehended ideal expression.

Now let us remember that, in both cases, the artist must have been disturbed by everyday distractions before the piece was completed; perhaps a visitor to entertain, or a business letter to write. Can it be conceived that the creative current (the be-all and end-all of these two different men's lives) would not be running along unchecked underneath, still concerned with the theme so dear to it? And on the (no doubt impatient) return to the manuscript, would not the old *personal* feeling of grief, concerned with the death of a hero, come flooding back as powerfully as ever, possibly giving a new impetus to continue with another aspect of that obsessive emotion?

Let us admit what is obvious to common sense: that Beethoven used the traditional language of music to express his own personal emotions, and that everyday interruptions did not prevent these emotions from persisting throughout the composition—and beyond it, indeed, for *Egmont* was still to come, and *Coriolan*.

We must now turn to the second part of Hindemith's theory—that concerning the emotional reaction of the listener. He says: 'If music does not express feelings, how then does it affect the listener's emotions? There is no doubt that listeners, performers, and composers alike can be profoundly moved by perceiving, performing, or imagining music, and consequently music must touch on something in their emotional life that brings them into this state of excitation. But if these mental reactions were feelings, they would not change as rapidly as they do, and they would not begin and end precisely with the musical stimulus that aroused them. If we experience a real feeling of grief—that is, grief not caused or released by music—it is not possible to replace it at a moment's notice and without any plausible reason with the feeling of wild gaiety; and gaiety, in turn, cannot be replaced by complacency after a fraction of a second. . . . The reactions which music evokes are not feelings, but they are the images, memories of feelings. . . . We cannot have musical reactions of emotional significance, unless we have once had real feelings, the memory of which is revived by the musical impression. Reactions of a grievous nature can be aroused by music only if a former experience of real grief was stored up in our memory and is now again portrayed in a dream-like fashion. . . .'[1] Again, he says: 'Paintings, poems, sculptures, works of architecture . . . do not—contrary to music—release images of feelings; instead they speak to the real, untransformed, and unmodified feelings.'[2]

It is difficult here to know where to start—there are so many fallacies. Let us return to the *Eroica* Funeral March, and consider the listener's reactions. In the slow, heavy, dragging rhythm, the minor key, and the mournful melody, he will recognize the type of the funeral march, and Beethoven's own individuality of expression, with its indefinable grandeur, will convey that it is a funeral march written by a noble mind in connection with a noble ideal. Will the music awaken 'former experience of real grief, stored-up in the memory, and now portrayed in a dream-like fashion'? Surely nothing of the sort: the listener's capacity for feeling grief (certainly intensified by any strong personal grief he has experienced) will be aroused by the music into feeling (through the distorting medium of his own temperament, admittedly) the personal grief of Beethoven, made incarnate by him in that music. *He will feel as he has never felt before.* (In listening to Chopin's Funeral March, he will experience another quite different personal grief, belonging to a quite different man—a grief more loaded with despair—and again, he will feel as he never felt before.) The listener thus makes direct contact with the mind of a great artist, 'interpreting' his expres-

[1] Ibid., p. 38.   [2] Ibid., p. 49.

sion of emotion in the same way that he will 'interpret' an
emotional letter from a friend: in both cases, mind meets mind,
as far as is possible. And if the listener has no capacity for feeling
real grief (as opposed to petty chagrin), he will, of course, not
really comprehend the Funeral March at all.

Hindemith's two reasons why musical emotions are not 'real'
feelings will not hold water. In the first place, emotions called
forth by music do *not* 'begin and end with the musical stimulus
that aroused them': begin, yes, since a specific emotion cannot
be awakened without a stimulus; but end, no, since it is many
people's experience that the feelings aroused by a piece of music
can persist for days afterwards, without memory of the actual
notes that caused them. In the second place, the idea that diverse
emotions cannot succeed one another swiftly is applicable only
to placid temperaments: Hindemith himself is no doubt possessed of remarkable equanimity, but more volatile people
often find themselves switching suddenly from depression to
gaiety with or without external stimulus. And this is found quite
commonly in art itself—in literature for example. One has only
to consider the violent transitions of mood, from deep gloom to
joyous ecstasy, in such a poem as Keats's *Ode to a Nightingale*.

In any case, what is meant by saying that the emotions
aroused by the other arts are more 'real' than those of music?
In what sense, for instance, is the feeling of grief evoked by the
Ode on the Death of the Duke of Wellington more 'real' than that
evoked by the *Eroica* Funeral March? Surely not that Tennyson
exhorts us, in explicit words, to 'bury the Great Duke', whereas
Beethoven 'only' expresses the inner feeling of grief on a hero's
death? In both cases, the feeling of grief is stimulated by the
use of an emotionally affecting language in a particular way.
And how far, in both cases, can the grief be said to be 'real'?
Not in the sense that one's own grief for a personal loss is real,
but in the sense that all great art stimulates our own real emotional capacities to partake vicariously of the artist's experience,
as we do of our friends' experiences when they speak to us of
them. In one sense, emotion conveyed through music is more
real than that conveyed through the other arts—because it is
more *pure*, less bound down to a 'local habitation and a name'.
The true expressive difference between the arts is that painting
conveys feeling through a visual image, and literature through a

rationally intelligible statement, but music conveys the naked feeling direct. As the composer felt, so we may hear, and feel: what he saw, or thought, does not interfere.

This brings us to a further difficulty; the supposed vagueness of the emotions expressed in music. Hindemith, like those of whom Mendelssohn spoke, finds music ambiguous. 'One given piece of music may cause remarkably diverse reactions in different listeners. As an illustration of this statement, I like to mention the second movement of Beethoven's Seventh Symphony, which I have found leads some people into a pseudo feeling of profound melancholy, while another group takes it for a kind of scurrilous scherzo, and a third for a subdued kind of pastorale. Each group is justified in judging as it does.'[1]

Hindemith is undoubtedly right in his observation that people react in different emotional ways to a given piece of music, but his statement that each reaction is equally justifiable fails to take a simple psychological point into account. Could it not be that some listeners are incapable of understanding the feeling of the music properly?[2] This can even happen in the explicit world of literature: I have seen Edmund in *King Lear* played as a superficially cynical butterfly, and the audience reacted accordingly, with giggles; but a close reading of Shakespeare's text does not justify this conception in the least. Similarly, the great German actor, Gründgens, plays Goethe's Mephistopheles as a self-tormenting fallen angel. And if actors can so distort the emotional make-up of a part, one wonders how many people read, say, Shelley's *Ode to a Skylark* as a pretty and pleasing piece of poetry, or take *Moby Dick* to be merely a stirring sea-story.

The fact is that people can only react to the emotions expressed in a work of art according to their own capacity to feel those emotions. Hindemith describes what too often happens (taking it as a general rule for all listeners): 'The difference in interpretation stems from the difference in memory-images [of emotions] the listeners provide, and the unconscious selection is made on the basis of the sentimental value or the degree

---

[1] Ibid., p. 40.
[2] The answer is, of course, yes; and this explains why 'tests', in which the reactions of a random collection of individuals are classified and analysed, prove nothing. Sympathetic understanding is a pre-requisite: what would be the use of applying such a test to, say, one of Blake's prophetic books?

of importance each image has: the listener chooses the one which is dearest and closest to his mental disposition, or which represents a most common, most easily accessible feeling.'[1] Such people, whom one knows to exist, are just plainly unmusical: suppose that such a listener's 'memory-image' has no connection with the emotions expressed by the music at all? If someone were to declare the *Eroica* Funeral March to be a sanguine piece, we should unhesitatingly accuse him of being emotionally undeveloped. Such a person would understand *Hamlet* as a tragedy only by virtue of the explicit meaning of the words, and remain utterly oblivious of the dark emotional undertones of the poetry. The truly musical person, with a normal capacity to respond to emotion, immediately apprehends the emotional content of a piece of music to the degree that he can experience it.

Ought we not always to be trying to expand our capacity for comprehending what the composer is trying to express, rather than accept the first 'stock response' of our emotions? One is not entirely at the mercy of one's superficial feelings; it is always possible to penetrate deeper. For example, my own (and others') experience of Mozart's major-key music has been: (1) in childhood, pretty music; (2) in adolescence, graceful and elegant, but trivial music; (3) in maturity, graceful and elegant music often shot through with deep and disturbing emotions. Here I would unhesitatingly maintain that in cases 1 and 2, we were not really understanding Mozart at all.

Let us now examine the second movement of Beethoven's Seventh Symphony. It is in the minor, has a heavy monotonous rhythm, and its theme opens with twelve repetitions of the same note, marking that rhythm; also, the movement has a 'trio' section in the major. It should hardly be necessary to point out that these are the emotive elements of the Funeral March. Consider Beethoven's own *Marcia Funebre* in the Piano Sonata in A flat, Op. 26, and that of Chopin in his Sonata in B flat minor. Consider also Schubert's later use of exactly the same rhythm (again to repeated notes) in his 'Death and the Maiden'. The two main differences between the *Allegretto* of the Seventh Symphony and the genuine funeral march is that the rhythm is not dotted, and the tempo is rather quicker. (Much depends on the con-

[1] Ibid., p. 40.

ductor's tempo, of course; Beethoven is reported to have said he should have marked the movement *Andante*, which would bring it nearer to the real funeral march tempo.) The absolute individuality of the movement is that it is a rather lighter, more gentle type of funeral march: it is, in fact, a restrained elegy, rather than a heavy lament. But a 'scurrilous scherzo'? A 'subdued pastorale'? One is bound to regard anyone who reacts in this way as either superficial, unmusical, or unsympathetic to Beethoven. If anything is needed to clinch the argument, there is that forceful opening and closing minor chord, with the fifth uppermost—one of the most 'tragic' chords in music. Compare the *Marcia Funebre* in the Sonata in A flat, Op. 26, the 'Fate' motive in *The Ring*, the horn chord preceding Rudolph's outcry on Mimi's death, in *La Bohème*, and the opening of 'Sanctus fortis' in *The Dream of Gerontius*: different colours, different registers, different dynamics, different contexts, but the essentially painful connotation is obvious in them all.

This interpretation of the *Allegretto* cannot be dismissed as being out of keeping with the mood of the symphony, since the movement fulfils a musical and 'extra-musical' function similar to that of the Funeral March in the *Eroica*. Of course, no words can ever describe precisely the emotion of this movement, or any other. The emotion is, in Mendelssohn's words, 'too definite' to be transcribed into the ambiguous medium of words. However, the emotion is there, is real; and unless the listener recognizes, consciously or unconsciously, the relationship of the movement to the basic conception of the funeral march, his experience of the music will be false; and once this relationship is pointed out to one who is quite unaware of it, it can revolutionize his whole emotional response to the work, unless he sincerely cannot (or obstinately will not) feel the connection.

Of course, to a more subtle degree, a piece of music does convey something different to each normally responsive listener. Here is how Aaron Copland puts it: 'Listen . . . to the forty-eight fugue themes of Bach's Well-Tempered Clavichord [sc. Clavier]. Listen to each theme, one after another. You will soon realize that each theme mirrors a different world of feeling. You will also soon realize that the more beautiful a theme seems to you the harder it is to find any word that will describe it to your complete satisfaction. Yes, you will certainly know whether it is a gay theme or a sad one. . . . Now study the sad one a little closer. Try to pin down the exact quality of its sadness. Is it pessimistically or resignedly sad; is it fatefully sad or smilingly sad? Let us suppose that you are fortunate and can describe to your own satisfaction in so many words the exact meaning of your chosen theme. There is still no guarantee that anyone else will be satisfied. Nor need they be. The important thing is that each one feel for himself the specific expressive quality of a theme, or, similarly, of an entire piece of music. And if it is a great work of art, don't expect it to mean exactly the same thing to you each time you return to it.'[1]

Indeed, the same applies in the more explicit field of litera-ture: the idea that there are various layers of feeling and mean-ing in a poem, say, is a commonplace of literary criticism. Or again, listen to two actors of widely differing temperaments reciting the same poem: it will have quite a different emotional effect in each case. And are we not still arguing as to the precise emotional and intellectual significance of Goethe's *Faust* and Kafka's *The Trial*? Nevertheless, the broad general feeling, in both literature and music, gets over; and some, by intuitive sym-pathy, get nearer to it than others. *Faust* and Beethoven's Fifth Symphony are felt to be (using the broadest possible terms) 'optimistic', whereas Kafka's *The Trial* and Tchaikovsky's Sixth Symphony are felt to be 'pessimistic', and all four works have many facets to which all react differently, but in the same general way.

But anyone who conceives a quasi-funeral-march movement to be a 'kind of scurrilous scherzo' must be considered emotion-ally abnormal (or simply unmusical) to a degree.

One final difficulty remains. Is the traditional language of music, to which we have referred, a genuine emotional language, whose terms actually possess the inherent power to awaken cer-tain definite emotions in the listener, or is it a collection of *formulae* attached by habit over a long period to certain verbally explicit emotions in masses, operas, and songs, which produce in the listener a series of conditioned reflexes?

It seems most likely that the answer is simply 'both'. It would be useless to deny that the continuous and consistent use of cer-

[1] Aaron Copland, ibid., Chap. 2.

tain terms of musical language throughout five centuries or more must have conditioned us to accept them without question; and it must have helped to intensify their effect, pinpoint their character, and codify them clearly. But it is difficult to believe that there is no more to it than that. In the first place, one can only wonder how (to quote Hindemith) 'certain patterns of tone-setting' ever came in the first place to 'correspond with certain emotional reactions on the listener's part', unless the correspondences were inherent, as are, for example, those between certain faces that we pull and certain emotions we intend them to express—delight, scorn, or disgust. Again, it seems surprising that throughout five centuries or more all European composers without exception—some of them violently revolutionary in other respects—should have accepted the established connotations of the various terms without demur (see the music examples in Chapters 2 and 3), and that this has proved the only unchanging aspect of music. One might have expected a revolutionary composer to try and cut loose from these connotations—to insist on using, say, the major 1–3–5–6–5 of innocent joy to express some dark and evil emotion; but nothing of this kind has been attempted.[1] In fact, it is possible to discover, as Chapter 2 tries to show, close natural correspondences between the emotive effects of certain notes of the scale and their positions in the acoustic hierarchy known as the harmonic series; it seems improbable that the 'strength' of the fifth and the 'joy' of the major third, for example, should not be inherent in their 'basic' positions in the series.

Ultimately, it is for the reader to make up his own mind; in the meantime, the foregoing may perhaps be taken as reasonable support for the view that music is a language of the emotions, and we may proceed to consider in more detail the analogy between music and literature.

The analogy between music and literature, then, is that both make use of a language of sounds for the purpose of expression. But the analogy is only valid on the plane of emotional expression, since abstract intellectual statements such as 'I think,

---

[1] Actually, with the advent of atonal and twelve-note music, we have at last witnessed a revolution which implies a total break with the past, a repudiation of even the old terms of musical language, and an attempt to recondition the listener to a new set. Whether it will be successful is not yet clear.

therefore I am' are outside the scope of music, and the power to describe the outside world belongs to the analogy with painting in the case of both arts ('tone-painting' and 'word-painting').

The analogy can best be understood on the primitive level. The most feasible theory of the origin of language is that it began as inarticulate, purely emotional cries of pleasure and pain; and some of these utterances still survive in the two languages— speech and music—which have grown out of them. A groan of 'Ah!' uttered by a character in an opera on a two-note phrase of definite pitch is hardly different from a groan of 'Ah!' uttered by a character in a play at indefinite pitch; the effect is equally emotive in both cases. An example is the wailing of Mime in Scene 3 of *The Rhinegold*: transfer these notes to an instrument, as Wagner does, and one can say that here is a basic term in the emotional vocabulary of music, stemming from a basic term in the emotional vocabulary of speech. It is, in fact. our two-note figure mentioned earlier (flat sixth falling to fifth).[1]

Beyond such simple cases, however, the analogy becomes less close, though still close enough to be fruitful. In literature, the inarticulate cries of primitive man have become elaborated into words, i.e., sounds which possess associations with objects, ideas and feelings—clear, rationally intelligible, but arbitrary associations; whereas in music, they have become elaborated into notes, i .e. sounds which have clear but not rationally intelligible associations, rather inherent associations, with the basic emotions of mankind. Nevertheless, the diverse effects of these two different kinds of sound have a close connection in that they both awaken in the hearer an emotional response; the difference is that a word awakens both an emotional response and a comprehension of its meaning, whereas a note, having no meaning, awakens only an emotional response.[2]

A note? A single note? Certainly. The capacity to react to an isolated musical sound is a testing-point for a listener's emotional apprehension of music. Hindemith's matter-of-fact indifference to music's mysterious emotive power is entirely explained

---

[1] See Ex. 62f.

[2] Actually, an unknown (foreign) word can awaken a purely emotional response: for example, hearing one foreigner abuse another by a single insulting word, one would react emotionally to the word without understanding its meaning. Here the purely emotional effect of language is isolated.

when one reads his flat statement that music cannot exist in a single note: he is completely impervious to the sensual and emotional impact of music's basic n ░░ .ial—a single sound of definite pitch. He says: 'The truth is that as single tones they are mere acoustical facts which do not evoke any genuine musical reaction. No musical effect can be obtained unless the tension between at least two different single tones has been perceived'.[1]

Of course, a piece of music cannot be made out of one note; but one note, like one word, can make an immediate artistic-emotional effect, before other notes or words follow. Let us take an example. Browning's poem *Pippa Passes* opens with a little mill-girl springing out of bed, crying 'Day!' This is the *first line* of the poem, and anyone reading it aloud would make a pause before continuing 'Faster and more fast . . .' In the listener, aware of the situation through the initial stage-direction, the single word calls forth at once an intellectual understanding that dawn has broken, and an emotional response to the ecstatic joy that the young girl feels at her experience of this natural phenomenon. There is poetry here already if not yet a poem.

Now turn to a musical equivalent—Wagner's *Rienzi*. The audience is sitting in the theatre, and the overture begins. A solo trumpet plays the single note A—starting it quietly, holding it, swelling out to a *forte*, and dying away again into silence. This sound is at once beautiful, mysterious, and thrilling—the tone-colour of the trumpet evokes military and heroic associations, the length of the note gives a sense of solemnity, the coming and going of the volume gives a sense of something growing out of nothing and fading whence it came. Not being a word, the sound has no intellectual associations, but merely awakens the emotions of awe and wonder, and a subdued expectancy of heroic events to come. There is music here already, if not a piece of music. (The fact that, in this case, the piece of music, when it does come, flagrantly disappoints the expectations aroused by the magical opening need not disturb us here, even if it does in the theatre.)[2]

[1] Ibid., p. 68.
[2] Cf. Aaron Copland, *What to Listen For in Music*, Chap. 2: 'You may be sitting in a room reading this book. Imagine one note struck on the piano. Immediately that one note is enough to change the atmosphere of the room—proving that the sound element in music [a few lines earlier he calls it more explicitly 'the sensuous plane'] is a powerful and mysterious agent, which it would be foolish to deride or belittle.'

Hindemith's main point is, of course, correct. A piece of music is made up of aggregations of notes, just as a poem is made up of aggregations of words. And here the analogy with literature breaks down completely in one sense, since there is no connection between the intellectual-emotional organization of words into coherent statements by means of the logic of verbal syntax, and the intellectual-emotional organization of notes into coherent statements by means of the logic of musical syntax. Nevertheless, the analogy is still valid in another sense, for the overall emotional organization of a piece of music is often quite similar to that of a poem or a drama. This can be seen clearly in the case of a song or an opera. Everyone can hear how Schubert, by the use of different types of melody, different rhythms, and subtle tonal modulations, follows the emotional progression of the poem, in such a song as *Gretchen at the Spinning-Wheel*; and, *pace* Hindemith, the conflicting emotions of poem and music follow in swift succession—restless anxiety, joyous ecstasy, a cry of pleasurable pain, restless anxiety—yet the emotions of the one are as 'real' as those of the other. Again, Wagner's musical construction, in such a work as *The Ring*, goes hand in hand with his verbal-dramatic construction; in fact, as is well-known, they were in places conceived as one indissoluble musico-dramatic whole.

But what of 'pure' music—music without words? Not music of the purely 'architectural' type, but music which is clearly intended as the expression of the composer's emotion? A more detailed comparison of the *Eroica* Funeral March and the *Ode on the Death of the Duke of Wellington* will throw some light on this question.

The death of a hero arouses conflicting emotions in the artist who feels such an event deeply: grief at the plain fact of death; a feeling of tender consolation in the thought that death brings peace; joy and triumph at the memory of the great things the hero has done; a fierce, determined courage inspired by his example. (It need hardly be said that, treating a theme like this, an artist feels himself to be the mouthpiece of national or universal emotions.)

Now Tennyson's Ode begins with three brief stanzas expressing a heavy, universalized grief for the hero's death. In a longer fourth stanza, he turns to 'remembering all his greatness in the past . . . great in council and great in war . . . that tower of strength which stood four-square to all the winds that blew'. In a fifth stanza of equal length, more tender feelings emerge: 'Under the cross of gold that shines over city and river, there shall he rest for ever among the wise and the bold'. The sixth and longest stanza is a proud and triumphant paean of praise of the hero's mighty deeds: 'with blare of bugle, clamour of men, roll of cannon and clash of arms'. The seventh and eighth stanzas bring the feeling of courageous determination: 'A people's voice! We are a people yet . . . not once or twice in our rough island-story, the path of duty was the way to glory'. The ninth and last stanza turns to a more serene grief: 'Peace, his triumph will be sung by some yet unmoulded tongue . . . speak no more of his renown, lay your earthly fancies down, and in the vast cathedral leave him. God accept him, Christ receive him.'

This is necessarily a broad general outline of the poem: Tennyson weaves these conflicting emotions in and out of one another in the kaleidoscopic way which words permit. Take for example, the lines:

> *O peace, it is a day of pain*
> *For one, upon whose hand and heart and brain*
> *Once the weight and fate of Europe hung.*
> *Ours the pain, be his the gain!*

It can be seen that three 'real' feelings—grief, admiration, and a sense of triumph—here succeed one another with extreme rapidity; yet there is no sense of what Hindemith, speaking of the way emotions follow one another in music, calls 'their delirious, almost insane manner of appearance'.

Nor is there anything insane in the way in which Beethoven's similar emotions (devoid of any intellectual associations, any 'meaning') succeed one another in the *Eroica* Funeral March. As with Tennyson, the opening section (the Funeral March proper) presents the feeling of heavy, universalized grief, though taking in the tenderer, consoling emotion in the passage in E flat major, and in the momentary appearance of the chord of D flat major, which is immediately contradicted (cf. 'Peace, it is a day of pain'). The second section (the C major trio) moves from joy to triumph, backwards and forwards, and breaks off, for the third section (the re-statement of the first section) to resume the feeling of grief. Here, however, after the first few bars, the mighty fugal passage begins, inverting the E flat 'consolation' theme, and putting it into the minor: this whole section presents the feelings of fierce determination—moving to an inspiriting courage (horns in E flat) and back again, picking up the grievous feeling once more in the resumption of the funeral march proper. After a sudden switch to the tenderer feelings (strings in D flat), the movement ends in hushed grief, with broken references to the opening theme.

Words are poor things, except in the hands of a poet. The emotional adjectives I have used above are only feeble labels to indicate the general feeling of the music. To return to Mendelssohn, words are 'so ambiguous, so vague'; in every attempt to express the emotions of the music in words 'something is right, but something is unsatisfying'. No one, least of all myself, would want to attach verbal labels to the deep feelings aroused during a performance of the *Eroica* Symphony. Nor would I be misunderstood concerning my comparison with Tennyson's Ode: the last thing I would think of when listening to Beethoven's Funeral March is this poem, which obviously expresses the same basic emotions, but through the agency of another man of another race with another attitude towards life, and through another artistic medium. Each says what it has to say in its own way, and there is no such thing as translation or equivalence. My only reason for a comparative verbal analysis of the two works is to endeavour to indicate that music functions very much like poetry in making a coherent and unified statement out of conflicting emotions. Nor am I concerned with the rights and wrongs of Beethoven's and Tennyson's conceptions of a hero, or with comparing the artistic value of the two works: I only chose the instances because of Hindemith's particular reference to 'an extremely funereal piece'.

We have another difficulty to meet here. It is usually objected, when one offers an analysis of the emotions expressed in a musical work, that music has a logic and constructive method of its own, that it ultimately has to stand or fall as a piece of music. With this no one would disagree, and one would hardly bother to make an emotional analysis of a work which one did not already know to be technically excellent. Actually, there is no conflict of ideas here at all. Any artist has to weave the emotions he is expressing into an intellectually and emotionally coherent statement; and emotions woven together in this artistically formal way do not cease to be emotions because they do not float about vaguely as in everyday life; in fact, they become even more 'real' by their isolation and sensitive combination in a great work of art. The great artist makes a supremely 'right' statement of the emotions one feels oneself but cannot organize into a satisfying expression.

Music is no more incapable of being emotionally intelligible because it is bound by the laws of musical construction, than poetry is because it is bound by the laws of verbal grammatical construction. In fact, in both cases, it should be a truism to say that the construction of a work of art is guided both by the feelings and the intellect: the intellect brings craftsmanship to bear on realizing the overall shape which is *felt* before it is intellectually apprehended. Let us turn to the *Eroica* Funeral March once more. We have seen how the C minor tonality and the slow march-rhythm must have crystallized unconsciously in Beethoven as the main theme. Equally unconsciously, the tenderer feelings for the dead hero would give rise to a complex of notes in E flat (the natural key for the end of a first strain beginning in C minor); the feeling of joy would naturally find outlet in brighter complexes of notes in C major (the natural key for the Trio section); and the feelings of triumph in the G major and C major climaxes of the trio—the central point, farthest away from the mournful opening and ending. The conscious craftsman in Beethoven would see to it that these unconscious compulsions were realized to the full.

A single example will suffice to show that the laws of musical construction aid rather than impede emotional expression, exactly in the same way as the laws of poetical construction. Both a funeral march and an ode on a dead hero, by the logic of human feeling, will normally move from grief to triumph and back. In Beethoven's case, as we have seen, the triumph was bound by the laws of musical logic to be the G major and C major climaxes, with trumpets and drums, in his C major trio—the central point of the movement; and the result is supremely right and satisfying, formally and emotionally. In Tennyson's case, the laws of language demanded a climax word to form his central point—and the finest word one can use to praise a dead hero in the English language is 'honour'. In the centre of Tennyson's Ode, the following lines appear twice on separate occasions, at a distance roughly proportionate to that between Beethoven's G major and C major climaxes, in so far as such a thing can be measured:

> *With honour, honour, honour, honour to him,*
> *Eternal honour to his name.*

I am not trying to say that these things could not have happened differently—in Chopin's Funeral March the brief moment of triumph is in the first section, in the relative major, and the consolation entirely in the trio, also in the relative major: I am only intent on demonstrating how a musician and a poet have obeyed the laws of their respective arts in a certain natural way, and in each case achieved a tremendous *formal* and *emotional* impact, *which are one and the same thing.*

In this way, one can explain how those who have a feeling for music but no technical knowledge can justifiably be said to 'understand' a piece of music—the form is apprehended as an emotional shape, as it must have originally been conceived by the composer. And one should not need to justify this approach to music (though the present *Zeitgeist* is utterly against it): music can hold up its head as the supreme expression of universal emotions by the great composers, and also be interesting from the point of view of craftsmanship to the technically-minded, in the way that a poem, emotionally absorbed by many readers, may be dissected by a student of poetic technique.

But still, it will be objected, we have not proved any inherent connection between the notes and the emotions they are supposed to express. That is, of course, the task of the rest of the book. At this point, we may sum up the foregoing, before proceeding to our examination of the way in which music functions as a language of the emotions.

The argument of this first part may be stated in brief as follows. Music naturally has its own technical laws, concerned with the organization of notes into coherent forms, but considered as expression, it has three separate aspects, related to the arts of architecture, painting, and literature. (1) The purely 'architectural' aspect is found in a limited number of contrapuntal works built out of material which is not emotionally expressive; though this 'inexpressiveness' is relative, scarcely ever absolute. The appeal of this kind of music is largely to the aesthetic appreciation of the beauty of pure form. (2)The purely 'pictorial' aspect of music is found in a limited number of works, and passages in works, which imitate external objects belonging to the natural world; and it is more valuable when the imitation is so approximate as to leave the composer considerable latitude to choose his own notes to embody his subjective experience of the object imitated. The appeal of this kind of music is through the aural imagination to the visual imagination and thence to the emotions. (3) The 'literary' aspect of music is to be found, to a greater or less extent, in most Western music written between 1400 and the present day, since music is, properly speaking, a language of the emotions, akin to speech. The appeal of this music is directly to the emotions and, to be fully appreciated, should be responded to in this way.

The widespread view of music as 'purely music' limits the listener's understanding of the great masterpieces to their purely aural beauty—i.e. to their surface attraction—and to their purely technical construction. This latter is no more (and no less) than the magnificent craftsmanship whereby composers express their emotions coherently: it is forever unintelligible to the layman, except emotionally, and ultimately inexplicable to almost anyone but a potential composer. Music is, in fact, 'extra-musical' in the sense that poetry is 'extra-verbal', since notes, like words, have emotional connotations; it is, let us repeat, the supreme expression of universal emotions, in an entirely personal way, by the great composers.

2

THE ELEMENTS OF MUSICAL EXPRESSION

The task facing us is to discover exactly how music functions as a language, to establish the terms of its vocabulary, and to explain how these terms may legitimately be said to express the emotions they appear to.

Beginning with the basic material—notes of definite pitch—we must agree with Hindemith that musical works are built out of the *tensions* between such notes. These tensions can be set up in three dimensions—*pitch, time,* and *volume*; and the setting up of such tensions, and the colouring of them by the *characterizing agents* of *tone-colour* and *texture*, constitute the whole apparatus of musical expression.

Let us now distinguish between the various ways in which these dimensions can function, beginning with that of *pitch*. Pitch-tensions can be regarded in two different ways—as *tonal tensions* (what the actual notes of the scale are) and as *intervallic tensions* (in what direction and at what distance the notes are from one another). Three examples will make this clear:

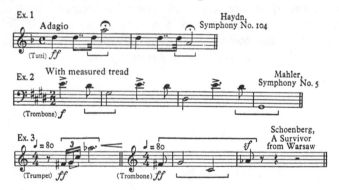

To explain, by using figures to indicate notes of the scale. In Ex. 1, the single tonal tension between 1 and 5 in the key of D is presented as two different intervallic tensions working in opposite directions—rising fifth and falling fourth. In Ex. 2, the single tonal tension between 5 and 1 in G sharp is presented as two different intervallic tensions working in the same direction —falling fifth and falling twelfth. In Ex. 3, the single series of tonal tensions between sharp 4, 5, 1, and flat 6, in the key of C, is presented as two different series of intervallic tensions: (a) rising semitone, rising fourth, rising minor sixth; and (b) rising semitone, falling fifth, rising minor sixth. In each example, there is clearly a similarity of expressive quality due to identical tonal tensions, and a difference of expressive quality due to diverse intervallic tensions. In Ex. 1, the 'launching-off' character of 1–5 is seen in its assertive (rising) and oppressive (falling) aspects. In Ex. 2, the conclusive, clinching power of 5–1 is seen in its oppressive (falling) aspect, but the effect is much emphasized in the second case by adding an octave to its fall. In Ex. 3, the painful effect of sharp–4–5–1–flat–6 is at its most acute when the series of notes is stretched out in ascending order to cover a range of over an octave (we may ignore the rhythmic difference between the two phrases for the moment).

These two kinds of tension, which are the only possible expressive functions of the dimension of pitch, have been disentangled from one another here for the purpose of analysis, but they are in reality always indissolubly united into a single expressive whole. Thus, in Ex. 1, we do not really have 1–5 presented as two different intervals, or two different intervals which are 1–5, so much as (a) 1–5-as-rising-fifth; and (b) 1–5-as-falling-fourth; and each is a single entity in itself.

It should also be mentioned that these two kinds of tension can of course occur not only between notes played successively (melodically) but between notes played simultaneously (harmonically).

The dimension of time functions in a greater variety of ways, as perhaps might be expected.

First of all, music can exist without setting up any strong time-tension at all. Plainsong, for example, uses time not as a dimension in which to set up tension, but as a continuum in which to flow freely. Such fluid, unmeasured rhythm is, properly speaking, outside the scope of this investigation, since we are concerned with the measured music of the harmonic period. However, we may mention the familiar fact that it is just this lack of a measured rhythm which removes plainsong from the human categories of time into those of 'other-worldliness', and gives it its spiritual quality. And occasionally, unmeasured rhythm has been brought back into more recent music, to free it from all trace of purely human expression (Holst's 'other-worldly' *Hymn of Jesus*, for example, and the 'elemental' *melismata* in some of Vaughan Williams's nature-music). Also, even in music with a measured rhythm, the regular beat can be obliterated by various means—a very slow tempo, syncopation, rubato, etc.—until 'timelessness' is come again (e.g., the opening of Wagner's *Parsifal* or the end of Mahler's *Song of the Earth*).

Turning to measured time, time-tensions are made possible by setting clear fixed points to measure them by; and these points are fixed by having a succession of 'beats', real or implied, spaced out at regular intervals of time, and by making one out of every so many 'strong' by accenting it—drawing on the tension available in the volume-dimension (that of making one note louder than others) to do so. Thus is produced the first expressive function of measured time—*rhythmic accent*—by which one note can be made more important than another. There is of course a sub-category here—that of *syncopation*: the accent is removed from a strong to a weak beat (by means of making the note on the weak beat louder than the note on the strong beat) and the unexpectedness of this procedure gives the note concerned a greater importance than the normally accented note.

The regular tensions set up by accent are of two kinds—that between one strong and one weak beat (*duple rhythm*) and one strong and two weak beats (*triple rhythm*). Out of these two basic rhythms all the different 'times' of music are derived: four-four is two twos, six-eight two threes, five-four a two and a three, etc., etc. It is obvious that these two basic kinds of rhythmic tension, and their various combinations and permutations, will all function differently from the expressive point of view, and their effects as part of musical language will have to be analysed.

The only other kind of time-tension besides that of accent is *duration*—notes may be longer or shorter than one another. This tension functions in three ways: as *tempo* (slow-fast), *movement* (even-jerky), and *phrasing* (*staccato-legato*).

The fundamental one is of course *tempo*. It may seem strange to define it as a function of duration, but it is obvious that a slow tempo is created out of beats of long duration, a quick tempo out of beats of short duration. We say of anyone who moves slowly that he 'takes his time'; and when the beats take their time, the tempo is slow. The effect of tempo on the musical expression is obviously of great importance, and will need analysing.

Movement is also extremely important. There is clearly a great expressive difference between an even stream of notes of equal length and a jerky, agitated succession of notes alternately long and short (dotted rhythms).

Phrasing in general is quite as much a product of volume-tensions as of time-tensions; but the *staccato-legato* antithesis belongs mainly to the time-dimension, being a matter of the actual length of a note compared with its rhythmic length. For example, a note that rhythmically lasts the whole of a four-four bar may in fact only be sounding for the first quarter or the first eighth, or it may be sustained right up to the end of the bar. Again, this will make a considerable difference to the expression.

Having begun this section on time by referring to the un-measured rhythm of the earliest period of our musical history, we may end it by mentioning the highly irregular and broken-up rhythm of much modern music; for just as there is an antithesis between measured and unmeasured rhythm, so there is between regular rhythm (dealt with so far) and irregular. Irregular rhythm is at the opposite pole from unmeasured: it is meti-culously measured down to the last fraction of a beat, so as to assure the maximum irregularity, expressing that modern affliction, a high state of nervous tension.

The remaining apparatus of musical expression need not detain us for the moment. As we have already said, *volume* is simply the dimension in which one note can be louder or softer than another; and *tone-colour* and *texture* are characterizing agents, which modify, by 'colour', the tensions set up in the dimensions of pitch, time, and volume.

We are now faced with the problem of disentangling the multifarious interactions of all these elements one upon another. If we are to bring order out of chaos, we must discover which of them is the fundamental one, on which the others merely act (however powerfully) as qualifying influences. Tone-colour and texture we have already admitted to be mere characterizing agents, and volume clearly cannot be regarded as fundamental in any sense (there has first to be a note, before one can consider whether it is loud or soft). This leaves us with pitch and time: which is fundamental?

Both, one might say. Melody can exist without rhythm (in plainsong), and rhythm without melody (African drum music). But the latter lies outside our experience, whereas plainsong does not; so it is reasonable to assume that, in *our* music, pitch is the fundamental element.

And ultimately, the fundamental element of pitch is *tonal tension*, in so far as it can be separated from intervallic tension: for example, '5–1' does mean something vital and all-important apart from its incarnation as a rising fourth or falling fifth; whereas 'a falling fifth' does not mean anything very concrete unless we know whether the tonal tension is, say, 8–4, 7–3, or 5–1. *What the actual notes of the scale are*—this is the basis of the expressive language of music: the subtle and intricate system of relationships which we know as tonality. In this system we shall find the basic terms of music's vocabulary, each of which can be modified in countless ways by intervallic tensions, time-tensions, and volume-tensions, and characterized by tone-colour and texture.

The bed-rock nature of tonal tensions can be seen in this way. A group of four adjacent descending notes, played slowly and quietly, *legato*, to the rhythm 1–2–3–1 in triple time, is a description that means precisely nothing, unless we know exactly what notes they are:

But once we make clear the tonal tensions between the notes, by putting, say, a treble or bass clef in front of them, all becomes clear. A treble clef gives 8–7–6–5 in the major scale—and the opening of Dowland's 'Awake, sweet love'; a bass clef gives 8–7–6–5 in the minor scale—and the opening of Bach's 'Come, sweet death' (slightly ornamented):

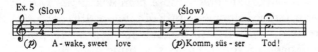

Of course, the qualifying agents do have a kind of general expressive quality of their own. In both phrases in Ex. 5, the slow tempo, the quiet dynamic level, the legato phrasing, and the even rhythm, do combine to produce a general effect of quiet acceptance; but the particular expressive effect in each case is entirely individual, there being all the difference in the world between falling from 8 to 5 via semitone-tone-tone and doing the same thing via tone-tone-semitone.

On the other hand, let us admit that the basic terms of the tonal language have no more than a general significance until brought to life by the action of the qualifying agents. Take, for example, the term 8–7–6–5 in the major scale: its latent power to express a mood of fulfilment can be brought out in quite different ways according to the way in which it is brought to life by the qualifying agents:

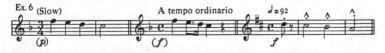

The three phrases, from the aforementioned Dowland song, Handel's *Messiah*, and Mahler's First Symphony, are all the same basic term in the system of tonal tensions, and all have the same basic sense of fulfilment, but the qualifying agents make each quite different in its specific effect. In fact, as can be seen, the qualifying agents are really *vitalizing* agents, for they give the basic emotional connotation of any given set of tonal tensions a vivid and entirely individual life of its own.

To disentangle and isolate the expressive powers of all the various elements of musical language, it will be necessary to deal with them in the following order. (1) Tonal tensions, because, as we have said, they convey the basic emotional moods, which are brought to life in various ways by the vitalizing agents of pitch, time, and volume. (2) Volume, since this is the simplest of the vitalizing agents in its functioning, working largely independently of time and pitch-as-direction. (3) Time, since this, although much more complex in its working, still functions largely independently of pitch-as-direction. (4) Pitch-as-direction, left till last because its expressive powers very much depend on tonal tensions, volume, and time.

We turn first, then, to an examination of the emotive powers inherent in the various tonal tensions.

THE TONAL TENSIONS

This section brings us to the heart of the problem of musical language, the persistent neglect to tackle which is responsible for the meaninglessness of most attempts to elucidate the 'emotional content' of music, and also for the widespread belief that any such attempts are futile, music being emotionally ambiguous. The simple but amazing fact is that, although certain general directional movements of pitch have occasionally been analysed as 'symbols' (Schweitzer on Bach, for example), no one has ever tried to analyse the expressive qualities inherent in the tonal relationships between the different notes of the scale. No one has seriously got down to the business of discovering, in each particular context, *exactly what the notes of the scale are and what tensions exist between them.*

The expressive basis of the musical language of Western Europe consists of the intricate system of tensional relationships between notes which we call the tonal system: in a given context, it is essential to know whether the important note is, say, the major or minor sixth of the scale. And whence does this system derive? Simply from the vertical structure of music peculiar to Western Europe which we call harmony: there are, of course, 'major' and 'minor' thirds and sixths outside the orbit of Western European harmony, but our investigation is confined to the 'harmonic' period of musical history. And whence does this harmony itself derive? From the natural phenomenon which we call the harmonic series.

As is well-known, when a note is sounded by vibrating a
string, not only does the whole string vibrate, producing the
fundamental note which is all that the untrained ear can hear,
but the two halves of the string vibrate in their own right at
the same time; and so do the thirds, the quarters, the fifths,
and so on, producing the rising succession of notes called the
harmonic series. Taking the note C below the bass clef as
fundamental, the first twenty-four notes of the series are as
follows:

(The starred notes are 'out of tune' to our ears.) The fractions
of the strings which produce the different notes are obtained
by putting a figure 1 over each of the numbers in Ex. 7: note 2
is produced by ½ the string, note 3 by ⅓, etc., etc. A practical
demonstration of this natural phenomenon can be made by
depressing the damper pedal of a good piano, striking the low C
and listening hard; there should be no difficulty in hearing
notes 2, 3, 4, and 5—the strings of these notes are set faintly
vibrating in sympathy with the halves, thirds, quarters, and
fifths of the low C string.

This means that in nature itself, a single note sets up a
harmony of its own; and this harmonic series has been the
(unconscious) basis of Western European harmony, and the
tonal system.

The reader should here be warned that this statement, which
was for long regarded as a truism, is being severely challenged
by modern theorists, especially those of the twelve-note school.
The reason is as follows. Twelve-note music has broken away
from the tonal system, producing harmony of acutely dissonant
effect; conservative opponents of this music declare that it goes
against the 'natural laws of harmony'; twelve-note theorists
have retaliated by maintaining the derivation of the tonal
system from the harmonic series to be pure illusion, much being
made of the practical inaudibility of the harmonic series. The
argument is still going on, and the truth will not be found in
a hurry. One feels that both sides are misguided, since it is

possible for a music based on the harmonic series to give way eventually to a music not based on that series, if that new music can establish its right to exist by achieving new kinds of beauty and significance. Some of man's greatest achievements have been made by going against natural laws; flying, for example, flouts the law of gravity—though only by enlisting the aid of other natural laws. Perhaps twelve-note music will eventually justify its 'naturalness' by discovering another 'natural law' of music on which it is unconsciously based. In the meantime, let us be content to say that it is most unlikely that the close correspondences between the natural harmonic system and the tonal system can be pure coincidence.

These correspondences are as follows. The earliest harmony we know of, that of the Greeks, used only note 2 of the series; i.e. their 'harmony' moved entirely in parallel octaves. This happens naturally, of course, when male and female voices sing the same tune; and the feeling is that they are singing the 'same' notes. Thus is established the naturalness of the octave, which is felt to be the same note as the fundamental, but at a higher pitch; this interval is the span of all the scales of Western music—the modes, the major and minor scales alike.

The earliest recorded attempts at harmony in Western Europe, in the ninth century, at first added only note 3 of the series: *organum*, as this type of harmony was called, moved in parallel fifths and fourths. This too can happen naturally: although most people can hear that note 3 of the series is a 'different' note, unlike note 2 which is 'the same', some people, singing or whistling a tune with others, quite naturally pitch it a fifth above or a fourth below, in blissful ignorance that they are not producing the same notes as the rest. It may well be that the fifth arose in this way, on the 'same note' principle of the octave; but once recognized and exploited as a different note, it opened up the way for harmony. So is established the naturalness of the fifth note of the scale, and the interval of the fifth, which spans the 'halves' of all our scales.

By about the twelfth century, the next different note began to establish its right to a place in harmony—note 5, our major third—and so was established the triad, which was to become the basis of Western European harmony:

Ex. 8

Another close correspondence is that notes 8 to 16 in Ex. 7 give us our major scale, with the addition of one extraneous note—note 14, B flat, the *minor* seventh. And in this note is to be found one of the closest and most complex correspondences of all. As will be seen, this is its second appearance in the series; it first occurs an octave lower, as note 7, in which capacity it is the next different note after the triad-forming note 5. This B flat may be legitimately described as the parent of the system of key-relationships we call tonality. It works in this way: turning to our scale of C, we can build up, as the composers of *organum* did, seven parallel fifths:

Ex. 9

The first six of these seven sounds are all 'firm' and 'stable', the tension between the two notes being the same in each case (the tension between notes 2 and 3 of the harmonic series, which we call the 'perfect fifth'); but the seventh sound is 'unstable', the fifth being imperfect, and not corresponding to any of the simple tensions of the harmonic series. This interval, the diminished fifth, was proscribed by medieval theorists as *diabolus in musica* (the devil in music) because of its 'flawed' sound. And when it was sung, the B was flattened (the procedure was called *musica ficta*) so as to obtain once more the firm sound of the perfect fifth:

Ex. 10

There is clearly a direct connection between this procedure and the fact that the B natural of the harmonic series (note 15) is outbalanced by the B flat (notes 7 and 14, and especially note 7, which can be picked up by a trained ear).

It was, of course, always possible to solve the diminished fifth problem in the opposite way—by sharpening the F:

Ex. 11

Now this too corresponds with a peculiarity of the harmonic series. Note 11 is not really F at all, but between F and F sharp, and slightly nearer to F sharp. This note occurs an octave higher (as note 22), together with a nearly-true F (note 21) and a nearly-true F sharp (note 23); behaving, in fact, rather like the 'out-of-tune' B flat (note 7) which appears an octave higher (note 14), together with a B natural (note 15). Obviously, the incompatibility of B and F as a harmonic interval derives from the ambiguity surrounding the B flat, B natural, F, and F sharp of the harmonic series; in other words, the 'flaw' in our harmonic system is a result of the 'flaw' in the harmonic series.[1]

Now the medieval composers' treatment of these two ambiguous notes B and F had surprising consequences. Their B flat became the first 'accidental' in Western European music: it turned the Lydian mode (F to F on the white notes of the piano) into our scale of F major, and the Dorian mode (D to D on the white notes) into our scale of D minor. Their F sharp likewise turned the Mixolydian mode (white-note scale G to G) into our G major scale, and the Phrygian mode (white-note scale E to E) into our E minor Scale. Thus, since the white-note scales on C (Ionian mode) and A (Aeolian mode) were already our C major and A minor scales, all the modes eventually became major and minor scales (except for the Locrian—the white-note scale on the fatal note B—which was never used anyway); and so arose our key-system.

Clearly, this system is the product of Western Europe's individual reaction to the 'flaw' in the natural harmonic series: the key-system 'corrects' it.[2] This is further confirmed by the

---

[1] This flaw also manifests itself in the fact that to tune a keyboard instrument in pure fifths puts some notes of the chromatic scale badly out of tune to our ears, an 'error' corrected by equal temperament. Looking at it another way, to tune by perfect fifths round the whole cycle of twelve brings us back not to our original note, but to one slightly sharp of it. Expressing it mathematically, we may say that whereas musically we want the equation $\dfrac{(3/2)^{12}}{128} = 1$, the correct mathematical equation is: $\dfrac{(3/2)^{12}}{128} = 1.014$.

[2] This musical 'correction' of nature is at one with the overall domination of nature by Western European man since the Renaissance.

fact that the system of key-relationships is also fundamentally based on the behaviour of the notes B, B flat, F, and F sharp. In C, the flattening of the B takes us into the key of F, as we have said, and we have to make it natural again to return to C:

Ex. 12

Likewise, the sharpening of the F takes us into the key of G, and we have to make it natural again to return to C:

Ex. 13

It can be seen that Ex. 13 is the same process as Ex. 12, working the opposite way, a fifth higher. Now the relationship of the keys of F (subdominant) and G (dominant) to the key of C (tonic), is the whole basis of the tonal system of Haydn, Mozart, and Beethoven. And the very behaviour of the notes derives from the harmonic series: note 7 is slightly flat of our B flat, so there is a tension pulling B flat downwards, whereas its off-shoot of B natural (note 15) pulls upwards (see Ex. 12); and note 11 is nearer to F sharp than F, hence the tension pulling F sharp upwards, whereas its offshoot of F (note 21) pulls downwards (see Ex. 13). Again, the well-known fact that it is 'easy' to 'fall' into the subdominant, and requires 'effort' to 'rise' into the dominant must be due to the fact that note 7 ('B flat') is a lower, more primary, and more audible note in the harmonic series than note 11 ('F half-sharp'). As Tovey pointed out, if a composer begins by hammering out the note C, you grow more and more certain that it will prove to be, not the key-note of C, but the dominant of F: the 'B flat' of the harmonic series must be responsible.

So, of the twelve notes we use, we have derived from the harmonic series nine: the seven notes of the C major scale, plus a B flat and an F sharp. What of the others? Returning to the harmonic series (Ex. 7), note 13, the note A, is also out of tune, being between A and A flat. If we resolve its ambiguity by treating it as A, it becomes our major sixth; if we treat it as A flat, it becomes our minor sixth. Coupled with the B flat and the B natural (notes 14 and 15), we get the upper part of our melodic minor scale, in its ascending and descending versions, a source of much expressive power in the music of the Elizabethan composers:

Ex. 14

Going up in sequence, the notes were usually natural, coming down usually flat.

Two notes remain unaccounted for—the minor third (E flat) and the minor second (D flat). Neither of these is a 'natural' note: the minor second does not really belong to either of our two modern scales, but is a survival from the Phrygian mode; and the minor third is a special case, a 'false' harmonic third, to be dealt with later. Both can be derived from the old scales, however: the scale was originally divided into two groups of four notes, called tetrachords, a fifth apart; and by transposing Ex. 14 down a fifth, we get:

Ex. 15

So, although neither E flat nor D flat can be derived from notes 8 to 16 of the harmonic series, we can say that they are justified by analogy. And so we account for the twelve notes of the chromatic scale:

Ex. 16

This scale is, of course, to be found in the higher reaches of the harmonic series (between notes 16 and 32, together with other, 'out of tune' notes); but the fact that, as we have seen, certain notes occur much earlier, nearer to audible range, explains their 'basic' quality, and the tensions by which they attract the 'subsidiary' notes to 'resolve' on to them.

Now the tensions between these notes are as follows. C is fixed, the fundamental note, known as the *tonic*. So is G (note 3 in the harmonic series), the fifth note in the scale, known as the *dominant*; though there is a tension pulling it back to C.

So is E (note 5 in the harmonic series), the *major third* of the scale; though again there is a tension pulling it back to C. The other notes have tensions pulling them back to these three: D flat and D (the *minor* and *major seconds*) are pulled towards C; F (the *fourth*) is pulled towards E; F sharp (the *sharp fourth*) and A flat and A (the *minor* and *major sixths*) are pulled towards G; B flat (the *minor seventh*) is pulled down to A and thence down to G; B natural (the *major seventh*) is pulled towards the upper C. The note E flat (the *minor third*) is an unusual case: it has a tension pulling it towards E, which was respected for centuries, but it was eventually regarded as fixed, in a way that will be explained when we consider its expressive quality. There is, of course, a tension pulling every note back to the fundamental, C.

We have decided to confine our investigation of the expressive language of music to the Western European 'harmonic' period; and we must now determine the limits of that period. It is easy to fix the latter date, which is, at the time of writing, *now*, since composers such as Britten are still using tonal harmony to good effect, and so of course are the best writers of popular music. If, in the meantime, the twelve-note school and others are devising and using new systems, these have not yet ousted tonality from our everyday experience.

The earlier date is more difficult to settle on. It is generally fixed at about 1600, when the 'figured bass' began to appear: before that, we are often told, composers wrote entirely contrapuntally, deploying their horizontal lines without thinking of the harmonic aspect of the result. Much nonsense has been talked on this subject. For example, the opening of Palestrina's *Stabat Mater* was once described as being actually a piece of pure counterpoint; despite its chordal aspect, it was declared to be a concatenation of horizontal lines:

Ex. 17   Palestrina, c. 1590

Sta - bat ma - ter do - lo - ro - sa

This opinion will not hold water. What a strange coincidence that Palestrina's flowing lines happened to form by accident a series of chords with a 'key-centre' of D minor! Obviously, the

best way of describing the passage is to say that the contrapuntal lines are woven into a harmonic framework. Yet *were*
all the lines conceived purely melodically? A definite 'no' is
given to this question by the lowest part: whereas the other
three move in more or less conjunct motion, as melodies, the
lower part functions in the second bar as a harmonic bass,
with the same kind of 'unmelodic' rising and falling fifths,
creating the roots of triads, that we find in the high harmonic
period, say in Mozart's *Marriage of Figaro*:

Ex. 18   Mozart, 1786
                                           (reduced)

Cor - riam tut - ti a fest - eg - giar!

The Palestrina example, and the thousands of others to be
found in sixteenth-century music, might be dismissed as mere
'foreshadowings' of the harmonic period, but further examples
will take us back across the centuries:

Ex. 19   Josquin,
                                           c. 1490

O____   Do - mi - ne Je - su Chris - - te

Ex. 20   Dufay, 1433

Eu - ge - ni - us, et rex Si - gis - mun - dus!

Ex. 21   'Beata
                            Viscera', c. 1300

Ex. 19, the opening of a motet published in 1503, is clearly
'in F major', and its bass is conceived harmonically as a series
of triad-roots. The same may be said of Ex. 20, a 'D minor'
passage from a motet written by Dufay to celebrate the signing
of a treaty between Pope Eugenius and the Emperor Sigis-
mundus in 1433. Ex. 21, from a Worcester manuscript dating
from about 1300, is rather different: clearly 'in F major', it is
an example of what is known as 'English descant'—a harmonization of a melody largely as a progression of 'six-three' chords,

variety being obtained by moving the bass up and down in fifths or fourths to produce an occasional root-position triad.

The above examples prove conclusively that our harmonic tonal system dates back much further than is generally admitted; its seeds are to be found in the thirteenth century. There is no intention here of denying that much great medieval music, by Pérotin (d. 1235), Machaut (1300–77), and others, was conceived entirely contrapuntally, with vertical clashes between the parts which arose purely out of the horizontal movements of those parts, and which had no harmonic intention at all. What *is* claimed, is that such composers still worked loosely within an implied harmonic and tonal framework, and that this framework was already *implicit* when the first medieval composers, in the ninth century or earlier, literally began to put two notes together as harmony, and immediately encountered the problem of the incompatibility of B and F as a harmonic interval. When they first 'corrected' this 'flaw' with a B flat, or an F sharp, all the modes were destined to become our major and minor keys by the addition of more and more accidentals: the principle of *musica ficta* had already produced B flat, F sharp, E flat, C sharp, and G sharp, *by about 1325*. So we may fix the limits of the harmonic period, not between 1600 and 1900, as is generally done, but between a vague date somewhere in the twelfth or thirteenth century, and a hypothetical date in the twenty-first century, when composers abandon the harmonic conception and the tonal system altogether.

The reasons why theorists have always set the limits at 1600 and 1900 are easy to understand. Before 1600, counterpoint tended to be more independent of the harmonic framework than afterwards, and composers fought hard to preserve the 'white-note' modes against the erosion of *musica ficta*; after 1900, the tonal system seemed to have 'broken down' because some outstanding composers abandoned it altogether for atonal, linear counterpoint. Nevertheless, the harmonic framework was always conditioning early contrapuntal writing, and the tonal system was unavoidable even in modal compositions; and in the twentieth century, the system has still been used to produce fine and original music.

For the practical purposes of our analysis of musical language, owing to the unavailability, unfamiliarity, and occasional unintelligibility of some early music, and to the non-existence of the music of the future, let us take the harmonic period as being roughly between 1400 and the present day; between say:

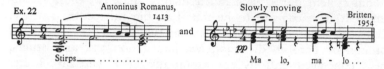

And let us admit that music of the harmonic-tonal kind (in its widest sense, including contrapuntal and modal music), written during these five-hundred-and-fifty years, constitutes nearly the whole of Western Europe's great musical achievement, and is what has most satisfied Western European humanity at large. But let us not deny the possibility that a new kind of music, based on an entirely new system, may arise (may have arisen, indeed), and may achieve equally great things.

MAJOR AND MINOR

Having established the fact that Western European music from at least 1400 to the present day is based on the harmonic tensions arising from the harmonic series, we can turn to our investigation of the expressive functioning of these tensions.

The twin poles of expression are the two interdependent systems known as major and minor, based on the major and minor triads:

and the major and minor scales:

Four notes of the scale—1, 2, 4, and 5—are common to both; the antithesis derives mainly from the other three—3, 6, and 7, each of which exists in two versions, major and minor. It is a commonplace (though a much-disputed one) that the positive emotions (joy, confidence, love, serenity, triumph, etc.) are expressed by major music, and the negative emotions (sorrow, fear, hate, disquiet, despair, etc.) by minor music. Using Freud's basic categories of human emotion—pleasure and pain—we may say that there is a tendency to equate the major system with pleasure, the minor system with pain. Why should this be?

Before trying to answer this question, one must assure the reader that the ambiguities of the major-minor opposition will not be overlooked. The Dead March in *Saul* and the 'pessimistic' ending of Mahler's *Song of the Earth* are both in the major; the fairy music of Mendelssohn's *Midsummer Night's Dream* Overture and the almost flippant *Badinerie* from Bach's Suite No. 2 for flute and strings are both in the minor. People often single out a lively minor piece from the eighteenth century and say, 'Here is proof, if proof were needed, that minor music need not be sad'. The fact that proof does seem to be needed shows the inherent connection between the minor system and painful emotions; exceptions will have to be dealt with when the time arises. In the meantime, let us think for a moment of the effect that a slow tempo and/or chromatic inflections can have on the major system, and the effect that a swift, jaunty, or lilting tempo and a purely diatonic framework can have on the minor system; and pass on to establish and account for the basic pleasure-pain opposition between major and minor. This can only be achieved by an examination of the different tensions existing in the major and minor systems; let us begin with the all-important third.

THE THIRDS, MAJOR AND MINOR

That the major third should be found to express pleasure should surprise no one, since it is present, as we have noticed, early on in the harmonic series: it is nature's own basic harmony, and by using it we feel ourselves to be at one with nature.

This is another old truism which has been much disputed. In the first place, the major third was for two or three centuries treated as a discord. However, there is some reason to believe that this attitude towards it was not so much a musical as a theological one: the Ionian mode (the major system) belonged to secular music—as is obvious from its prevalence in the troubadours' songs—but the church preferred to adhere to the sterner modes. A decree like the following, issued in 1322 by Pope John XXII, at the age of eighty-two, shows how far ecclesiastical conservatism strove to prevent the perfectly natural tendency of the modes to crystallize harmonically into the major and minor systems: 'Certain disciples of the new school . . . truncate the melodies with hocquets, deprave them with discants, and sometimes even stuff them with upper parts made out of secular songs. So that often they must be losing sight of the fundamental sources of our melodies in the Anti- phoner and Gradual . . . *they may become entirely ignorant concerning the ecclesiastical tones, which they already no longer distinguish.* . . . In consequence, devotion, the true end of worship, is little thought of, and wantonness, which ought to be eschewed, increases. . . . Yet, for all this, it is not our intention to forbid, occasionally—and especially on Feast Days or in solemn cele- brations of the Mass—the use of some consonances, for example, *the octave, fifth, and fourth,* which heighten the beauty of the melody: such intervals therefore may be sung above the plain cantus ecclesiasticus, yet so that the integrity of the cantus itself may remain intact. . . . Used in such a way, the consonances would much more than by any other method both soothe the hearer and arouse his devotion, and also would not destroy religious feeling in the minds of the singers.' (My italics.)

Pope John was, of course, perfectly right. The 'other- worldly', non-tensional modal melodies could only retain their character when harmonized in octaves, fifths, and fourths. Even here, accidentals began to be used; and once the third was allowed, all the different modes began to transform themselves into the more 'human' Ionian and Aeolian (major and minor) modes by the inexorable logic of *musica ficta*: *one could not any longer distinguish between one ecclesiastical tone and another.* That some composers continued to do so until about 1600 was a triumph for their determined 'spirituality': in general, in music as in life, the natural tendency was towards secularity.

Pope John's references to 'secular songs' and 'wantonness' suggests that there was a long (unwritten) secular tradition of music in the major system: that popular musicians were singing and playing major music years before its insidious influence crept into the church. Strong support for this theory is given by the famous round 'Sumer is icumen in'. Scholars continue to argue, but its most probable date is about 1240. It consists of *a catchy tune, in jigging rhythm, in four-bar periods, in F major* (the original is actually notated with the key-signature of one flat); and when sung as a round, with its simple drone bass, it creates a harmony consisting of two alternating chords, the two chords produced by 'blow' and 'suck' on the modern mouth-organ—*tonic major triad* on the strong beats, and *second inversion of the dominant seventh, with added ninth,* on the weak ones. Such a straightforward combination of major tune, regular four-bar rhythm, and major harmony, does not turn up again in musical history until late in the fifteenth century, in the *chansons* of Binchois, for example.

The piece exists in the handwriting of a monk of Reading Abbey, with religious words written beneath the secular ones (which are in Wessex dialect); and on this account, attempts have been made to claim it as a piece of art-music by the monk himself. One can only say that such a theory goes all against the feel of the music, which is entirely 'secular' and 'folky'; and it is unaccountable that, if such an unusual masterpiece were produced by a church musician, it should have had to wait for two-and-a-half centuries before begetting any progeny. Common-sense supports the original theory about this work— that it was a piece of popular music, which so intrigued the Reading monk that he noted it down, and added ecclesiastical words, wondering whether it could be adapted to church use. One fears that if it ever was tried out, the effect on the Abbot must have been disastrous, and it must have been shelved. (This was a century *before* Pope John's decree!)

It seems most likely then, that popular musicians in Western Europe were already using the major triad naturally, to express joy, at a time when the church-composers were treating it as a 'discord', in an attempt to stave off the secularization of ecclesiastical art-music. But there is another, more serious reason offered against the equation 'major = pleasure'—the fact that in other systems of music, pleasure is apparently expressed by music of a decidedly minor character; in African and Oriental music, for example, and even in Spanish, Slav, and Balkan folk-music. An examination of this point will lead us straight to the heart of the problem.

It is clear, and needs no arguing, that the development of Western European music has gone hand in hand with the development of Western European man. Now, as has often been pointed out, the essential difference between Western European thought and that of other cultures is the concept of humanism: the belief in the individual's right to progress towards personal material happiness, which came to the fore at the Renaissance, and had its roots in still earlier times. The insistence on the 'rightness' of the sense of happiness has been accompanied by an insistence on the 'rightness' of the major third (see, for example, the finale of Beethoven's Fifth Symphony, written at the height of the period of confidence). It was for this reason that the church wished from the beginning to keep the note right out of ecclesiastical music. The major triad (and the major scale) belonged to the popular, secular life founded on the desire for pleasure; and this always threatened to undermine the religious ideal of a humble, God-centred existence, in which the emphasis was on the acceptance of one's lot in 'this vale of tears', and to replace it by the concept of a proud, man-centred existence, in which the emphasis was on personal happiness. In fact, of course, this eventually happened: with the increasing secularization of life, from the Renaissance onwards, the modes, with their lack of strong tensions, gave way more and more to the powerful tensions of the major and minor systems; eventually the centre of musical life moved from the church to the opera-house (seventeenth-century) and concert-hall (eighteenth century), and an increasingly secular society expressed its sense of human pleasure and pain by means of the major and minor systems, regular rhythms, and four-bar periods—until the tide turned. Ever since about 1850—since doubts have been cast, in intellectual circles, on the possibility, or even the desirability, of basing one's life on the concept of personal happiness— chromaticism has brought more and more painful tensions into our art-music, and finally eroded the major system and with it the whole system of tonality.

Only those who still believe strongly in the concept of happiness cling to the major triad. It is significant that the 'disruption of tonality', now in progress in Western European and American art-music, has not spread to the 'pop music' of the pleasure-biassed population at large, which still continues to thrive on the major triad. So does the 'average concert-goer', with his tendency to stick to the Bach-to-Brahms period. And in Soviet Russia, where the official philosophy is one of progress towards material happiness, experiments in non-tonal music are banned, and composers such as Shostakovich have been obliged to persevere with the major triad, to express 'optimism'.

Hence we may say that such diverse bodies as the medieval ecclesiastics, the seventeenth- and eighteenth-century aristocrats, the nineteenth-century late romantic composers, the contemporary *avant-garde* composers, the modern masses, the average concert-going public, and the official Soviet musical theorists—whatever their differences of opinion—all concur in the principle of equating the major triad with pleasure. Wherefore it is only natural that, outside the orbit of Western European civilization, and outside the period of its belief in the individual's right to progress towards material happiness, people whose lives have not been based on this attitude have not insisted on the major third, but have expressed their own assertion of vitality in different ways. This would explain the fierce 'minor' liveliness of some of the folk-music of the Spanish, Slav, and Balkan peoples, inured to a hard life; the melancholy minor tunes to gay words to be found in some of the folk-music of our once-oppressed peasantry; and the stern minor Glorias and Osannas of the God-fearing, self-abasing medieval church-composers. Explanations of the expressive qualities of utterly alien music, such as that of the Indian, African, Chinese, and Japanese peoples, would have to come from experts on such music: it suffices to say that, wherever Western European civilization has penetrated another culture, and set the people's thoughts along the road to material happiness, the tonal music of Western Europe has begun to oust the music of that culture from the people's affections. This is quite definitely going on at present in India, for example; and it is significant that, in a recent improvisation on a *raga*, by one of India's leading sitar-players, the normal 'bare fifth' drone bass of this purely indigenous music had taken unto itself a major third, and become a major triad.

It would seem, then, that our major third has established itself naturally as an expression of pleasure or happiness. Its character is so well-known that it hardly needs demonstrating (any music in a major key is bound to make much use of the major third); but a few examples may serve to isolate its basic expressive effect:

Ex. 25 (a)

In all the above quotations, the operative note is the major third. The 'Alleluia', the refrain of the early English part-song 'Now wel may we mirthes make', needs no comment. The Monteverdi is from his opera *L'Incoronazione di Poppea*; Drusilla, believing that Ottone loves her, sings 'Joyful is my heart'. Handel significantly turns to the major third, in *Saul*, when David sings of 'sweetest harmony'. The Beethoven is, of course, from the Ode to Joy in the Choral Symphony: the whole tune revolves round the major third. The Verdi is from the convivial *brindisi* in *La Traviata*. Wagner, like Handel, uses the major third to express the very idea of harmony—the pleasurable, amoral state of nature itself which begins *The Rhinegold*: in fact, he makes a musical demonstration of the natural 'rightness' of the harmonic series, for the horn-call is preceded by the low E flat on the basses, the harmonic series of which one can actually hear sounding before the horn picks out notes 2, 3, 4, 5, 6, 8, and 10 of the series as a theme. The Mahler is from his Second Symphony('I am from God, and to God will return'); the Stravinsky from his *Symphony of Psalms* (that paean of praise, Psalm 150). The extract from the finale of Shostakovich's Fifth Symphony is included as an example of 'optimistic' Soviet music: he himself said that the finale 'resolves the tragic and tense impulses of the earlier movements into optimism and the joy of living'. 'Polly-wolly-doodle' shows the use of the major third on a popular level.

What of the minor third? As we have seen, this note is not to be found in the lower reaches of the harmonic series; but it was soon used harmonically, sandwiched between the tonic and dominant, by analogy with the major third, to form a minor triad, and its effect was found to be quite different. Being lower than the major third, it has a 'depressed' sound, and the fact that it does not form part of the basic harmonic series makes it an 'unnatural depression' of the 'naturally happy' state of things (according to Western ideas). Western composers, expressing the 'rightness' of happiness by means of the major third, expressed the 'wrongness' of grief by means of the minor third, and for centuries, pieces in a minor key had to have a 'happy ending'—a final major chord (the 'tierce de Picardie') or a bare fifth. But eventually, the need to express the truth—cases of unrelieved tragedy—led composers to have an 'unhappy ending' in the minor.

If, at this point, it is wondered exactly what is meant by saying that the minor third functions expressively as a depression of the major third of the harmonic series—whether such a thing has a genuine aural significance, one cannot do better than indicate a context in which its effect is isolated, and can be clearly heard. In Act 2 of Wagner's *The Valkyrie*, when Wotan's world has collapsed about him, he laments his fate, i.e. gives vent to his sense of the 'wrongness' of his suffering, in a low-pitched recitative (*Als junger Liebe*) in A flat minor; this is supported only by a sustained low A flat on cellos and basses, the harmonic series of which can actually be heard sounding (in a 'live' performance) as far as note 5, i.e. as a ghostly major chord; and the minor third of the vocal line can be heard jarring with the major third of this chord, as a gloomy depression of it. Here one can experience the musical expression as an acoustical phenomenon, just as one can at the opening of *The Rhinegold* (Ex. 25f).

It is an undeniable fact that composers throughout the centuries, including those medieval[1] churchmen who used the minor key to express a stern, sedate, or sober satisfaction, have expressed painful emotions by bringing the minor third into prominence, melodically or harmonically (Ex. 26).

The *Dies Irae* needs no comment. The Josquin is the opening of his chanson 'Full of woe, and of melancholy'; it is 'in A minor', and the overlapping voices all arrive on the minor third for the word 'woe'. The Dowland is from his Second Book of Airs; the Bach from the St. Matthew Passion ('If my tears prove unavailing . . .'). The reliance on the minor third at the beginning of the 'doom-laden' first movements of Beethoven's, Tchaikovsky's and Mahler's fifth symphonies is characteristic (see also Ex. 28a and 28c). The first Verdi is the 'last trumpet' in the Dies Irae of his Requiem Mass; the second the opening of Iago's 'Credo' of hatred in *Otello*. The Richard Strauss is from *Till Eulenspiegel*—the point where Till is sentenced to death. The Stravinsky extracts are both from *Oedipus Rex*: in the first,

---

[1] I am using the word 'medieval' to describe a state of mind, not an exact historical period; church-music remained 'medieval' in outlook through much of the period of the Renaissance—certainly till near the end of the sixteenth century.

Jocasta, full of foreboding, inveighs against the oracles in a mad fury; the second is the fanfare heralding the announcement of her death. The 'St. Louis Blues' is a reminder that the minor third is one of the operative notes in the mournful blues style.[1]

The strong contrast between the 'natural' pleasurable major third and the 'unnatural' painful minor third has been exploited throughout our musical history. Inevitably, it suggests a sudden switch from pleasurable to painful feelings, or *vice versa* (Ex. 27).

The Dufay is from his last work, the *Salve Regina* composed on his deathbed, and sung at his funeral: 'Hail Queen of Heaven, hail Mistress of the Angels'—sung 'in C major' by tenors and basses—'have mercy'—here the striking in of the two upper parts with the trebles on the minor third, is electrifying—'on thy dying Dufay and let him not be cast into the burning fire!' The Weelkes is the opening of one of his Madrigals to Five Voices. The Monteverdi is from *L'Incoronazione di Poppea*: Ottone having undertaken to rid Ottavia of her enemies, she asks him to kill Poppea, whom he loves; she urges him on confidently, reminding him of his promise, and he replies bitterly, 'Did I promise that?' The Haydn is from a little part-song he wrote towards the end of his life, 'Gone is all my strength'—the first line of which he had printed on a card, to give visitors he was too tired to see: the words of the extract are, 'The roses have faded from my cheeks, Death is knocking at my door.' The Schubert is the piano postlude of the song 'Pause' in *Die schöne Müllerin*: the young miller, having heard the strings of his lute faintly vibrating in the breeze, has just been asking, 'Is it the echo of my love's sorrow? or the prelude to new songs?' The Verdi is from the last scene of *La Traviata*: Violetta, on her death-bed, sings, 'Let us go to a temple, Alfredo, and give thanks for your return', but the last word of

---

[1] This note actually originated as a kind of half-flat third (which would of course be none the less a depression of the 'natural' major third), owing to the tendency of the untrained Negro voice to 'worry' the third note of the scale, slurring or wavering between major and minor. When W. C. Handy wrote down the old blues tunes from his memory of how the Negroes had sung, he represented this strange sound by the minor third, either as a slow or quick grace-note leaning on to the major, or on its own. This minor third (often played simultaneously with the major one on the piano) became known as 'the blue note'; and the more of such notes, the 'meaner' the blues. (See Abbé Niles' early essay on the blues, published in 1926 as an introduction to a collection of pieces by Handy: reprinted in *Frontiers of Jazz*, ed. Toledano).

Ex. 27 *(a)*

the extract coincides with the last stage of her illness, and her vocal line resolves on to the minor instead of the major third, as the fatal fit of coughing seizes her. The Stravinsky is from *The Rake's Progress*: Anne is saying good-bye to her sweetheart Tom as he sets off for London (A sharp is indistinguishable from B flat as an expressive tonal tension, and the alternation of major and minor thirds reminds us that 'parting is such sweet sorrow'). The Britten is from *The Turn of the Screw*: the Governess, arrived on her dubious mission, walks towards the nurse and the two children, screwing up her courage (the tensely rhythmic violin theme, harmonized in B major, is derived from her previous utterance 'A strange world for a stranger's sake'), when suddenly her confidence deserts her (the violin goes on to the minor third unaccompanied, and plays the theme of her previous cry of 'Oh, why did I come?'). The Irving Berlin tune, from his music for the film *Follow the Fleet*, is a rare example of minor 'pop' music: the situation here concerns the projected suicide of a dancer, and the words continue with what is the song's actual title—'Let's face the music and dance'. (See also Ex. 26n, and Ex. 31a, d and f.)

Latterly, composers have discovered a different way of exploiting the expressive power of the opposition between the major and minor thirds: leaving the third fixed, and altering its character by shifting the tonic and dominant, or the tonic alone (Ex. 28).

The Tchaikovsky is the opening of his Fourth Symphony: the 'fateful' minor third of F (A flat) becomes for a moment the brightly glittering major third of E (as G sharp) before the music plunges back into the gloom of F minor. The Britten is from *Peter Grimes*: Ellen tries to coax Peter out of his bitter humour with a soothing phrase in E major; Peter treats her major third of E (G sharp) as the minor third of F (A flat), and sings her own phrase in F minor, hanging on to his bitter mood. The

Vaughan Williams examples are the opening and closing bars of his Sixth Symphony, which has aroused so much controversy as to the exact significance of its violently emotional impact. The opening telescopes both ways of placing major and minor thirds in opposition. It begins by rising up the scale of F as far as the minor third, which is immediately transformed into the major third of E (as G sharp) by the intrusion of a tonic E; but the E has a G natural (minor third) attached to it, and this pulls the theme's G sharp down to G natural; the gloomy opening minor third (the A flat) has become a major third falling to *its* minor third—an extraordinarily dark saying. The Symphony ends with alternations of E flat major and E minor triads, with the third uppermost—G in both cases; it is finally retained as the minor third in the final triad of E minor, 'which is, after all', as the composer said, 'the home key'—an even darker saying. (Incidentally, it is odd that all the passages quoted in Ex. 28 should be involved with the key of E; perhaps it is due to the old Phrygian scale—see Ex. 35f, g, and h.)

We can now consider the question of the specific kind of pleasurable and painful effects inherent in the major and minor thirds—their individual characters as emotive notes. They have one thing in common—their fixedness. In the triad, both function harmonically as an initial, intermediate, or final concord; used melodically, they are still fixed, in that they do not have to 'resolve' on to another note—so long as they retain their basic character as part of the triad, either by harmonization or implication. In this triadic context, they have a definite, settled quality; and so the major third expresses a feeling of settled, enduring pleasure, the minor third a feeling of settled, enduring pain. Hence the major third, when emphasized strongly in the triadic context, is the supremely satisfied, straightforwardly and contentedly joyful note, firmly 'looking on the bright side of things'; the minor third, emphasized strongly in the triadic context, is the supremely stern, straightforwardly and dignifiedly tragic note, firmly 'looking on the dark side of things'. (The effect of harmonizing the major and minor thirds as 'inessential' notes needing resolution—as in Ex. 25g, 26c, and 26n—will be dealt with later.)

THE SIXTHS, MAJOR AND MINOR

When we turn to the second most common note in the major-minor antithesis—the sixth—we find that the contrast functions in much the same way as with the third. Again, the major interval is used for pleasure, the minor one for pain. Here are a few examples of the expressive use of the major sixth (Ex. 29).

Ex. 29a is from a *rondeau* by a thirteenth-century French trouvère, who was executed in Paris in 1303: the words of the song are 'À vous douce' (To you, sweet lady) and the phrase quoted is sung to the word 'debonair'. The Morley is from the first of his Three-Part Canzonets of 1593, the Handel examples from *Saul* and *Messiah* respectively: none of these requires any comment. The Schubert is the ending of the song 'Rückblick' from *Die Winterreise*: after a stormy outburst of bitterness in G minor, the young man longs to return to the village he has left and to stand at peace outside the house of his faithless sweetheart. The Verdi is from the end of the love-duet in *Otello*, at the point where the lovers embrace and kiss: it is reintroduced at the end of the opera with a pathos which arises entirely out of dramatic considerations. The Mahler is the 'infinitely yearning' end of *The Song of the Earth*; the Delius, the opening of the first of the *Songs of Farewell*, reminds us that the 'lushness' of

his music is often due to his use of the chord of the 'added sixth'. The Britten is from *Peter Grimes*: amid the storm, Peter dreams of finding peace with Ellen. 'Roll out the Barrel' is quoted as an example of popular reliance on the major sixth.

The minor sixth has an entirely opposite effect:

The Machaut is from his motet 'With sighing heart, grieving I lament': the tone-painting of sighing will be noted in the broken vocal line. The De Salinis is from a three-part setting of the *Salve Regina*: 'Hail, Queen of Mercy . . . to thee we call, the exiled sons of Eve, weeping in this vale of tears. O holy one, pray for us.' The Donato is from his First Book of Madrigals: the words begin 'We unhappy nymphs'. The Monteverdi examples are from Arianna's Lament ('Leave me to die') and *L'Incoronazione di Poppea* (Seneca's friends plead with him: 'ah, to die, Seneca, no!'). The Bach quotations are the beginning of the St. John Passion, and the arioso 'O grief' from the St. Matthew Passion respectively (these two works are permeated with the minor sixth). The Beethoven is the opening of the uproar which begins the finale of his Ninth Symphony. The Schubert is from the song 'Gefror'ne Thränen' in *Die Winterreise*: 'O tears', sings the despairing lover, 'my tears'. The Verdi is from the 'Willow Song' in *Otello*. The Strauss, from the end of *Don Juan*, pinpoints the acutely painful effect of the minor sixth superbly: Strauss is said to have been tone-painting the stabbing of Don Juan in a duel, but the effect is of course an emotional (almost physical) one of anguish. The Debussy is from *Pelléas et Mélisande*: Mélisande begins to cry at the point where the minor sixth enters, and her husband Golaud asks her why she is unhappy. The Stravinsky is from *Oedipus Rex*: the chorus implore Oedipus 'save the city of Thebes from the plague of which it is dying'. For an example of popular use of the minor sixth, see Ex. 27j. See also the 'reveille' fanfare in the concentration camp in Schoenberg's *Survivor from Warsaw* (Ex. 3), and Palestrina's *Stabat Mater* (Ex. 17).

As in the case of the minor third, composers have exploited the effect of using the major and minor tensions in opposition (Ex. 31).

The Wilbye is from his Second Set of Madrigals: first 'My life so ill from want of comfort fares', then 'Draw on sweet night, best friend unto those cares . . .' The Beethoven is from *Fidelio*: Leonora sings of bitter tears, Marcellina of sweet tears. The Wagner is from *The Rhinegold*: the first phrase is the cry of delight of the Rhine-maidens for the joy-giving gold; the second is connected with the evil, oppressive and sorrow-giving power of the ring forged from the gold by one who has renounced

love. The Strauss is from *Don Quixote*: first, the sprightly, fantastic character of the simple country-gentleman of La Mancha; secondly, his transformation into the 'knight of the sorrowful countenance', prepared to battle and suffer in the cause of righting the world's wrongs. The Debussy is from *Pelléas*: it portrays the elusive, ambiguous character of Mélisande, who at one point in the opera says, 'I am happy, but I am sad' (cf. Ex. 30k). The Britten is from *Peter Grimes*: first, Peter describing his anguish on 'that evil day' when his apprentice died in his boat; secondly, his yearning for peace, against the background of the storm (the culmination of this phrase is shown in Ex. 29h). Incidentally, Ex. 31a, d, and f, above, also exploit the opposition between the major and minor thirds.

Now to consider the individual characters of the major and minor sixths. They differ from the thirds in that they are not fixed as concords in the triad, but have to 'resolve': hence when either is used in its basic character as a dissonance in relation to the tonic triad, it expresses, not a sense of pleasure or pain fixed and accepted, but of being in a state of flux, in a pleasurable or painful context. This effect is enhanced by the fact that in both cases the resolution is on to the dominant—the 'open' note in relation to the 'final' tonic. The feeling is thus not one of possession or acceptance, like the third, but of non-possession, non-acceptance, need.

The expressive effect works differently in the two cases. The minor sixth is an acute dissonance, due to its semitonal relationship to the dominant, and when it is exposed against the minor triad unresolved, it engenders a feeling of acutely painful dissatisfaction—a feeling of *anguish*, in fact. The extract from Strauss's *Don Juan* (Ex. 30j) shows this clearly, as does the ferociously dissonant climax of the first movement of Beethoven's *Eroica* Symphony, where the chord is the same (considered not technically, but expressively)—the A minor triad with added minor sixth. See also the extract from the Choral Symphony (Ex. 30f). When the minor sixth does resolve (Ex. 30b, f, and g; Ex. 31a, b, c, and f), the total effect of dissonance and resolution is of a burst of anguish.

The major sixth functions differently. It is not an acute dissonance, but a mild one, its relationship to the dominant being that of a tone, not a semitone. Nevertheless, when it is exposed against the major triad unresolved, it produces a pleasurable feeling of being unsatisfied; i.e. the feeling of a continuous pleasurable longing, or longing for pleasure. This is shown clearly by Peter Grimes's yearning for peace with Ellen (Ex. 29h); Delius's persistent use of the 'added sixth' to express nostalgia for past or otherwise unattainable joy (Ex. 29g—the words continue, 'how sweet the silent backward tracings . . .'); and Mahler's 'infinite yearning' (Ex. 29f). When the major sixth does resolve, the effect is of a burst of pleasurable longing: the trouvère's longing for the 'debonair' lady (Ex. 29a), the winter-journeyer's longing for peace with his beloved (Ex. 29d), Othello's longing for Desdemona's embrace (Ex. 29e), Marcellina's longing for Leonora, alias Fidelio (Ex. 31b), the Rhinemaidens' intense attraction towards the joy-giving gold (Ex. 31c).

One or two points remain to be clarified. The degree and exact nature of the joy, tragedy, pleasurable longing, or anguish which is conveyed in the various uses of the major and minor thirds and the major and minor sixths, is of course dependent on the vitalizing agents of time, volume, and intervallic tensions: we must leave these for the time being, while we establish the basic characters of the various tonal tensions. Returning to the sixths themselves, when either is used in a melodic pattern so that it does not resolve on to the dominant, the effect is merely of a brightening or darkening of the feeling of pleasure and pain: see the *Don Quixote* themes (Ex. 31d). With regard to the major sixth, we have already taken a slight step towards understanding the ambiguity of the 'major = pleasure' equation: longing for pleasure, although in one sense a pleasurable feeling, is in another sense a sad feeling, especially when the longing is not satisfied by resolution—hence the pleasurable sadness of Delius's added sixths. Hence also the luxuriant sadness of the ending of Mahler's *Song of the Earth*: the chord of the added sixth ends the work on a note of eternal, unsatisfied longing, for the sixth has been trying to rise through the major seventh to the tonic, and has failed (Ex. 29f).

The chief point needing clarification is the way in which harmony affects the expressive qualities of the thirds and sixths, making them partake of one another's characters. For example, when the minor third is harmonized, not by the tonic triad, but by the dominant major triad, it functions harmonically as the minor *sixth* of that triad, and the element of anguish enters in. In Dowland's 'Sorrow, stay' (Ex. 26c), the first note in the melody is B flat, and it is harmonized by the chord of G minor, as the minor third; but it has hardly established itself in this character, setting the basically tragic atmosphere, when the harmony immediately changes to the chord of the dominant—D major—making it *harmonically* a minor *sixth* of D: it resolves normally, moving down a semitone on to A, and the feeling of anguish is unmistakable. Likewise, when the minor sixth of a key is harmonized by the subdominant minor chord, it becomes the minor *third* of that chord, and takes on the more stoic character of that note, while still keeping the sense of anguish due to its melodic need for resolution: see the Donato quotation (Ex. 30c), where the minor sixth (F) would be more anguished if the harmony remained on A minor throughout. Incidentally, it is amusing to note that Browning, so often derided by musicians for his excursions into musical terminology, hit this nail right on the head in his poem 'On a Toccata of Galuppi's':

> *What? Those lesser thirds so plaintive, sixths diminished,*
> > *sigh on sigh,*
> *Told them something? Those suspensions, those solutions—*
> > *'Must we die?'*

Remember that Browning was writing of an Italian, and knew Italian; that *minore* means literally 'lesser'; and that, being a poet, he would not repeat the word but seize on a (regrettably ambiguous) synonym—'diminished'; and his 'faulty terminology' disappears, to reveal a remarkable insight into the expressive effect of the minor third and minor sixth treated as 'suspensions' needing 'solution'.

Again, when the major third is harmonized not as the third of the tonic triad, but as the major *sixth* of a dominant chord, particularly the chord of the dominant seventh, it becomes that well-known romantic stand-by, the 'dominant thirteenth', the 'yearning' effect of which is notorious: see the theme from Mahler's Second Symphony (Ex. 25g). (See also Ex. 27f.) Conversely, when the major sixth is treated harmonically as the major *third* of the subdominant chord, it acts quite firmly and joyfully *as* a third, and the feeling of longing is entirely removed from it: see Handel's Hallelujah Chorus (Ex. 29c). The effect is now of an increase of the sense of joy due to the sense of moving from one firm major third to another, harmonically speaking. Whereupon it becomes obvious that any note of the scale functions, from the expressive point of view, either melodically or harmonically, or in both ways at once. This ability to change the expressive quality or a note from moment to moment, and to give it two (or more) expressive qualities simultaneously, is the whole basis of the extraordinarily subtle emotional language of music. There are, of course, an infinite number of possible combinations and permutations, which would require not a book, but a library of books, to analyse. However, such an exhaustive investigation, even if possible, is not really desirable: the intention of the present book is not to provide an encyclopedia of every single term of musical expression, but merely to show, on the simplest possible level, that music does function as a language; hence our investigation will be confined to the basic elements. In consequence, even such fascinating elementary procedures as minor-triad-plus-major-sixth, and major-triad-plus-minor-sixth, will be ignored, not to mention such subtleties as the 'mystic chord' of Scriabin, and the dominant-minor-ninth-plus-eleventh (first inversion) that permeates Wagner's *Götterdämmerung* with a sense of ruin.

THE SEVENTHS, MAJOR AND MINOR

With the sevenths, there is no such clear antithesis as with the thirds and the sixths. Perhaps it is best to begin by showing that the minor seventh, like the minor third and sixth, is expressive of painful feelings:

The Binchois is from his *Missa de Angelis* (it is the only 'D minor' passage in the 'F major' Credo); the Morley from his little motet *Nolo mortem peccatoris* (I would not die a sinner's death); the Bach from the St. Matthew Passion (the contralto strikes in immediately with the words 'Ah Golgotha, unhappy Golgotha'). The Mussorgsky is from *Boris Godunov*: it is the orchestral passage ending the Simpleton's lament for the unhappy fate of Russia (note also the anguished minor sixths resolving on to the dominant). The Fauré is, of course, from his Requiem. The Puccini is from *La Bohème*: Mimi cries out woefully at Rudolf's groundless jealousy. The Debussy is the piano epilogue from his Charles d'Orléans setting 'Pour ce que plaisance est morte' (Since pleasure is dead). The Britten is the very end of *The Turn of the Screw*: the Governess, holding the child's dead body, utters woefully a snatch of the pathetic little Latin rhyme he used to sing, leaving the minor seventh floating in the air (the whole tune of this rhyme is permeated with minor sevenths; see Ex. 22). The Gershwin is the opening of his nostalgic song, 'The Man I Love', and is a reminder that the minor seventh is a subsidiary 'blue' note, and that this very phrase is a *cliché* of the blues style.[1]

The minor seventh can be seen above functioning in two different ways: with the major triad and with the minor. With the major, it is of course note No. 7 of the harmonic series (see Ex. 7)—one of the 'flaws' in nature's harmony, which undermines the stability of the tonic triad by pulling it down to the

[1] Abbé Hines, in the essay already quoted, mentions the Negroes' 'characteristic fondness for the flattened seventh'.

subdominant, and which Western European music has optimistically 'corrected' by insisting on the 'rightness' of note 15
to preserve the tonic triad's integrity (see Ex. 12). Consequently
when it is exposed in relation to the major triad and left unresolved (Ex. 32c, h, and j), it has a sad, empty sound: the
'flaw' is made apparent, and nothing is done to set it right.
In relation to the triad, it cannot rise to the upper tonic, but
is drawn towards the dominant; hence it is a kind of 'lost' or
homeless minor third on the dominant, whose immediate
resolution (on to the major sixth) brings no satisfaction. And
being only a mild dissonance (compare the acute minor sixth
with its fierce need for resolution) it is not expressive of violent
anguish, but of a gentle mournful feeling, which is made the
more woeful by its undermining of the normal joyful feeling
of the major triad supporting it. We have here another element
of ambiguity in the 'major = pleasure' equation: the Dead
March in *Saul* makes use of this very note both melodically
(B flat as the minor seventh in the key of C major, falling to
the major sixth and the dominant), and harmonically (F, the
fourth of C, is harmonized as the minor seventh on the chord
of G, and falls to *its* sixth and dominant):

Ex. 33

In other words, if the major third of this movement, *pianissimo*
and *grave*, establishes the joy that is perfect peace, the minor sevenths, harmonic and melodic, introduce the mournful element.

Used in relation to the minor triad, the minor seventh has
an even more melancholy character. Unable as ever to rise to
the upper tonic, it cannot even perform its normal though
unsatisfying resolution on to the major sixth, for this note has
no inherent connection with the minor triad; it is drawn down
further on to the minor sixth, note of anguish, and thus almost
immediately on to the dominant. Often enough, it does not
bother with this intermediate step, but falls the whole interval
of the minor third straight on to the dominant, with a woeful,
hopeless effect (Ex. 32d, e, f, and g; see also Ex. 58d).

The major seventh, of course, provides an antithesis to this

melancholy note, turning upwards optimistically to the tonic.
It was often thrown into harmonic battle with it by the Elizabethans (see Morley's use of it, Ex. 32b), but the minor seventh
always won the day, expressively speaking, through the very
fact that it jarred so 'painfully' (the word Morley used it to
illustrate) with the major seventh and was forced down on to
its melancholy resolution through the minor sixth to the
dominant. Its miserable defeat was far more powerfully expressive than the major seventh's simple and logical rise to the
tonic. In other words, the Elizabethans opposed the two notes
to bring out to the full the mournful character of the minor
seventh and give it a more painful quality, not to intensify the
optimistic character of the major seventh.

In fact, the major seventh has rarely been isolated expressively, apart from its natural function of being a stepping-stone
for the major sixth to rise optimistically to the tonic. This is
due to the fact that its tension in relation to the triad is a semitonal one upwards to the tonic, so that when it is exposed in
relation to the major triad, the 'longing for pleasure' it evokes
is so violent as to be almost painful. It is, moreover, a longing
for pleasure in a context of finality, aiming at the tonic, as
opposed to the major sixth's longing for pleasure in a context
of flux, aiming at the dominant. A single example will suffice:

O ter-ra ad-di-o, ad-di-o O val - le   di   pian - ti!

In this final duet of the two lovers in *Aida*, who are about to
die immured, they bid 'farewell to this vale of tears'; their
violent longing for joy finds painful expression in the initial leap
of a major seventh: the hopelessness of their longing is conveyed by the resolution to the upper tonic being immediately
nullified by a fall to the dominant; by the process being
repeated a fourth *lower*—still a leap to the *major seventh* on the
dominant, this time resolving quite definitely up to *its* tonic,
which is, however, immediately felt to be still only the dominant
of the main key; and lastly by the fall to the *minor* seventh on
the dominant, a semitone *below* the last major seventh, and the
'hopeless' fall to the lower tonic. Clearly, by choosing the right

tensions, a composer can make the major key express a considerable intensity of pain. However, the equation 'major = pleasure' remains true, in the sense of a basic context; just as Handel's Dead March moves from peace to triumph, through mournful feelings, so Verdi's lovers are glad to die together, painful though their unsatisfied longing to live may be. In the same way, we may say that Mahler and Delius both enjoyed their nostalgic longing for the infinite, embodied in the major triad with unresolved major sixth.

One last word about the major seventh: Delius, of course, found it most useful, added to the major triad, *pianissimo*, unresolved, to express his obsessive nostalgia (the opening chord of *On Hearing the First Cuckoo in Spring*). And Sibelius found it an admirable note to add to the tonic triad, *fortissimo*, and to resolve, to end his Seventh Symphony in a mood of intense aspiration and affirmation.

Once again, we must mention that our two contrasted intervals, like the thirds and the sixths, can change their character by being harmonized by a chord other than the tonic triad. The major seventh, of course, features mainly as the major third of the dominant chord, and acts joyfully as a major third in its own right. The minor seventh is often harmonized as the minor third of the dominant minor chord, and acts sternly as a minor third in its own right: this use of the note accounts for the austere nature of modal and neo-modal music (see Ex. 32a).

THE SECONDS, MAJOR AND MINOR

As with the sevenths, there is no clear-cut antithesis between the major and minor seconds. And again, we may begin by showing the painful nature of the minor interval (Ex. 35).

Ex. 35a is from a fourteenth-century Mass 'Le Serviteur'; the Josquin from one of his motets, 'Tribulation and anguish came upon me'. The Luzzaschi is from a madrigal published in 1594: the words are: 'Grievous sufferings . . . unhappy I lament'. The Purcell is the 'Plaint' from *The Fairy Queen*: 'O let me for ever weep'; the Mozart from *Così fan tutte*—the point where Ferrando is in a fury of grief at his betrayal by Dorabella. The Strauss is from *Don Juan* again: either portraying Don Juan's death, or, according to others, expressing the feeling of

Lenau's lines on the ageing libertine, which preface the score—
'the fuel is burnt out, and all is cold and dark upon the hearth.'
The Stravinsky is from the *Symphony of Psalms*—a setting of a
verse from Psalm 39: 'Hear my prayer, O Lord, and give ear
unto my cry; hold not thy peace at my tears.' The Vaughan
Williams is from the enigmatic finale of his Sixth Symphony
(in E minor) which commentators have found evocative of lost
worlds, the end of mankind, and general desolation. The Britten
is from *The Turn of the Screw*: that lost soul and sinister ghost,
Miss Jessel, sits brooding on past wrongs, and revenge to come
(G flat actually forms the bass throughout).

Properly speaking, as we have mentioned, the minor second
is not part of our minor scale at all (see Ex. 24). It is a survival

from the old Phrygian mode (white-note scale on E), the only one to begin with a rise of a semitone (Ex. 35f, g, and h avow this in their different ways, by being 'in E minor'); but composers of all periods have drawn on its intensely expressive quality. Its tension is obviously akin to that of the minor sixth: it is an acute dissonance in relation to the minor triad, but whereas the sixth is drawn by semitonal tension down to the dominant, the minor second is drawn by semitonal tension down to the tonic. This means that whereas the minor sixth is an expression of anguish in a context of flux, the minor second is an expression of anguish in a context of finality; in other words, the minor sixth expresses an active anguish, the minor second a hopeless anguish. The contrast between the two is shown in the Josquin quotation: the E flat falling to D has a much more despairing quality than the B flat falling to A. The Stravinsky isolates the note in its true character. The movement opens with the tonic triad of E minor, but the second remains a minor one throughout: the music is definitely in the Phrygian mode seen through modern eyes, and the falling of the minor second to the tonic admirably expresses the weeping supplication of the psalmist. The Strauss example is a subtle use of the note in its dual character: the F begins as both an 'anguished' minor sixth in A minor (by harmonic implication), and a 'hopeless' minor second on E major (by actual harmonization), but when it falls to the tonic of an E minor chord, its true quality of final despair is isolated in retrospect. The Vaughan Williams example shows the sense of unrelieved hopelessness to be obtained by exposing the minor second in relation to the tonic triad, unresolved (note the fact that it is coupled with the mournful minor seventh). The Purcell, Mozart, and Britten examples demonstrate the poignant effect derived from bringing the minor second into close conjunction with the 'yearning' major seventh; and the Faugues and Luzzaschi phrases show how, by harmonizing the minor second as a minor third on the minor seventh, the same procedure can be given a sense of dignity (both of these are minor thirds, becoming minor seconds retrospectively, by means of the Neapolitan modulation).

The major second is rarely isolated as an expressive tension: it is largely a neutral note, common to both major and minor systems, bridging the melodic gap between the tonic and the third, and strengthening the context, but not functioning expressively in its own right. In latter times it actually has been isolated, and is found to function similarly to the major sixth. A mild dissonance in relation to the major triad, drawn towards the tonic by the tension of a whole tone, it has the same 'longing' quality as the major sixth's tension towards the dominant; except that, being connected with the 'fixed' and 'final' tonic, its longing is not in a context of flux, but in a context of finality. Mahler has used the major second in this way:

The first phrase is from the end of *The Song of the Earth*: the final movement is called *The Farewell*, and symbolized for Mahler his own approaching farewell to the world (he knew he had not long to live); the last section expresses his infinite longing—'The lovely earth, everywhere, blooms in spring and grows green again, everywhere and for ever shines the blue horizon, for ever, for ever' (the words of this section are Mahler's own). The major second that will not resolve down to the tonic, as well as the major sixth that has been trying to push up through the major seventh to the upper tonic and failed, and still will not resolve on to the dominant (Ex. 29f), remain suspended on the air at the end of the work, expressive of infinite yearning, at once glad, peaceful, and sorrowful. The second phrase is the same procedure carried forward into the main theme of the first movement of the valedictory Ninth Symphony, the work which followed.

Also in latter times, the major and minor seconds have been used in antithesis:

The Wagner is the 'grave old tune, with its sound of lament' that awakens Tristan in Act 3 of the opera. The theme is unaccompanied, but the major second is 'harmonized' by implication as a dominant on the dominant, and has the strong, 'open' character of that note; it falls melodically to the minor second, using it expressively as a depression of the major one, exposing it long enough for its sadness to take good effect, and letting it fall poignantly to the major seventh. (Incidentally, the whole theme makes powerfully expressive use of all four minor tensions—third, sixth, seventh, and second.) (See also Ex. 27h, last bar.) The Debussy, from the end of Act 1 of *Pelléas*, works the other way round: Pelléas remarks to the newly-arrived Mélisande that he will be leaving to-morrow, and she replies, regretfully, 'Oh! why are you leaving?' The minor second expresses her regret; the major second takes over, expressing her hope and longing for Pelléas to stay; and remaining suspended, together with the major sixth, keeps open that longing towards the future. For his last chord, Debussy makes use of the same procedure as Mahler, but much more reticently: Mahler leans heavily on to the major second in a drawn-out appoggiatura, over and over again, with the contralto (or baritone) voice; Debussy merely places the note, quietly, once, with a light soprano voice. The basic effect is still one of (gentle) longing; and again the context is one of finality, hinting at what is going to happen—Pelléas stays.

THE FOURTHS

Here we move away from the major-minor antithesis, for the normal fourth is common to both systems, and has no minor equivalent; but it has a companion in the form of the sharp fourth. Before examining the expressive effects of these two notes in relation to the triad, it will be best to treat them in their more prevalent character—as minor and major sevenths on the dominant.

A glance at Exs. 12 and 13 will show what is meant. Just as the minor seventh on the tonic (B flat in the key of C) pulls us down to the key of the subdominant, and the major seventh (B natural) lifts us back to the tonic, so the sharp fourth (F sharp) lifts us up to the key of the dominant, and the normal fourth

(F), pulls us back down to the tonic. Now we have mentioned that, owing to the importance of the minor seventh in the harmonic series (B flat, note 7), it is 'easy' and indeed 'defeatist' to fall into the subdominant; quite possible to stay in the tonic, by 'optimistically' insisting on the major seventh (note 15); and extremely 'difficult' to rise into the dominant, insisting on the 'optimistic' version of note 11 (F sharp) against the 'pessimistic' version of it (F natural) and the 'defeatist' note 7 (B flat). Hence, the sharp fourth, F sharp, acts as an accessory and more powerful major seventh on the dominant, its semitonal tension towards the dominant being alone capable of performing the 'heroic' task of lifting us into the key of the dominant. Beethoven pinpoints this character of the note unmistakably in the finale of his Fifth Symphony:

Ex. 38

Allegro

Beethoven, 1804

ff (Clarinets, oboes, bassoons, horns)

Functioning in this way, the sharp fourth obviously expresses the same violent longing (upward semitonal tension in a major context) as the major seventh, but not in a context of finality; rather in a context of pushing outwards and upwards, aspiring towards something higher. It is significant that the use of the note in this way reached a climax with Beethoven and his intense humanistic aspirations.

By contrast, the normal fourth preserves the *status quo*, keeping the music in the tonic key. Often, it functions as a neutral note, bridging the melodic gap between the third and the dominant; otherwise, it falls, like the minor seventh, by a semitone, the difference being that it falls on to the contented third. It is in fact the only note in the major scale that has a downward semitonal tension in relation to the tonic triad, and it almost invariably acts, in reality or by implication, as a minor seventh on the dominant; thus it takes on a little of the mournful character of the minor seventh, while remaining essentially untragic, since melodically it resolves on to the contented major third. Hence it is one means of achieving a feeling of pathos in the major key, which we have already seen in the Dead March in *Saul* (Ex. 33). Here are a few more examples:

Ex. 39(a)
(Slow)   Thibaut, King of Navarre, 13th cent.
(*mf*) Tuit mi de - sir et tuit mi___ grief tor - ment...

(b)
(Slow)   English song c. 1500   (c) Largo   (Violins)   Handel, 1741
(*p*) A - dieu, a - dieu, my har-tis lust...   (*p*) He was des-pis-ed...

(d)
Andante mosso   espress.   Verdi, 1852
(*f*) L'a - mo - re d'Al - fre - do___ per - fi - no___ mi man - ca

(e)
Molto adagio   Mahler, 1909
(Violins) *P*   *molto espress.*

(f)
Moderato   Irving King, 1925
(*mf*) Show me the way to go home,

Ex. 39a is a troubadour song: the words are 'All my desire, and all my bitter grief'. Since this has no harmonic implications, the simple melodic semitonal tension is obviously sufficient to express pathos: a downward semitonal tension, in any context, will always be found to convey at least a slight feeling of sadness. The Handel example, from *Messiah*, needs no comment, except that it is repeated over and over; the music then uses the true minor seventh, and eventually plunges into real anguish, with a threefold repetition of the minor third harmonized as a minor sixth in the dominant ('A man of sorrows and acquainted with grief'). The Verdi is from the closing scene of *La Traviata*; Violetta, on her death-bed, believing that Alfredo has deserted her, sings 'His love fails me at the end'. The Mahler, the main theme of the finale of his valedictory Ninth Symphony, uses the fourth to pathetic effect: in bar 4 it is harmonized as a minor sixth of the B flat minor triad, clashing with the dominant of the triad, F. Note also the melodic appearance of the minor third, disguised as E natural; moreover, the second F in the theme is harmonized as the 'yearning' dominant thirteenth, and the bass-note below the first D flat in the theme is B double-flat, the minor sixth. These subtleties show clearly how the major system not only contains an element of pathos in the 4–3 suspension, but can be packed full of pathos by introducing, melodically or harmonically, tensions from the minor-system. 'Major = pleasure' can only be true on a large scale when the music is entirely diatonic and steers clear of the 4–3 suspension. 'Show me the way to go home' demonstrates the pathetic use of the fourth on a popular level. (See also Ex. 27f.)

This is the proper place to mention the only other downward semitonal tension in the major scale—that between the tonic and the major seventh. When the major seventh is harmonized as a major third on the dominant, and the tonic is suspended on to it, the effect is akin to that of the 4–3 suspension, and has a similar effect of pathos, especially when the dominant chord takes its own *minor* seventh, i.e. is a dominant seventh. The sense of pathos of 8–7 is more acute than that of 4–3, since the 'resolution' is on to the major seventh, which is itself a dissonance requiring resolution.

Ex. 40 *(a)* — Andante con moto — *(p)* Che fa - rò sen-za Eu - ri - di - ce? Che fa - rò? Dov' an - drai? — Gluck, 1762

(b) Largo — *(p)* (Oboe and cello) — Haydn, 1787

The Gluck, Orpheus's lament for his lost Euridice, is a well-known crux in the problem of musical expression. How can such a simple, diatonic, major melody express grief? In fact, it achieves a purely classical pathos, by suspending the tonic on to the major seventh, as a 4–3 progression on the dominant, in the essentially pleasurable context of the major key. The pathos is even enhanced, in a purely classical way, by being in a major context; since this conveys the natural joy of life which is undermined by the pathetic suspension. The same effect is noticeable in the Dead March in *Saul* (Ex. 33): it is significant that both pieces are in the key of C, so often used to suggest the 'simple light of common day'. Tne superb Haydn melody, the main theme of the Largo of his 88th Symphony, has the same effect of classical pathos, derived from both 8–7 and 4–3 (and later 2–1 on G); it is rendered most expressive by the accent on the 'inessential' note, yet remains nobly serene owing to its slow, even rhythm and the logical sequence of its phrases. This melody can move a listener almost to tears that have nothing to do with tragedy or anguish; in fact it brings to mind Wordsworth's phrase about the 'thoughts that do often lie too deep for tears'. No wonder that Brahms, on hearing it, should say, 'My Ninth Symphony must be like that!'

THE AUGMENTED FOURTH OR DIMINISHED FIFTH

The augmented fourth and the diminished fifth are, of course, the same note; and this note is the same as the sharp fourth, but treated in a different way—as a note on its own, unconnected with the major and minor triads or scales, but simply related to the tonic. Its relationship to the tonic is that particular tension which we have mentioned earlier as embodying the 'flaws' in the harmonic series, and in the whole musical scheme of things—*diabolus in musica*. The interval may be seen in Ex. 9: there it appears as the tension between the major seventh and normal fourth of the major scale (B and F in the key of C); but, as we have seen, these notes were always carefully integrated into the system of tonal tensions as 'inessential' notes resolving on to the tonic and the major third (C and E)— the 'flaw' was always corrected. When composers have wished to isolate this tension, they have usually done so by taking the interval between the tonic and the sharp fourth: this should normally act as a modulation to the dominant (see Ex. 38); but when it is exposed without any resolution of any kind, and becomes an 'essential' note, a tension in its own right, it becomes *diabolus in musica* indeed, for it acts as a 'flaw' which destroys the integrity of the tonic key—thus removing the music outside the categories of human joy and sorrow inherent in the major and minor systems. *Diabolus in musica;* the flaw in the scheme of things; it is hardly surprising that composers should have used it to embody 'Old Nick' himself, his deputies, substitutes, and influences:

The absence of medieval examples here is not surprising: the old Catholic composers naturally shunned the devil and all his ways. The Buxtehude is from his *Last Judgment*—the wailing of a lost soul in hell (minor seventh, minor sixth, augmented fourth, the latter being resolved according to the niceties of those days). The Mozart is from *Don Giovanni:* the Don offers the Statue his hand—'Here it is'—but when he grasps it he cries out in horror, moving to the diminished fifth. The chord accompanying his cry—the chord of the diminished seventh— is, of course, made up of two interlocking diminished fifths. The Weber quotations are from *Der Freischütz:* the opera is in C, the 'Wolf's Glen' scene opens in F sharp minor; here the music moves from F sharp minor (in the bar's rest, the clock strikes midnight), via the diminished fifth A to E flat (in the next bar's rest Caspar calls on the Black Huntsman Samiel to appear) to C major (that key is not conclusively established until the arrival of Samiel ten bars later). The second Weber example is from the 'Wild Hunt' in the same scene. The first Berlioz is the opening of the 'Dream of a Witches Sabbath' in the Fantastic Symphony; the second and third are from *The Damnation of Faust*—Mephistopheles' entrance, and his invocation to the spirits of fire 'I require your aid'. The Liszt extracts are the openings of his Dante Sonata and Dante Symphony (both begin in the Inferno) and of his Mephisto Waltz No. 2. The Wagner quotations all portray elements of evil in *The Ring:* the cursing of the ring by Alberich, the devil in the work's cosmology; the dragon Fafner; and the call to arms by Hagen, Alberich's misbegotten son. The first Gounod is from *Faust*—the Church Scene, with Mephistopheles standing inside a pillar, enjoining the praying Marguerite to despair. The second is the main theme of his oratorio *Mors et Vita:* of this phrase, Gounod said in his preface, 'Its sternness gives expression both to the sentences of Divine Justice and to the sufferings of the condemned' (in other words, to damnation, as experienced from both ends). The Saint-Saëns is Death 'tuning' his fiddle, calling the skeletons from their graves, in *Danse macabre;* the Dargomijsky is from *The Stone Guest,* which tells the Don Juan story (the phrase quoted is connected with the Statue, and occurs *ad nauseam*); the Elgar refers to the demons in *Gerontius.* The Boito examples are from *Mefistofele:* the first is from the 'wild hunt' in the *Walpurgisnacht* scene; the second occurs where Mephistopheles stands behind the ageing Faust 'like an incubus'. Busoni is represented by *Doktor Faust:* Faust's invocation, 'Lucifer, hither to me!', and Faust's question to Mephistopheles, 'Will you serve me?' The first Stravinsky is the penultimate phrase of the Triumphant March of the Devil which ends *The Soldier's Tale*: the second occurs in *The Rake's Progress*, where the rake, Tom, is in the graveyard with Nick Shadow (the devil), who has come to claim his soul. Both the Bartók phrases are from his *Cantata Profana*, which tells of the nine sons of one father who went roving in the forest, and fell under an evil enchantment that turned them into deer; the second phrase accompanies the words 'they got lost in the forest'. The Vaughan Williams quotations are: first, Satan's Dance of Triumph in *Job*; second, Christian's cry in the City of Damnation in *The Pilgrim's Progress*. All three Britten examples are from *The Turn of the Screw*: Mrs. Grose's description of the horrible death of the evil valet, Peter Quint; the appearance of the ghost of Miss Jessel, the equally evil late governess; and the latter's luring call to the child Flora.

It is unnecessary to go into the various ways in which the augmented fourth (or diminished fifth) is used above: they all work to the same end. They are not isolated fragments, but, except for the Buxtehude, Mozart, Saint-Saëns and second Stravinsky, are thematic and pervasive. Almost all of them set the tension between the *tonic* and *its* sharp fourth. What is extraordinary is that two-thirds of them are concerned with the notes B, B flat, F and F sharp—the 'flaws' in the harmonic series on C (the 'Ionian' white-note key of 'natural' joy), or with C itself and *its* augmented fourth, F sharp. Of thirty-seven uses, above, of the augmented fourth or diminished fifth, ten are C to F sharp; eight F to B; seven B flat to E; and only twelve are divided amongst the other three possibilities. Note that the second Boito uses E to B flat (A sharp), B to F (E sharp) and F sharp to C; the first Vaughan Williams combines F and B with C and F sharp; the first Britten B and F with B flat (A sharp) and E.

All of which makes one wonder how much composers have been influenced by the phrase *diabolus in musica*. Only Gounod had anything to say about his augmented fourth; but he did not mention it by name, and was obviously under the illusion that he had made a profound discovery! To try and elucidate the point, I am forced back on to my own experience; I trust

I shall be forgiven if for a moment I mention small music in connection with great. When I made a setting of Burns's poem *Tam O'Shanter*, I had led Tam as far as the church and reached the key of F; I expected some 'inspiration' to descend on me to express the *diablerie* of the 'witches and warlocks' dancing Scots reels in the house of God, and it descended in the shape of a bagpipe drone not of F and C, but of F and B natural. The interval became pervasive, and as the dance got wilder, the music moved into B major, apparently of its own accord. At that time, although the term *diabolus in musica* was of course familiar to me, I had not yet begun to investigate the properties of the augmented fourth or diminished fifth as an expressive tension, much less made the above collection of musical demonology. Hence, if it is admitted that the mysterious thing known as 'inspiration' functions in the same way with composers of no account as with the great, the all-important difference lying in the quality of it and the ability to build on it, it would seem likely that composers have turned unconsciously to this interval to express the devilish, *for its actual sound*, which derives from the 'flaw' in the harmonic series, just as they have turned instinctively to the major third for its naturally joyful sound.

There is an extension of the connotation of the augmented fourth, in that composers have also used it to express alien, eerie, hostile, and disruptive forces. For example, Vaughan Williams employed it for the frozen wastes of his *Sinfonia Antartica*; Britten for the icy winter which opens his *Spring Symphony*; Holst for his 'Mars, the Bringer of War' in *The Planets*. In as much as these forces are inimical to mankind, they may be regarded as springing from the 'negative' principle of the universe. With regard to Mars, nothing need be said in this age; as for the spirit of the cold, we may remember that Mephistopheles, in Goethe's *Faust*, expresses a desire that life shall dissolve into nothingness; and, as we know, when that happens, the sun will have burnt out, and cold will conquer all.

We have now isolated the basic expressive functions of all twelve notes of our scale, and it would be best to summarize them here:

Tonic: Emotionally neutral; context of finality.

Minor Second: Semitonal tension down to the tonic, in a minor context: spiritless anguish, context of finality.

Major Second: As a passing note, emotionally neutral. As a whole-tone tension down to the tonic, in a major context, pleasurable longing, context of finality.

Minor Third: Concord, but a 'depression' of natural third: stoic acceptance, tragedy.

Major Third: Concord, natural third: joy.

Normal Fourth: As a passing note, emotionally neutral. As a semitonal tension down to the major third, pathos.

Sharp Fourth: As modulating note to the dominant key, active aspiration. As 'augmented fourth', pure and simple, devilish and inimical forces.

Dominant: Emotionally neutral; context of flux, intermediacy.

Minor sixth: Semitonal tension down to the dominant, in a minor context: active anguish in a context of flux.

Major sixth: As a passing note, emotionally neutral. As a whole-tone tension down to the dominant, in a major context, pleasurable longing in a context of flux.

Minor Seventh: Semitonal tension down to major sixth, or whole-tone tension down to minor sixth, both unsatisfactory, resolving again down to the dominant: 'lost' note, mournfulness.

Major Seventh: As a passing note, emotionally neutral. As a semitonal tension up to the tonic, violent longing, aspiration in a context of finality.

THE AMBIGUITIES OF THE MINOR SYSTEM

Before proceeding to an analysis of the expressive functions of volume, time, and pitch-as-direction, one more question remains to be answered. It has been shown how the naturally joyful effect of the major system can be undermined by two of its own tensions—4–3 and 8–7—and more powerfully by introducing tensions from the minor system; hence the ambiguities inherent in the equation 'major = pleasure' need no longer trouble us. But what of the ambiguities of the 'minor = pain' equation?

It has been said above that the *degree* of emotion expressed by a particular note depends on volume, time, and intervallic tensions. Hence, if the minor third 'looks on the darker side of things' this may function as tragedy, as stoic acceptance, as sternness; or to a lesser degree, as gravity, soberness, seriousness. No one would deny that it is possible to experience a grave, sober, or serious pleasure; and herein enters the ambiguity. Thus, the medieval church composers, setting the Gloria or Osanna, usually employed a fairly lively tempo, but often felt it incumbent upon themselves to use the minor system, remembering that they were not angels or blessed spirits enjoying the pleasures of heaven, but men praising God from this 'vale of tears':

Ex. 42

Likewise, to a philosophic mind, pleasure must not be unbounded, and sometimes becomes so sober that it loses the sense of joy altogether.

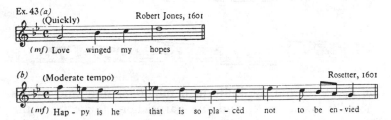

The words of both the poems set here are worth quoting, as examples of 'taking one's pleasures sadly':

JONES: *Love winged my hopes and taught me how to fly*
        Far from base earth, but not to mount too high;
        For true pleasure
        Lives in measure . . .

ROSETTER: *Though far from joy, my sorrows are as far,*
           And I both between.
           Not too low, nor yet too high
           Above my reach would I be seen.
           Happy is he that is so placèd,
           Not to be envied, nor to be disdained or disgracèd.

Here we face a philosophy that conflicts with Western Europe's general insistence on the 'right to be happy', regarding such an insistence as *hubris* inviting the inevitable *nemesis*; and to express the idea that 'true pleasure lives in measure', the major system is shunned in favour of the minor one, *with a light rhythm and moderate tempo*. The Rossetter, however, like so many of his ayres, falls unmistakably into pathos. Sometimes, of course, we must beware of jumping to conclusions. Morley's madrigal, 'Hark, Alleluia', is in the minor, and quite definitely sorrowful: but naturally so, for it is a requiem for Henry Noel, who is imagined making music with the angels in heaven, while Morley laments his loss on earth.

Moving outside the realm of the golden mean, we shall find that composers have expressed a lively but still essentially serious pleasure by the minor system plus a lively or jogtrot tempo, and a light texture and tone-colour:

The *Badinerie* from the Suite in B minor for flute and strings is usually taken *presto*, and the harpsichord fugue from the 'Forty-Eight' at a jogtrot *moderato*. The former uses none of the really painful tensions of the minor key; in the latter, no one will deny that there is a slight sense of sadness in the 'dying fall' from the minor sixth.

Again, Handel expresses a sense of the grave pleasure of being religiously comforted, by the minor key plus a lilting tempo:

This heart-easing melody from *Messiah* again uses none of the really painful minor tensions, and in fact by the end of the phrase quoted is already in the relative major of B flat, and stays there much of the time.

Monteverdi uses the minor system in two superficially pleasurable contexts, in *L'Incoronazione di Poppea*:

Ex. 46(a)
(Moderate tempo)   Monteverdi, 1642

(p) A - pri, a - pri un bal - con, Pop - pe - - - a . . .

(b)
(Slow)   Monteverdi, 1642

(p)
O - bli - vi - on so - a - ve

The first example is Ottone's serenade to the sleeping Poppea: 'Open, open a window, Poppea.' Serenades are very often in the minor system, and this one, like Schubert's and many others, may be taken as expressing the lover's pangs, the desire which is a pain to him until it is satisfied: he is attempting to arouse the lady's pity, by letting her know of his sad and lonely state without her. The second example is the lullaby sung to Poppea by her nurse, Arnalta; it is accompanied by the descending phrase 8–7–6–5 in the minor, a term of musical vocabulary normally expressing a falling-away from the joy of life, as we shall see later. We must remember that sleep, at that period, was often called 'Death's brother' (here it is called 'oblivion'); and that, in any case, to fall asleep is to lose all vitality. Moreover, in the opera, it seems likely that Poppea's sleep will be the sleep of death, for Ottone is on his way to kill her.

One last example is perhaps the most subtle of all the uses of the minor system for apparently pleasurable effect:

Ex. 47
Allegro di   Mendelssohn, 1827
molto
(Woodwind)   (Violins)
pp

Mendelssohn's fairies in *A Midsummer Night's Dream*: nothing tragic, stoic, grave, sober, or serious here! Why then is the minor system so superbly right? First, it should be said that the tempo is swift, the volume *pianissimo*, the tone colour and texture as light and feathery as possible: in such a context the seriousness of the minor system is reduced to a minimum. Nevertheless, a faint whiff of melancholy is present; yet we imagine that fairies are entirely 'happy'. Could it be that there is, for human beings, an infinitesimal trace of pathos attached to these tiny creatures, who certainly cannot experience human joy? Perhaps Mendelssohn's inspiration provided him with this minor music because he had an unconscious feeling of the strangeness and very slight sadness evoked by even the brighter manifestations of the spirit world. Or perhaps we may leave this as an isolated miracle of musical expression, entirely inexplicable in words.

Apart from this miracle, the foregoing examples clarify the ambiguities of the 'minor = pain' equation. And we can see now that a composer does not express pleasure or pain simply by using the major or minor system, but by bringing forward and emphasizing certain tensions in these systems, in certain ways. This emphasis and these ways derive entirely from the use of the vitalizing agents—volume, time and intervallic tensions. In each of our examples of the uses of a single tonal tension by different composers, the differences may seem more important than the resemblances (which explains why the fact that music is a language has been obscured for so long): these differences are due to the use of the vitalizing agents, and it is through these that a composer, and indeed a whole generation of composers, stamp their decisive individuality on the raw material of the tonal tensions.

THE VITALIZING AGENTS

The tonal tensions are the purely musical thing about music; so, in a less fundamental way, are the characterizing agents of tone-colour and texture. The *vitalizing agents*, however, also function in another field—that of speech; and we can get a broad idea of their effect by briefly considering their behaviour in this field. If we think of a group of people talking, it is obvious that, the more excited they become, the louder, quicker, and higher their voices will get; the more relaxed they become, the softer, slower, and lower they will speak. And the effects of the three different elements can be roughly isolated as follows. The *louder* a person speaks, the more *emphasis* he gives to what he is saying; the *quicker* he speaks, the more *animated* he is becoming; the *higher* his voice rises, the more he is *asserting* himself.

The same correspondences exist in the field of physical action:

compare the high state of excitement inherent in running up-hill, quickly and noisily (by stamping one's feet), with the state of relaxation inherent in walking downhill, slowly and quietly (by stepping gently). Again, upwards = more assertion; faster = more animation; louder = more emphasis. Hence it is that the high, rising, loud, swift scales at the climax of Beethoven's Overture *Leonora No. 3* are about the most invigorating sound in all music, representing life at its most vital; whereas the deep, falling, soft, slow phrases that end Tchaikovsky's *Pathétique* symphony are about the most dispiriting, representing life at its lowest ebb. Of course, the all-important tonal tensions clinch the matter, the Beethoven being major and diatonic, the Tchaikovsky minor and harmonized chromatically.

The above is nothing more than a broad generalization. In the field of speech, it does not take into account the effect of emphasis gained by whispering or measuring out one's words in a low, quiet voice; in the field of physical action, it ignores such things as knocking a pole down into the ground, or pressing down to close a portmanteau. And in the musical examples, it does not mention that Tchaikovsky is giving the maximum emphasis to what he has to say, by other means than loud volume. Moreover, the effects of one of the agents can cancel out those of another: the rising scales of the Beethoven are preceded by some falling ones, but there is no sense of relaxation, the tempo being so quick.

Nevertheless, it will serve as a general rule, exceptions to which will be made clear as we proceed.

VOLUME

Volume will be considered first, since its effects hold good whatever the tonal tensions or the other vitalizing agents may be doing. It does not matter whether the music is major or minor, quick or slow, 3/4 or 2/4, even or jerky, *staccato* or *legato*, high or low, up or down: the louder the music gets, the more *emphasis* is given to what is being expressed; and naturally, the converse holds good—the softer, the less emphasis. Thus the so-called 'Treaty' Motive in *The Ring* is first heard *piano* in *The Rhinegold*, while Wotan and Fricka discuss the question of the treaty with the Giants; but when Wotan tries to evade the treaty, and the Giants hold him to it furiously, the motive is thundered out *fortissimo*. However, beyond a certain point of softness, a new kind of emphasis appears. When we get to *pp* (as soft as possible) or *ppppp* (which must mean three times softer than possible), the composer (or sometimes only the conductor) achieves the emphasis of secrecy, forcing what he has to say upon our attention by making us strain our ears. In this way, Tchaikovsky stresses his despair at the end of his *Pathétique* Symphony, and Delius emphasizes the unutterable nostalgia which ends most of his works. This procedure can also function as the emphasis of understatement: when, in Debussy's *Pelléas*, an orchestral crescendo is followed by Pelléas' murmur, 'I love you', the maximum emphasis is given to this avowal by the unexpectedness of a soft dynamic level. No such reversal takes place at the other end of the scale: louder and louder always means more and more emphasis—one has only to think of the self-advertizing character of a Rossini crescendo, or the rhetorical power of Wagner working up to a climax. An excellent example of the emphasis to be gained from loud volume is that over-worked trick of the film-composer—the single dissonant chord, *fortissimo* on brass, as the camera, wandering around a dark, empty room, suddenly switches dramatically on to a dead body. What effect could a quiet chord have here, when the intention is to emphasize the gruesome discovery?

Such are the simple, straightforward functions of the volume-tensions, louder and softer. It may be mentioned that the development of these functions has been a direct outcome of the development of Western European man. In the Middle Ages and early Renaissance, when humility was still enthroned as a virtue, and art-music lived mainly in the church, self-abasing composers ignored the extremes of volume, and, so far as is known, had no idea of *crescendo* or *diminuendo*. But with the growing urge for human self-realization, the growing harmonic expression of the rightness of happiness and the wrongness of pain, and the removal of the musical centre from church to opera-house and concert-hall, composers began to enlist the rhetoric available in the volume dimension to stress their points. It is certain that if a medieval church-composer could hear the finale of Beethoven's Choral Symphony, or Siegfried's Funeral

March in Wagner's *Götterdämmerung*, he would shrink from them as blasphemous examples of *hubris*.

TIME

Measured time is no less a product of Western Europe's march towards self-realization. First of all, as an element of art-music, it was the direct outcome of the discovery of harmony: once a number of voices began to sing different parts simultaneously, it became necessary to measure the exact moment when each singer was to change to his next note, otherwise chaos would have reigned. Of course, measured rhythm had existed from time immemorial, in the shape of the march and the dance; but it was the gradual incursion of these into liturgical art-music that heralded the end of the 'other-worldly' rule of the church, and the advent of humanism. We have to remember, for example, that the closing movements of Bach's St. Matthew and St. John Passions are sublimated examples of a once-lascivious dance—the sarabande—and that they are purely human in expression, compared with the freely flowing monody of plainsong. Plainsong is timeless, like the Christian eternity; humanistic music is time-ridden, like human life. And time functions in music as in life: it is a dimension in which things occur in succession. Hence in music it expresses the speed and rhythm of feelings and events—in other words, the state of mental, emotional, or physical *animation*.

Turning to our detailed examination, the first expressive antithesis of the time-dimension is that between *duple* and *triple* time—one strong beat and one weak beat, and one strong beat and two weak beats. Its basic effect can be seen as the contrast between the regular, rigid, masculine rhythm of the two feet marching or running, and the looser, swinging or lilting, feminine rhythm of the dance: the contrast between the 'wooden' slow march and the 'graceful' minuet; between the 'controlled' quick march and the 'abandoned' jig; between the 'stilted' *galop* and the 'whirling' tarantella. As a general rule we may take it that duple rhythm is more rigid and controlled, triple rhythm more relaxed and abandoned. In art-music this antithesis can be seen clearly: compare the rock-like inner strength of the 4/4 Air from Bach's Suite No. 3 in D with the easy grace of the 3/4 Minuet from Handel's *Berenice*; the rather rigid force of the first movement of Beethoven's 'Emperor' Concerto with the relaxed power of the 3/4 first movement of his *Eroica* Symphony; or the comparatively controlled gaiety of the duple-time *scherzos* of Brahms's Fourth, Tchaikovsky's Fourth, or Borodin's Second Symphony, with the abandoned excitement of the triple-time scherzos of Beethoven's Seventh and Walton's First.

But this antithesis only works *when other things are equal*. When tonal tensions, tempo, volume, and phrasing function in the opposite way, they make any distinction between duple and triple time practically meaningless. Compare the relaxed serenity of the slow, soft, *legato*, major 4/4 of the Adagio of Beethoven's Choral Symphony with the rigid power of the fast, loud, staccato, minor 3/4 of the Scherzo in the same work. Putting other things equal again, however, we see that the 3/4 sections of the Choral Symphony's Adagio are more relaxed than the 4/4 ones; and the 2/4 finale of the Seventh Symphony is more rigid in its violent rhythmic force than the 3/4 scherzo of the Choral. So we are left, after all, with our general rule: other effects accounted for, duple rhythm gives an effect of control or rigidity, triple rhythm of relaxation and abandonment. But the other effects will definitely have to be accounted for, before the effect of duple or triple rhythm is considered.

The second expressive function of the time-dimension— *rhythmic accent*—needs little explanation. Rhythm, aided (often infinitesimally) by louder volume, throws a spotlight on to the 'strong' beat, or on to a weak beat by the procedure known as syncopation. In either case, the way in which accent functions is perfectly clear: it throws *emphasis* on to a given note in the scheme of tonal tensions, and thus qualifies the emotional expression of a phrase of two or more notes. Thus, in the case of the two-note figure mentioned earlier as being expressive of a burst of anguish (minor sixth falling to the dominant), the accent is often on the minor sixth, the dissonant note, as in Schubert's 'Erl King'—'my father, my father', emphasizing the effect of anguish:

Ex. 48

But when the same figure occurs with the accent on the dominant—the consonant note—the anguish is less emphasized, as in the first vocal phrase of Schubert's 'Gretchen at the Spinning Wheel'—'My peace is gone':

(Note, of course, the effect of the softer dynamic level, the slower tempo, and the lilting 6/8 rhythm.)

The chief expressive power available in the time-dimension is *tempo*—the speed at which a piece of music moves. The equation is a simple one here: the faster, the more *animation*. (There is surely no need to expatiate on the connection with walking and running feet, and the beat of the heart.) The effect is to be seen most clearly in a theme which the composer used at different tempi: e.g., the main crochet theme of the finale of Beethoven's Choral Symphony, with its appearance near the end at a faster tempo, and at double speed, in quavers; or the opening theme of the slow introduction to Brahms's First Symphony, with its metamorphosis into the *allegro* first subject.

The effect of tempo on emotional expression is clearly all-important, since every basic emotion can be experienced at many different levels of animation. Thus the joy expressed by a certain progression of tonal tensions may be tumultuous if *allegro*; easy-going if *moderato*; serene if *adagio:* the despair expressed by another progression may be hysterical if *presto*, or resigned if *lento*. A single example will suffice: returning to our two-note anguish figure (minor sixth falling to fifth), compare its use at a fast tempo in Schubert's 'The Erl King' (Ex. 48) with its use at a slow tempo in the Crucifixus in Bach's B minor Mass:

Another strongly expressive factor in the time-dimension is the antithesis between an *even* rhythmic movement and a *jerky*

one—between a succession of quavers, for example, and a progression made up of dotted quaver plus semiquaver. The effect of even rhythm—that of a smooth, unimpeded flow of any particular emotion—is so obvious as to need no comment; but dotted rhythms function in a more complex way.

At a fast tempo, dotted rhythms give enormous tension and energy to the already animated emotional expression (the first movement of Beethoven's Seventh Symphony and some passages in the finale are perhaps the supreme examples); but at slow tempi they function in several different ways. (1) Softly, in the minor, they give a weary, dragging feeling to the emotional expression; e.g., 'It is enough', in Mendelssohn's *Elijah*, and 'Total eclipse' in Handel's *Samson*. They sometimes tone-paint at the same time the dragging of feet in the Funeral March, or in the Way of the Cross: e.g., the *Eroica* Funeral March, and 'Komm, süsses Kreuz' in Bach's St. Matthew Passion. (2) Loudly, in the minor, they arouse grave and solemn feelings connected with tragedy: e.g., the opening of the *Messiah* Overture, or the Qui Tollis in Mozart's Mass in C minor. (3) Softly, in the major, they give a lilting charm to the music: e.g., the Air in Handel's Water Music, and the siciliano movement in Brahms's St. Anthony Variations. (4) Loudly, in the major, they produce an impression of pomp and splendour, or courage and confidence (the two are linked by royal and military associations, and the rhythm is here derived from the ceremonial military drum); e.g., the typical French Overture, or 'Lift up your heads, O ye gates' in *Messiah*, or 'I am he that comforteth; be not afraid' from *Elijah*.

There are, of course, many subtle modifications of these four general procedures, and many interactions between them and the other qualifying agents (they are considerably affected by the duple-triple antithesis, for example); but in the main, we can say that dotted notes function chiefly in the ways detailed above. The important exceptions are that (1) and (3) can interchange, according as the 'pleasurable' major system is undermined by its more melancholy tensions, in a dead slow tempo, and the 'painful' minor system kept to a merely 'serious' level by the simple use of the minor third, in a not-too-slow tempo. Thus Handel's 'Lascia ch'io pianga', from the opera *Rinaldo*, though major, has effect (1) above, owing to its use of the pathetic suspension 4-3; and 'How beautiful are the feet' has effect (3)—as we have already seen (Ex. 45)—owing to its lack of the painful minor sixth, seventh, or second in any form whatsoever.

The reason why even and dotted rhythms function as they do is clearly connected with the human activities of walking and running (smooth motion, slow and quick); limping and skipping (jerky motion, slow and quick); and slow marching (jerky motion, ceremonial); and the antithesis needs no further elaboration.

But at this point, an unlimited field of rhythmic procedures opens up to our view. There are almost as many rhythmic procedures as there are compositions, and it would take a library of books to cover them all. However, we are concerned here with basic elements, and the four antitheses outlined above (duple *v.* triple, accent *v.* non-accent, fast *v.* slow, even *v.* jerky) are in fact the basic functions of the time-dimension, and every rhythmic procedure is ultimately derived from them.

There is still one remaining function of the time-dimension, which is not a matter of rhythm, but of phrasing—the *staccato-legato* antithesis. Actually this is only very strictly speaking a function of the time-dimension—a matter of the actual length of a note as compared with its rhythmic length; in reality, it acts very much in the same way as volume, giving or withholding emphasis. This is due to the fact that, as with volume, it depends on an expenditure of energy. And since it always requires more energy to perform instantaneous actions (punching or spitting) than sustained ones (pushing or blowing), *staccato* naturally gives more emphasis than *legato*. One need only think of the impact which *staccato* gives to the opening theme of Beethoven's *Egmont* Overture: without it, the music would still be music, but would lose most of its force. Or consider how entirely the grave, reflective character of the opening theme of Schubert's Unfinished Symphony depends on *legato*: played *non-legato*, it would still make sense, but would lose its brooding, withdrawn character. Another good example is again the so-called 'Treaty' Motive in *The Ring*: this descending scale sounds vague and slightly ominous on its early appearances in *The Rhinegold*, *piano* and *legato* on cellos and basses, and only takes its first step towards its full impact when played, still *piano* on cellos and basses, but with detached bowing.

Pitch is felt by everyone to be an 'up-and-down' dimension. I say everyone, though there are those who hold that this is an illusion; that there is no reason for calling notes with more vibrations per second 'higher', except in so far as they have always been written higher on the stave. In answer to this, it should hardly be necessary to point out the connexions between the following facts: (1) By the law of gravity, 'up' is an effort for man, 'down' a relaxation; (2) To sing 'high' notes, or play them on wind, brass, or string instruments, demands a considerable effort; (3) To tune a string 'upwards', one screws 'up' its tension; (4) Scientists, talking of 'high' notes, speak of a 'high' number of vibrations per second. There is a natural instinct in these matters, which the intellect should respect: surely the inventors of notation obeyed both common-sense and intuition when they put 'higher' notes literally higher on the stave.

Now let us try and analyse the various expressive powers inherent in rising and falling pitch, in so far as they can be disentangled from the almost infinite number of contexts—tonal, rhythmic, and dynamic—in which they occur. On the simplest level—that of tone-painting—we find that composers have been unanimous in accepting 'up' and 'down' in pitch as equivalent to up and down in the physical world: in settings of the Mass in all periods, the Resurrexit has been set to rising phrases, and 'descendit de coelis' to falling ones; and the music of many a Magnificat goes down and up at the words 'he hath put down the mighty from their seat, and hath exalted the humble and meek'. (Again, it seems quite unnecessary to assume, as some do, that these are visual symbols, due to the appearance of rising and falling notes on the stave: surely the sense of direction produced by the *sound* of rising and falling phrases is sufficient explanation?)

There is no harm in enjoying this naïve kind of tone-painting, so long as we do not try to persuade ourselves that it is the whole of the musical expression in itself. It is nothing more than symbolically appropriate: one cannot imagine a setting of the *Resurrexit* to descending scales, though of course it is possible to ignore the simple up and down progression altogether. It is, of course, the *tonal tensions* existing in the particular series of ascending or descending notes, which express what kind of ascent or descent is involved. A single superb example is the downward movement at the end of the Crucifixus of Bach's B minor Mass, to the words 'et sepultus est': the mere naïve 'descent' symbolism on its own could easily have ended the movement with a perfect cadence in the tonic key, E minor, and would have expressed nothing extraordinary; the mingled sense of awe and profound peace connected with death is conveyed by the tonal tensions—that totally unexpected but ineffably serene melodic and harmonic progression that leads the melody down below the tonic of E minor to the *third* of G *major*.

Returning to the simple question of 'up' and 'down' in pitch, and accepting the natural instinct for regarding them as equivalent to the same directions in space, we are brought up against the fact that pitch is the *only* directional dimension of music, and it has only these two directions, up and down. What of 'out' and 'in', or 'away' and 'back'?

Volume can, of course, help to suggest farness and nearness, but usually the effect is achieved through pitch: 'up' and 'down' are, by analogy, made to stand for all other directions, in an obvious way. By the law of gravity, as we have said, 'up' is an effort for man, 'down' a relaxation. Now, from a given starting point, to go out or move away implies an active effort; and to come in or come back implies a relaxation of the initial exertion. Consequently, composers have used 'up' in music to suggest 'out' and 'away'; and 'down' to suggest 'in' and 'back'. Thus, in Handel's *Israel in Egypt*, the theme of the chorus 'He led them through the deep' consists of two rising phrases each preceded by a leap down—they were led on an *outward* journey through the *depths* of the sea; and in Purcell's *King Arthur*, the theme of the chorus 'Hither, this way' consists of falling intervals. Similarly, 'up and down' is used to suggest 'to and fro', or 'hither and thither'; in fact, we use the phrase 'up and down' to signify this kind of movement. Thus in the Prelude to Act I of *The Valkyrie*, Siegmund's padding footsteps, as he runs hither and thither, are portrayed by the upward and downward movement of the bass.

But this is all tone-painting, whereas our particular concern is with the emotional language of music. What are the *expressive* effects of rising and falling pitch? They work by analogy with the 'up-and-down', 'out-and-in', and 'away-and-back' symbolism of tone-painting, and that is why the analysis was begun by establishing the instinctive naturalness of that symbolism.

First of all, 'up-and-down'. In the opening pages of the Prelude to *Tristan*, the general level of the melodic line rises with the 'mounting' passion; at the end of the *Liebestod*, it falls with Isolde's 'sinking' into oblivion. In Schubert's 'Gretchen at the Spinning-Wheel', the vocal line rises with her rising agitation, and returns to a lower level when she grows calmer again. In his song 'Gute Nacht' in *Die Winterreise*, the melody falls with the young man's 'drooping' despair; rises with his spirits as he remembers his erstwhile happiness; and in the third verse, rising defiance gives an upward twist to the falling phrases of despair. It is clear that rising and falling pitch can express a rising and falling vitality in a given emotional context.

Secondly, 'away-and-back'. The symbolism of moving away is connected with the beginning and continuing of activity, that of returning with coming to an end of activity. Consequently, in various emotional contexts, rising pitch can convey a sense of initiation or continuation, falling pitch a sense of fulfilment or finality. Thus, at the opening of the Prelude to *Tristan*, nascent and growing passion is presented by means of gradually rising pitch, but at the very end of the *Liebestod*, the sense of fulfilment and finality finds expression in falling phrases. In 'Gute Nacht', the falling vocal line expresses not only the young man's drooping spirits but also the finality of his despair; the rising phrases not only his rising spirits at memories of his lost love, but the sense of continuance felt in the emotion of love, in contrast with the sense of finality felt in the emotion of despair.

Lastly, 'out-and-in'. Here we come to the heart of the problem, for this symbolism sums up and includes 'up-and-down' and 'away-and-back'. (With the coming of space-travel, we shall become familiar with the fact that 'up-and-down', 'away-and-back' and 'out-and-in' are really all the same thing.) The expressive quality of rising pitch is above all an 'outgoing' of emotion: depending on the tonal, rhythmic, and dynamic context, its effect can be active, assertive, affirmative, aggressive, striving, protesting, or aspiring. The expressive quality of falling pitch is of an 'incoming' of emotion: depending on context, it can be relaxed, yielding, passive, assenting, welcoming, accepting, or enduring. These qualities clearly absorb the 'rising and falling vitality' of the 'up-and-down' symbolism, and the 'continuation and finality' of the 'out-and-in' symbolism. The passion of the *Tristan* Prelude is outgoing—active, assertive, striving; the fulfilment at the end of the *Liebestod* is 'incoming'—it is received, welcomed, accepted. The despair in 'Gute Nacht' is 'incoming'—passively accepted; the memories of lost love 'outgoing'—assertive; the defiance also 'outgoing'—aggressive, protesting. The whole thing is explained when we remember that falling notes are yielding to the tensional, 'gravitational' pull back to the lower tonic; rising ones are asserting themselves against that pull.

To confirm this hypothesis fully, it would be necessary to draw on our broad generalizations that 'major-minor' equals 'pleasure-pain', that tempo expresses the level of animation, that volume expresses the degree of emphasis given to the feeling, and permute 'up-down', 'major-minor', 'fast-slow' and 'loud-soft', producing sixteen types of basic context; and then to subdivide them further by taking into account the ambiguities of the major-minor antithesis, the various effects of rhythm and phrasing, and the shades of emphasis given by different levels of volume. Such an exhaustive analysis is beyond the scope of this book: a few general principles will have to suffice; they will be further particularized in the chapter on the basic terms of musical vocabulary.

To rise in pitch in the major is normally to express an outgoing feeling of pleasure. This may be an excited affirmation of joy (fast and loud—the climax of Beethoven's Overture *Leonora No. 3*); a suppressed joyous excitement (fast and soft—the working-up passage in Act 2 of *Tristan*, where Isolde sees Tristan approaching); a calm, emphatic affirmation of joy (slow and loud—the *Gratias* in Bach's B minor Mass); or a calm, quiet, joyful aspiration (slow and soft—the end of Vaughan Williams's Fifth Symphony). It can be many other things, of course, depending on chromatic inflexions, jerky rhythms, etc., but the basic effect is always pleasurable and assertive, even in 'revenge arias', expressions of courage, battle music, etc., etc. To fall in pitch in the major is normally to express an incoming feeling of pleasure. This may be an acceptance of soothing comfort (slow and soft—Dowland's 'Awake, sweet love, thou art returned; my heart which long in absence mourned now lives in perfect joy'); a majestic, triumphant acceptance of joyous fulfilment (slow and loud—'Lift up your heads, O ye gates, and be ye lift up, ye everlasting doors, and the King of Glory shall come in', from Handel's *Messiah*); an excited, triumphant acceptance of fulfilment (fast and loud—the closing pages of Mahler's First Symphony). (See Ex. 6.)[1]

To rise in pitch in the minor is normally to express an outgoing feeling of pain. This may be an excited, aggressive affirmation of, and/or protest against, a painful feeling (fast and loud—the rising bass theme accompanying Wotan's terrible cry of rage and protest in Act 2 of *The Valkyrie*, 'O heilige Schmach'); or a strong heroic self-assertion against impending tragedy (also fast and loud—the 'Valkyrie' motive from the same work). In these two cases, the tonal tensions (minor sixth and chromatic harmony in the one, simple minor third in the other) are the basis of the difference. It can also be a suppressed painful excitement (fast and soft—Osmin's muttered, impotent fury against Pedrillo, in the A minor section of his music, in Mozart's *The Seraglio*); or a subdued assertion of grief (slow and soft—the opening of Bach's St. Matthew Passion).

To fall in pitch in the minor is normally to express an incoming feeling of pain. This can be fierce despair (slow and loud—the opening of the finale of Tchaikovsky's *Pathétique* Symphony); or a powerful feeling of subjection to fate (also slow and loud—the so-called 'Treaty' Motive in *The Ring*, or the descending scale near the beginning of Tchaikovsky's Fourth Symphony). Tonal tensions and phrasing are the basis of the difference: the *Pathetique* uses chromatic harmony, legato; the Wagner and the Tchaikovsky Fourth examples are diatonic and non-legato. The same sense of subjection to fate can be expressed by the fast-loud combination (the opening of Beethoven's Fifth Symphony), the quicker tempo expressing greater agitation.

The above are only a few examples; but they demonstrate the

[1] See note on p. 167

general effects of rising and falling pitch, and give an idea how exceptions may be explained. They are mainly examples of step-wise movement; but there is another procedure in the pitch-dimension, which must be briefly examined—the leap of, say, a fifth or more. Naturally, this gives an added impulsiveness to the emotion concerned. The upward leap is often used to ex-press physical passion, whether by Mozart ('Dies Bildnis', in *The Magic Flute*), Wagner (the opening phrase of *Tristan*), or Britten ('Her breast is harbour too' in *Peter Grimes*—see Ex. 29h); it can also, of course, express violent joy, aspiration, protest, triumph, or fear, depending on the tonal tensions involved. Downward leaps are often used to express gushes of the more yielding types of emotion (Brangaene's consolation of Isolde in Act I of *Tristan* is full of them); though they can also express a sudden accept-ance of sorrow or yielding to despair. A striking example of upward and downward leaps used in conjunction is the opening of Richard Strauss's *Der Rosenkavalier*, with its first, upward-leaping theme standing for the assertive male character, Ok-tavian, and its second, downward-leaping theme representing the yielding female character, the Marschallin.

It should be made clear, at this point, that most music mingles rising and falling pitch so subtly that no broad expres-sive intention in the dimension of pitch is immediately discern-ible. The reason is that if the music aspires to the heights or sinks to the depths, it obviously cannot continue unchecked without passing beyond the limits of musical pitch as known to humanity. In other words, supreme human aspiration, for example, cannot find complete expression because of the limita-tions of the physical world, and the same may be said of the ultimate human despair; that is why the main theme of Beet-hoven's Overture *Leonora No. 3* has continually to take a step back before climbing up again, and why the main themes of the finale of Tchaikovsky's *Pathétique* Symphony have to fall over and over again from the same level, and even at the end the second one can only go *so* far down (though far enough, in all conscience!).

Generally speaking, however, it is true to say that within these natural limitations, pitch tends to fluctuate according to the ebb and flow of the emotions expressed. As an example, let

us take the beginning of the aria 'Total Eclipse' from Handel's
Samson:

Ex. 51
Larghetto

To - tal e - clipse!   No sun!   No moon!   all   dark,_____   all

dark_____   a - mid the   blaze__   of noon!

Total eclipse (downwards, slow, minor = despair); *No sun! No
moon!* (a terse, rising, two-note figure, twice = a more active,
'protesting' kind of grief); *All dark, all dark*—(returning to the
bottom again, a more gradually rising phrase, repeated higher
= return to despair, then growing protest); *Amid the blaze of
noon!* (the voice rises to a climax, only to fall again—the 'protest' finds fierce expression, then despair sets in again, ironically
in the 'blaze' of the major.

We can understand more clearly how the dimension of pitch
functions, perhaps, if we take this quotation and alter the intervallic tensions without changing the tonal tensions at all. Unfortunately, we shall have to ruin Handel's noble theme and
give the tenor something absurdly difficult to sing:

Ex. 51 *(bis)*
Larghetto

To - tal e - clipse!   No sun!   No moon!   all   dark,_____   all

dark_____   a - mid the   blaze__   of noon!

The tonal tensions are the same, but the intervallic tensions
are different. 'No sun! No moon!' is still sung to the notes B-E,
but the whole expression is changed by making this a falling
interval instead of a rising one: the first half of the 'tune'
expresses a dull obsession with despair, as opposed to Handel's
illuminating contrast of despair and protesting grief. The
second half of the 'tune', instead of rising to protest and falling
back into sadness, carries the protest still further to the point
of hysteria; yet the tonal tensions are still the same—D, E, F

sharp, G, C, B, A, G. The 'tune' is, of course, a ridiculous one; but it is significant that its failure is simultaneously one of musical form and expression. As Handel sees it, Samson moves between despair and protest, and the fluctuations in pitch convey the conflict of these two emotions within him. The alteration of the tune sees him veering almost neurotically from the most morbid despair to the most violent hysteria.

Some late romantic and modern music has in fact expressed neurotic states of mind by means of excessive pitch-fluctuation and very wide leaps (the vocal line in Richard Strauss's *Elektra*, for example). So once again, we find history at work behind musical expression: medieval and early Renaissance music tended to move in stepwise progressions at a normal, medium pitch, befitting man's humble subjection to the deity; but with the growth of human self-realization, music-drama, in the hands of Monteverdi and others, began to introduce more and more liberty of pitch-movement to express the rhetoric of human passion; until by the end of the nineteenth century, violent emotional unrest beat against the natural limits of audible pitch. Once more, could a medieval composer hear the high-pitched, anguished cries of Verdi's Othello, or the low-pitched despairing growls of Wagner's Wotan, he would be horrified at humanity making so much of itself; what he would think of the demented whinings of the Captain in Berg's *Wozzeck* cannot be imagined.

Sometimes, of course, pitch functions by not fluctuating at all —when the music consists of repetitions of a single note.

Such repetitions may be fast or slow. When they are slow, the level of animation is low, and there is no sense of outgoing or incoming emotion, but only of a monotonous deadness. In consequence this procedure is used in funeral marches (Beethoven's Piano Sonata in A flat, Op. 26, and Chopin's Piano Sonata in B flat minor) or in other music connected with the idea of death (some of the Statue's utterances in Mozart's *Don Giovanni*, Schubert's Song 'Death and the Maiden', and, to speak of lesser things, Sullivan's ballad 'The Lost Chord', written by the bedside of his dying brother). One may say that just as a man does not raise his voice in the presence of the dead, but keeps it low, at a level pitch, and talks slowly and quietly, so a composer will tend to do, musically speaking, when he composes with the idea of death as his inspiration. And so does the sexton, tolling his solitary bell. And the listener, hearing the voice, the bell, or the music, will feel those emotions aroused which are connected with the idea of death.

When the repetition is quick, the effect is quite different. The level of animation is now high, but again there is no sense of outgoing or incoming emotion: the effect is naturally one of continuous excitement without action. In consequence, it usually functions as pure rhythm, used at the beginning of a work, or section of a work, to set the listener agog for what is to follow (the opening of Mendelssohn's Italian Symphony, the Scherzo of Borodin's Second Symphony, the famous stamping chords in Stravinsky's *Rite of Spring*, and many quick movements by Bartók). If the swiftly-repeated note *is* used to generate a theme, it produces one of terrific drive (the opening of Beethoven's *Waldstein* Sonata). Relating the procedure again to the behaviour of the human voice, one may compare the sense of excited expectancy conveyed by the voice of a sports commentator, speaking rapidly at a level pitch, at moments when the race or game is still in the balance.

There are, of course, many other uses of the repeated note, of which we may single out two: moderately quick repetitions in an easy-going tempo, to convey a sense of jog-trot, rather uneventful continuity (the *Allegretto* of Beethoven's Eighth Symphony, and the *comodo* opening of Mahler's Fourth); and very fast, soft repetitions in a slow tempo (i.e. string tremolando), to create maximum mystery and expectancy (the opening of Bruckner's Fourth Symphony).

There is one other way in which pitch functions expressively— as an absolute region for a particular work, or passage in a work. The 'normal' pitch-range of music is an overall spread from just above the treble clef to just below the bass clef (i.e. the complete gamut of the human voice); but sometimes a given passage will lie at the top or bottom of this range, or even above or below it. Naturally, the upper reaches (defying 'gravity') have an effect of lightness, rarification, ethereality, or transcendence; while the lower reaches ('unable to leave the earth') evoke feelings of darkness, heaviness, earthiness, or evil.

A few examples are: (1) upper reaches—'Glory to God' in *Messiah* (angels), the *Lohengrin* Prelude (the Holy Grail descending from heaven), and the Introduction to Act I of Britten's *Peter Grimes* (the early morning air and sky); (2) lower reaches— 'The people that walked in darkness' in *Messiah*, the Prelude to Act 2 of *Siegfried* (the 'depths' of the forest where the dragon has his lair, and the evil 'depths' of his nature), the symbolic scene in the vaults in *Pelléas et Mélisande*, and the opening of Sibelius's *The Return of Lemminkaïnen* (the land of darkness and death—Tuonela—from which the hero is returning). The two are exploited simultaneously by Richard Strauss at the end of *Also sprach Zarathustra*, a high B major chord being supposed to represent man's highest aspirations, while a low C natural is intended to indicate his earth-bound nature. (The fact that few people take this piece of expression seriously proves nothing, since we are only concerned with the way in which Strauss used the dimension of pitch naturally as a part of musical language.)

More subtle examples of the way in which absolute regions of pitch function as musical expression are the end of Act I of *Der Rosenkavalier* and the Prelude to Act 3 of *La Traviata*. Just as the Marschallin's resignation is 'transfigured' by being lifted up to the heights of musical pitch, so the sadness of Violetta's approaching death is made more pathetic by being 'etherealized'—i.e. played on high strings. In this last case, let us indulge in a hypothetical transposition of register to make a point: if the Prelude were put down two octaves, would it not take on a dark, gloomy, brooding quality more suited to the death of a Wagnerian hero (cf. the Prelude to Act 3 of *Tristan*)? Conversely, if the opening of Tchaikovsky's *Pathétique* Symphony were transposed up three octaves, would not its dark, gloomy, brooding character be transformed into something sweet, sad, and gently pathetic?

Of course, it is obviously not enough to write a low chord for brass, woodwind, or strings, and label it 'evil' or 'hopeless grief'; nor to write a high chord for violins and label it 'aspiration' or 'transfiguration'—the example of Strauss's *Also sprach Zarathustra* shows this. But it can be said that if a composer is intent on expressing a dark, brooding evil, or a dark, brooding grief, his theme, with its tonal tensions expressing evil or grief, will naturally tend to occur to him in a low register, and the opposite will happen in the case of a composer intent on expressing an etherealized grief or a transcendent vision.

For the sake of completeness, we may briefly glance at the expressive effects of the characterizing agents of tone-colour and texture.

In one sense, *tone-colour* is analogous with volume as an expressive element: a theme introduced by the bass voice can later be made much more emphatic by being played on trombones (Alberich's 'Curse' motive in *The Rhinegold*, for example). In the main, however, it is music's chief means of dramatic characterization: one need hardly expatiate on the warmly passionate strings, the pastoral flute and oboe, the querulous or comic bassoon, the heroic trumpet, or the solemn trombone; or on such individual discoveries as Berlioz's shrilly vulgar E flat clarinet, Strauss's spiteful oboes, Mahler's viciously sardonic trombones, and Vaughan Williams's lachrymose saxophone.

Texture, in one way, is a function of the pitch-dimension— depth-in-pitch—but it is normally absorbed into becoming a function of the characterizing tone-colour. The connexion between thick texture and emotional emphasis (most of Wagner and Richard Strauss) and between spare texture and emotional understatement (most of Debussy and Stravinsky) is so obvious as to need no comment. There is also the spare texture of emotional emptiness (the 'empty sea' passage in Act 3 of Wagner's *Tristan*, and the second, 'all-passion-spent' theme of the finale of Mahler's Ninth Symphony); the hallucinatory texture of delirium (Schoenberg's *Erwartung* and Berg's *Wozzeck*); the velvety texture of sensuality (Wagner's *Tristan* and Debussy's *Prélude à l'après-midi d'un faune*); the hard, clear-cut texture of irony and realism (much of Satie and Hindemith), etc., etc., almost *ad infinitum*. Most great composers create a new texture of their own to express their new vision. In the analysis of the basic terms of musical vocabulary which follows, the tone-colour and texture will each have to be considered in its own right.

3

SOME BASIC TERMS OF MUSICAL VOCABULARY

So far, the attempt to analyse the functioning of musical language has necessitated that most dubious procedure, the breaking down of an indivisible unity into its component parts, which have no genuine separate existence. There are, strictly speaking, no such things as 'the major third', 'quick tempo', 'loud volume', etc., considered apart from the innumerable contexts in which they occur. Every piece of music is a whole, in which the effects of the various well-worn elements interpenetrate and condition one another from note to note, from bar to bar, from movement to movement, in an entirely novel way; in every context, each single element has newly merged its identity into a new overall expression.

Our justification is that this method is the only possible one, and that we are now going to try and put the parts together again with a better idea how they are likely to interfuse with one another for expressive purposes. The first step must be the examination of small-scale examples of the total functioning of musical language—combinations of two or more notes into those short phrases which are the basic terms of musical vocabulary. Once again, though, various uses of these terms will have to be separated from their contexts, and examples will have to be gathered from different periods and different composers, to establish the emotive significance of each term. In fact, as we shall now be dealing, not with single notes, but with melodic patterns, we shall be playing , a little more seriously than usual, the game known as 'twisted tunes'.

This piece of foolery, which crops up from time to time in professional musical circles, has afforded a good deal of harmless amusement in its time, as a radio feature, a parlour game, and a stand-by for anyone planning a musical quiz. It goes like this: having discovered a case of two composers utilizing the same bit of tune, one intrigues people by demonstrating the fact, or by trying to confuse them as to which is which. And there the matter usually ends: few try to puzzle out why such resemblances should be. Why, for example, the supreme moments of tragic anguish in Wagner's *Parsifal* and Verdi's *Otello* both found expression in the same triadic phrase— 1–3–5–6–5 in the minor system; especially since Verdi was unacquainted with *Parsifal*, Wagner died before *Otello* was written, and the two composers' aims, styles, and methods were utterly different.

From the expressive point of view, of course, the phrase is superbly right in both cases—a rising minor progression, as we have said, expresses an outward-going feeling of pain, and our phrases take in both the tragic minor third and the anguished minor sixth, placing much emphasis on the latter. Parsifal, after receiving Kundry's soul-seducing kiss, cries out in agony 'Redeem me, rescue me from guilt-stained hands!'; Othello, standing by the sleeping Desdemona, looks down at her, still loving her but determined to kill her, and says nothing. Many subtle psychological connexions between the two cases might be established, but as always, the exact situation is irrelevant to the musical expression, which is concentrated entirely on the painful emotion of anguish.

But how are we to explain the similarity, or rather the near-identity? Coincidence? There are an enormous number of them in music. Before trying to answer the question, let us first assemble our collection of such 'coincidences', as they have occurred throughout the ages. But although it is necessary to play at 'twisted tunes', a pledge is given that there will be no 'twisting' of the kind whereby you can prove anything. In giving examples of, say, 8–7–6–5, anything only approximate like 8–7–6–4, or 8–7–5–3 will be shunned like the plague. In any case, there are far too many exact similarities for us to bother with approximations.

ASCENDING 1–(2)–3–(4)–5 (MAJOR)

We have postulated that to rise in pitch is to express an outgoing emotion; we know that, purely technically speaking, the tonic is the point of repose, from which one sets out, and to which one returns; that the dominant is the note of intermediacy, towards which one sets out, and from which one returns; and we have established that the major third is the note which 'looks on the bright side of things', the note of pleasure, of joy. All of which would suggest that to rise from the tonic to the dominant through the major third—or in other words to deploy the major triad as a melodic ascent 1–3–5—is to express an outgoing, active, assertive emotion of joy. Composers have in fact persistently used the phrase for this very purpose (Ex. 53). We may as well clear up a thorny point at the start. It is not 'twisting' to say that 1–3–5 can materialize in composers' inspiration as 1–2–3–5, 1–3–4–5, or 1–2–3–4–5: Gastoldi and Mozart in Ex. 53h show this clearly, using both simple and ornate forms in the same breath, without changing the basic expressive effect. And it is obviously desirable to exemplify, not only the basic term itself, but the two or three different forms it can take. However, to jumble the different forms together in a block example might awaken suspicions that it had been difficult to find exact examples, and that variants had been dragged in to fill historical gaps. (The opposite is the case—it has been difficult to choose a few examples from the plethora of material.) Wherefore, the four different variants of the basic term have been separated, each with examples in chronological order.

Byrd's 'Blow up the Trumpet' shows the derivation of 1–3–5 from the naturally cheerful sound of a simple trumpet-call; a derivation which probably lies at the root of Purcell's 'O praise God in His Holiness', and is obviously integral to 'The trumpet shall sound' in *Messiah*. The three Mozart examples (Ex. 53b)

Ex. 53(a)

show that a composer can use a single term over and over again: there are many examples of this re-use of the same term in the works of every tonal composer. The first is the climax of Belmonte's opening aria in *The Seraglio*: waiting in joyful expectation of seeing his beloved Constanze again after long separation, he prays to Love to 'bring him to his goal'. The second is the orchestral opening of Fiordiligi's aria 'Come scoglio' in *Così fan tutte*: her fidelity to her lover is 'firm as a rock', she sings with glad confidence. The third is the greeting of the chorus to Tamino and Pamina in *The Magic Flute*, after they have passed through their ordeal triumphantly. In Ex. 53c, the Berlioz is the Easter Resurrection Chorus in *The Damnation of Faust*; the Liszt part of the *Magnificat*, as the Dante Symphony proceeds to the upper reaches of Purgatory, near to Paradise: the Johann Strauss needs no comment; the 'pop' quotation is the opening of the tune 'Rock around the Clock' which swept the world in

1956—as sung on the record by its exponent Bill Haley, who substituted 1-3-5, with unerring instinct, for the actual tune's less ebullient 1-2-3.

Example 53d shows 1-3-4-5 in a fifteenth-century *chanson* 'To my lady, kind and fair, I will give a rosary'; a well-known Morley ayre; the chorus of shepherds in Monteverdi's *Orfeo*, calling the nymphs from the mountains to the plains, to join them in dancing; and the music given to the Sons of the Morning in Vaughan Williams's *Job*, at the point where they triumph over Satan (for Satan himself, see the augmented fourths, Ex. 41n). In Ex. 53e, we have 1-2-3-5 from 'Every valley shall be exalted' from *Messiah*; 'For he is like a refiner's fire' from the same work (the psalmist may be regarded as expecting the forthcoming purification with a fierce joy—*forte, allegro*); and the phrase sung by Leonora in Beethoven's *Fidelio* when she turns her thoughts from the wickedness of the tyrant who has falsely imprisoned her husband, to express her hope that all will end well—'A many-coloured rainbow shines on me'.

In Ex. 53f, 1-2-3-4-5 is shown in Victoria's anthem telling of the Seraphim singing 'Holy, holy, holy'; two Byrd quotations, which need no comment; and the final chorus ('Praise the Lord') from Debussy's *Martyre de Saint Sébastien*. Ex. 53g, also showing 1-2-3-4-5, consists of the bass duet in Handel's *Israel in Egypt*, expressing a joyful satisfaction in the warlike Jehovah's drowning of the Egyptians in the Red Sea (or a phrase from 'The trumpet shall sound' in *Messiah*); the opening of the Gloria of Beethoven's Mass in D; and the only moment of joy in Stravinsky's *Oedipus Rex*, when Creon relates the words of the oracle— 'The God has spoken: avenge Laius, avenge the crime' (joyful satisfaction at having found the reason for the plague which is destroying Thebes, and being able to pursue a line of action which will remove it). In Ex. 53h, the Gastoldi is from *Il Trionfo di Dori*—'Amid the murmuring of crystal fountains, the nymphs and shepherds sang O happy joyful day'; the Mozart is the serenade which Don Giovanni sings with light-hearted malice to his discarded mistress, Donna Elvira—the light-heartedness is in the music, the malice in the dramatic situation. Ex. 53j—the Gloria from Bach's B minor Mass and the Overture to Handel's St. Cecilia Ode—is included to show how a simple basic term can be expanded into a longer phrase.

The joyful feeling of all the above phrases needs no stressing nor the fact that the feeling is outgoing, i.e. assertive or affirmative in all cases. Naturally the vitalizing agents express the degree and kind of joy: for example, the quiet, calm, assured joy of Berlioz's Resurrection Chorus—*piano* 4/4 *moderato*, even rhythm, *legato*; and the violently animated, vociferous joy of Beethoven's Gloria—*fortissimo*, 3/4 *allegro*, impulsive rhythm, *non-legato*. The effects of the vitalizing agents in these and succeeding examples as analysed in Chapter 2, can be related to the emotional expression by the reader, without fear of error. (For further examples of 1–3–5 major, and its variants, see Ex. 25a, b and j, and Ex. 39a, b and c; the last three are, of course neutralized, saddened in retrospect by the subsequent use of the 'pathetic' 4–3 suspension).

Looking ahead for a moment, does not Ex. 53 show how the opening of the finale of Beethoven's Fifth Symphony can be legitimately said to express triumph? (1–3–5 major, *fortissimo*, *allegro* 4/4, *alla marcia*, with a rhythm of three even hammer-blows, played on trumpets, *non-legato*, with a full orchestral texture consisting of the major triad). And can we not say that the opening of Brahms's Second Piano Concerto definitely expresses a serene, romantically dreamy, yet rock-firm feeling of joy? (1–2–3 (432) 3–5 major, *mezzo-piano*, *allegro non troppo* 4/4, evenly flowing rhythm, played on the 'romantic' horn, unaccompanied).

ASCENDING 5–1–(2)–3 (MAJOR)

To leap from the dominant up to the tonic, and thence to the major third, with or without the intervening second, is equally expressive of an outgoing emotion of joy. One might say that it is a partial synonym of 1–3–5, as the word 'joy' is a partial synonym of the word 'happiness'. It is not always easy to make a clear distinction between these two terms (see Bach's Gloria, Ex. 53j, in which 5–1–2–3, ornamented, is incorporated into an extended version of 1–2–3–4–5); but in general we may say that 5–1–3, aiming at the major third, is more expressive of joy pure and simple; and 1–3–5, launching farther out from the tonic, more expressive of a sense of exuberance, triumph or aspiration.

Ex. 54a consists of the opening of the Credo from Compère's

Ex. 54 (a)

Mass 'Allez regrets' ('I believe in God the Father Almighty');
the beginning of Byrd's anthem 'Unto the hills mine eyes I lift,
my hope shall never fade'; and a well-known 'aubade' madrigal
by Morley. In Ex. 54b we have a sixteenth-century chanson 'To
the woods I'll go'; the opening of Bach's Cantata No. 31 'The
heavens laugh'; and the first phrase of the Resurrexit from his
B minor Mass. Ex. 54c shows a phrase from the chorus 'The
heavens are telling the glory of God' in *The Creation* (the chorus
actually opens with 5–1–2–3, as do several other movements of
this work); the *idée fixe* from the Fantastic Symphony, depicting
'the beloved' (the pleasurable feeling towards her, expressed in
5–1–3, with an extra passionate leap from the dominant up to
the third, turns to pathos and longing as the melody goes
straight on to the 'pathetic' 4–3 suspension, and falls back
through two other 'longing' suspensions, 3–2 and 8–7); and the
Russian folk-theme which Mussorgsky used for the Coronation
Scene in *Boris Godunov*.

Ex. 54d shows Faust's 'O night of love' from Gounod's opera
(no 'pathetic' 4–3 suspension here, but the third is harmonized
as a dominant thirteenth, resolving on to the second, bringing
in the element of pleasurable longing); a phrase from the last of
Delius's uncharacteristically heroic and jubilant *Songs of Farewell* (Whitman's poems look forward to death in triumphant
mood—'Much, much for thee is yet in store'); and a popular
wartime tune, which needs no comment. Ex. 54e is included to
demonstrate the near-equivalence of 5–1–3 and 1–3–5, and the
fact that they can be telescoped into a single expressive unit:
the quotations are the opening of Bach's 'And I expect the
resurrection of the dead' from the B minor Mass; the heroic and
joyful Sword Motive from *The Ring* (see also the opening of the
work, Ex. 25f, from which this motive is clearly derived); and
the exultant climax of Britten's setting of Donne's sonnet 'Thou
hast made me, and shall thy work decay?' (up to this point, the
song is in E flat minor). Ex. 54f shows how 5–1–3 can be extended into a longer phrase, in quotations from the final triumphant Chorus of Loves from Monteverdi's *L'Incoronazione di
Poppea*, and the Resurrexit from Mozart's Mass in C minor.
(See also Shostakovich's 'optimism', Ex. 25j, and the Strauss
and Britten quotations in Ex. 56j).

Once again, would it be going too far to find a quiet, peaceful, assured joy in the opening of the Larghetto of Beethoven's Second Symphony? (Ascending 5–1–2–3 major, *piano*, 3/8 *larghetto*, evenly flowing rhythm, *legato*, played by violins as the upper part of a simple harmonic and diatonic string texture.)

ASCENDING 1–(2)–3–(4)–5 (MINOR)

Substituting the minor for the major third in the 1–3–5 progression, we shall expect to find the resulting phrase expressive of an outgoing feeling of pain—an assertion of sorrow, a complaint, a protest against misfortune—and we shall not be disappointed.

Ex. 55a quotes a fifteenth-century love-lorn madrigal 'I find no peace'; Robert Whyte's anthem 'Behold and see, all ye who pass

by, if there be any sorrow like unto my sorrow'; and a madrigal by Byrd, which juxtaposes 1–3–4–5 major and minor ('In fields abroad, where trumpets shrill do sound'—major—'where bodies dead do overspread the ground'—minor). In Ex. 55b, we have Morley's madrigals 'Why sit I here, alas, complaining?', and 'Miraculous love's wounding'; and the phrase 'But Jesus cried again in a loud voice, and gave up the spirit' from Schütz's St. Matthew Passion (note the minor sixth and minor seventh, unable to rise to the tonic—the melody does in fact fall after this phrase). Ex. 55c, from the opening chorus of Bach's St. John Passion 'Lord, our Governor, redeem us through thy holy passion', shows 1–2–3–4–5 in extended, ornamented form. Ex. 55d consists of the opening of the chorus from Mozart's Requiem, 'Lord Jesus Christ, save, we beseech thee, the souls of all thy faithful departed servants from fire everlasting'; and Tamino's terrified cry in *The Magic Flute*, where he enters, pursued by a serpent, 'Help me, or I am lost'.

Ex. 55e shows Schubert's well-known attachment to this phrase, in three quotations from *Die Winterreise*. First, 'Auf dem Flusse'; 'You who once rushed along so gaily, impetuous stream, how still you are now, with never a sound to greet me'—the river is frozen like the lover's heart, now that his sweetheart has deserted him. Second, 'Der stürmische Morgen'; 'How the storm has torn the grey garment of the sky'—the weather, the lover says, is suited to his own mood, in which there's nothing but 'winter cold and wild'. Third, 'Der Wegweiser': 'Why do I seek out the hidden pathways across the snowy crags' (there is only one sign-post that the lover cares for, he says—the one that points to the land from which no one ever came back). In Ex. 55f we see Mahler's 'wayfaring lad' in the same love-lorn frenzy—'I have a red-hot knife in my heart'; Debussy more reticently using the same phrase in setting Baudelaire's words 'Sorrow, give me your hand'; and Don Quixote, in Strauss's tone-poem, beginning to go crazed with thoughts of chivalric heroism, danger and death in defence of the oppressed. Ex. 55g quotes from *Belshazzar's Feast* ('For with violence shall that great city Babylon be destroyed'—a fierce assertion of intended revenge for suffering); Bartók's *Cantata Profana* (the father pleads anxiously with his spell-bound sons to return home to their mother, who is waiting for them; and that pathetic and bitter popular song 'Brother can you spare a dime'—the protest of the out-of-work American war hero. (See also Exs. 32g, 41n (with flattened fifth), 43a, 46b, 51 and 52a and b.)

In view of all this, it would seem that those writers who connect the opening of the slow movement of Schubert's Ninth Symphony with the feeling of *Die Winterreise* are not mistaken (1–2–3–4–5, minor, *piano*, *allegretto* 4/4 dotted rhythm, cellos and basses beneath marching minor triads on upper strings. And should we not understand the opening of Mahler's Second Symphony, then, as a fierce protest against suffering? (1–(7)–1–2–3, 3–(2–3)–4–5, minor, *fortissimo*, 4/4 *allegro*, spasmodic rhythm, marked 'wildly', played low down by cellos and basses beneath a fierce string tremolando on the dominant.)

ASCENDING 5–1–(2)–3 (MINOR)

If the major version of 5–1–3 stresses joy pure and simple, by aiming at the major third, the minor version expresses pure tragedy, by aiming at the minor third. And to move upward *firmly and decisively* from the lower dominant, *via* the tonic, to the minor third, gives a strong feeling of courage, in that it boldly acknowledges the existence of tragedy and springs onward (upward) into the thick of it, as composers have realized.

Ex. 56a begins unpromisingly with another love-lorn madrigal, but there is quite definitely something strongly accusing in this particular lover's reproach—try singing the words to 1–3–2–1 or even 1–3–4–5 (both minor), and it will be found that 5–1–2–3 has in fact much more strength of purpose. The example continues with Christ's words 'My God, why hast thou forsaken me?'—presented by Schütz in his St. Matthew Passion as a strong protest (we can see this as the moment when Christ becomes a purely human tragic hero, protesting against his fate). The words set to 5–1–2–3 by Purcell are basic to all uses

of the phrase: 'In the midst of life we are in death'—the tragic situation firmly acknowledged as the basis of life. In Ex. 56b, we have the brave assertion of the Christian soul in Bach's St. Matthew Passion—'I will watch beside my Lord', reflecting on the fact that the disciples slept when they should have been keeping guard; David's bold scorn of Saul's persecution in Handel's oratorio; and another basic use of the phrase—'As by man came death' from *Messiah*. Ex. 56c shows Electra, in Mozart's *Idomeneo*, fiercely enduring, as a Greek tragic figure should, 'the torments of Orestes and Ajax', after she has finally lost the hero Idamante to her rival Ilia; Schubert's winter-journeyer throwing off his grief for the first and only time in the whole cycle ('When the snow flies in my face, I shake it off again'—the song is entitled 'Muth' (Courage); and the two grenadiers in Schumann's Heine setting, who are willing to face death for their emperor, Napoleon.

In Ex. 56d, we see how Wagner turned to the phrase for the tragic heroes in *The Ring*: first, the opening of the 'Volsung' motive, attached to the brave but long-suffering hero Siegmund; second, the first notes of the phrase attached to him when the Valkyrie comes to announce his death (he sings it to her again and again, first questioningly, then defiantly); third, the beginning of Siegfried's heroic motive, perhaps the supreme example of the phrase (the plunge from the tonic of the major triad to the *minor* third, the buoyant rhythm, and the recoil and leap over the dominant on to the *minor sixth*, normally the note of anguish, but here transfigured into joy by being harmonized by its own major triad—these elements explain to some extent the extraordinarily indomitable character of the theme). Ex. 56e shows that Berlioz was equally dependent on the phrase in his heroic opera *The Trojans* ('cribbing'?—Berlioz didn't know a note of *The Ring* when he wrote his work). First, the ghost of the great Trojan hero, Hector, appears to Aeneas, bidding him set out to Italy and found a new Troy there; second, the tragic heroine Cassandra, during the sacking of Troy, scorns the weaker characters among the Vestal Virgins who wish to yield to the Greeks, being afraid to obey her injunction to commit suicide (she asks them if they really desire a life 'unworthy of noble hearts'). The Mussorgsky quotation is from *Boris Godunov*: the young monk, Grigory, about to leave his cell and become the 'pretender', to take arms against the usurper Boris, militantly apostrophizes his future enemy, saying that his misdeeds are written down in the monastery records and he will one day face the judgement of mankind.

Ex. 56f quotes Othello's defiant cry in Verdi's opera, as, supposedly disarmed, he draws an unsuspected dagger and stabs himself—'I have a weapon yet'. The second quotation is from Debussy's *Pelléas*, a work in which one hardly expects to find heroics. But everything is packed with symbolism in this subtle opera, and the words of Pelléas quoted here make an ominous reference to forthcoming disaster, which he feels to be inherent in his own destiny, and which he does nothing to avoid: watching the mysterious ship leaving the harbour for an unknown destination, he says 'We shall have a storm tonight; there has been one every night now for some time'. In Ex. 56g, we find Delius again unusually showing the heroic side of his character in the last of the *Songs of Farewell*—'Now land and life finale and farewell . . . depart upon thy endless cruise, old Sailor' (it is the minor version of the major 5–1–3 of Ex. 54d— the courageous plunge towards death, as opposed to the joyously triumphant hailing of it). The Stravinsky quotation is from his ballet *Orpheus*; it occurs several times in Orpheus' *Air de Danse*, in which he revolts against the acceptance of Euridice's death. 'Pop numbers' steer clear of heroics, but the fiercely warlike Russian march-tune shows a popular use of the phrase in question (repeated a fourth higher).

Ex. 56h is included to demonstrate that, as with the major triadic phrases, the minor 5–1–3 and 1–3–5 phrases can approach equivalence and merge into a single unit of expression: Cassandra, defying the Greeks in *The Trojans* as she tells them that Aeneas and his men have escaped to Mount Ida, and Wagner's Valkyries, created by Wotan to recruit armies of heroes against expected attacks from enemies, both use 5–1–3 (the 'heroic' element), 1–3–5 (normally the 'protest' element, but here merged by sequence into the 'heroic'), and go over into 1–3–5 in the relative major, into triumphant joy (a feeling common to Cassandra and the Valkyries).

Ex. 56j demonstrates two extensions of the use of 5–1–3. First, from Bach's Cantata No. 56 'I will gladly carry the Cross' (the sharp fourth is set against the minor triad as an accented dissonance—a painful, semitonal one—resolving *upwards*, i.e. *onwards*, to the dominant); and a phrase from Britten's first Donne Sonnet ('Thou'rt like a pilgrim which abroad hath done treason and durst not turne to whence he is fled')—the brave enterprise of a pilgrimage has gone astray and ended in the anguish of fear, i.e. the 5–1–3 phrase goes on to end on the *minor sixth*, which stays unresolved. The Richard Strauss quotation is the theme of that scapegrace hero, Till Eulenspiegel (the minor third of 5–1–2–3 turns slyly upwards to the major third—Till's tragedy is a tragi-comedy); the Britten example shows the use of the same procedure, when Albert Herring, in the opera which bears his name, is mentioned as candidate for the post of May-Queen (May-King)—Albert, too, is a tragi-comical hero.

Perhaps we can now get an idea of the mood of the finale of Brahms's First Piano Concerto. As is well-known, the material of the stormy first movement arose out of Brahms's grief at Schumann's madness and impending death, and over the slow movement he originally wrote the word 'Benedictus', which aptly sums up the serene and blessed feeling of consolation it awakens—see the section on 8–7–6–5 (major). Now, the opening theme of the finale begins 5–1–2–3–(5–1), ascending, minor, *forte*, 2/4 *allegro non troppo*, *non-legato*, thrusting rhythm, played by the solo pianist (the protagonist in the concerto-drama—Brahms himself at the first performance), without orchestra, but with a strenuous semiquaver accompaniment by the soloist's left hand. The movement is usually described as 'lively' and 'robust', and so it is, but does not the 5–1–3 phrase, shooting on up the minor triad to the upper tonic, deployed in thrusting rhythm, *forte*—does not all this convey the feeling of the grief-stricken youth's courageous, even heroic resolve to leave anguish and consolation, and get on with the business of life—in the midst of which, as Schumann's sudden extinction had made clear to him, we are in death? This interpretation was once suggested to me long ago by a friend; at the time, I could only *feel* he was right, but in view of the persistent 'heroic' use of the minor 5–1–3 phrase, shown in our examples, he would seem to be absolved from the sin of 'reading into the music what isn't there'.

DESCENDING 5–(4)–3–(2)–1 (MAJOR)

If to fall in pitch expresses incoming emotion, to descend from the outlying dominant to the point of repose, the tonic, through the major third, will naturally convey a sense of experiencing joy passively, i.e. accepting or welcoming blessings, relief, consolation, reassurance, or fulfilment, together with a feeling of 'having come home'.[1]

Ex. 57a quotes a phrase from John Danyel's ayre 'Grief keep within', at the point where the poet speaks of finding relief, not in shouting his sorrow abroad, but in experiencing it passively: the sorrow of the song resides in the prevailing D minor key— this D major refrain is the moment of consolation. The Handel is the opening vocal phrase of the aria 'Ombra mai fu' from his opera *Xerxes*: the great Persian warrior, at the opening of the opera, is represented as passively enjoying the delights of his garden, apostrophizing his favourite plane-tree with the words 'Never was the shade of a tree so dear to my heart'. The Schubert is the opening vocal phrase of his song 'Der Lindenbaum' in *Die Winterreise*: the jilted lover finds comfort and consolation in his favourite linden-tree, which seems to offer him a 'happy ending' to his sorrows—the peace of death beneath its shade. In Ex. 57b, two composers show, by differing instrumental and vocal forms of the same phrase, that 5–3–1 can appear as 5–4–3–2–1 and even 5–4–3–7–1 (such a radical case as the latter will not be taken as an excuse for any 'twisting' in our examination, though it demonstrates the perfect legitimacy of such twisting, within bounds). In his Cantata No. 53 Bach accepts with joy the comforting thought, for the devout Christian, of the bell striking the last hour of his life on earth; in the second quotation, Samson's father Manoah, in Handel's oratorio, says that if only his blinded son's life is spared, he will gladly comfort and console him in his old age. Ex. 57c shows Palestrina, in his *Missa Brevis*, using the phrase in connexion with the 'Lamb of God', in the way that composers have often employed it to express the receiving of consolation from the gentler manifestations of the Deity; and Bach, in Cantata No. 106, expressing the supreme sense of gratified fulfilment to be drawn from Christ's words 'This day shalt thou be with me in Paradise'.

In Ex. 57d the comforting aspects of the deity are again in-

[1] See note on p. 167

Ex. 57 (a)

voked: by Handel, in *Messiah*, the image of the Good Shepherd
tending his sheep; and by Mozart, in his C minor Mass, the
image of God the Son, the Lamb of God, the human inter-
mediary (after expressing the appeal to God the Father by
ascending 5–6–7–8 in D minor—see Ex. 69). There follows a
totally different kind of comforter, the minx Zerlina in Mozart's
Don Giovanni, pacifying her jealous lover Masetto. In Ex. 57e,
Elgar uses the phrase in the religious context: the dying Gerontius, having sung 'Jesu, Maria, I am near to death' in D minor,
with minor sixth, turns to the key of B flat and 5–4–3–2–(3)–1
for the feeling that death means being called home by Jesus and
Mary. The two Britten quotations are: first, in *Peter Grimes*,
Ellen sits by the sea on the bright Sunday morning following the
storm, speaking to the unhappy boy apprentice of the comfort
of letting themselves enjoy 'a holiday full of peace and quietness';
second, Lucia, in *The Rape of Lucretia*, sings a vocalise with the
other women as they fold the linen (the words of the other parts
are significant—'Time treads upon the hands of women; at
birth or death their hands must fold clean linen. . . . Home is
what man leaves to seek—what is home but women?'—this
whole scene represents women as home, the place of repose and
comfort to which one returns). (See also Ex. 27b, 31f and 53e.)
    In all the above, the vitalizing agents combine to make the
effect of the phrase gentle and tender; but 5–3–1 can be robust,
when played *allegro* and *forte*, with strong accent, as Ex. 57f
shows. In both cases, the upper tonic is used as a starting point,
and the effect is one of final fulfilment. The Mozart is the opening of the last act of *Don Giovanni*, which conveys a remarkable
sense of the wheel coming full circle (a critic has recently asked,
in a review, 'why is it that this phrase has such a feeling of
finality?') The Stravinsky is, like Ex. 53g, from the point in
Oedipus Rex where Creon announces that the oracle has spoken
('The God has replied')—bringing final relief after much suffering: again, the clinching sense of finality is unmistakable.
    Once more extending an interpretation drawn from musico-
verbal contexts to a purely musical one, can we perhaps now
account for the 'glorious' effect of the broad major theme in the
first movement of Carl Nielsen's Fifth Symphony? After some
exceedingly grim minor music, declared by the composer to
represent 'destructive forces', a G major tune enters, 5–4–3–2–

(7)–1, *mf*, *adagio* 3/4, flowing rhythm, *legato*, played by violas and bassoons, as the upper part of a simple diatonic and harmonic texture: it immediately gives a sense of joyful relief after the turmoil. But the music of the 'destructive forces' returns and grows to a shatteringly brutal climax; and when the G major tune emerges out of it, *fortissimo*, high up on the horns (and violins), supported by a firm texture, and a bass of rushing hemi-demi-semiquavers, its effect is naturally that of an excited welcoming of the relief which has been expectantly striven for, a triumphant acceptance of joyous fulfilment.

DESCENDING 5–(4)–3–(2)–1 (MINOR)

Substituting the minor for the major third in the descending 5–3–1 progression, we have a phrase which has been much used to express an 'incoming' painful emotion, in a context of finality: acceptance of, or yielding to grief; discouragement and depression; passive suffering; and the despair connected with death.

Ex. 58a quotes a famous song attributed to Dunstable; 'O lovely rose, my sweet love, alas, let me not die; alas, must I end my days in weeping, after serving so truly and so loyally?'. The Josquin is the opening of his chanson 'Incessantly I am forced to suffer torment'; the Gesualdo the ending of his madrigal 'Luci serene e chiare', (the lover describes the pangs of hopeless love as 'miraculous'—'one dies but does not pass away'). In Ex. 58b, we have the opening of the Qui Tollis from Bach's B minor Mass, which is a deeply sorrowful setting of the prayer 'O Lamb of God that takest away the sins of the world, have mercy upon us'; the opening of the minor verse of Schubert's song 'Der Lindenbaum', in which the lover rejects the consoling thought of dying peacefully beneath the linden-tree (cf. Ex. 57a),

Ex. 58 (a)   (Gently)   attrib. Dunstable, c. 1450   (Slow)   Josquin, c. 1501
(p)   O ro - sa bel - la   (p)   In - cess - a - ment. . . . . .
(Slow)   mo - - re e non lan - - gue.   Gesualdo, 1596
(f)   mo-re e   non___   lan - gue,   mo - re e non lan - - gue

saying that he must continue his hopeless journey 'into the deep night'; and the dramatic and despairing cry of Dido in Berlioz's *The Trojans*—'I am going to die'. Ex. 58c consists of the opening of Verdi's *Requiem*; another symbolic remark from Debussy's *Pelléas et Mélisande*, evoking thoughts of death—'The night falls very quickly'; and Faust's despairing utterance, in Busoni's opera, when he rejects the salvation evoked by the Easter Hymn, and signs the pact with Mephistopheles—hearing the choir sing of the 'quick and the dead', he cries out loudly

'Faust, you are now a dead man'. Ex. 58d shows us the despair
of Oedipus in Stravinsky's oratorio—'All is brought to light';
the statement of tragic irrevocability at the end of Britten's *The
Rape of Lucretia*—after Lucretia's suicide the question is asked
'Is this all?' and is at first answered in the affirmative; and the
despair of Serena in Gershwin's opera *Porgy and Bess*, as she
laments that her murdered husband will never come home to
her again—'My man's gone now'.

In Ex. 58e, there is a *chanson* by a fifteenth-century Belgian
composer—'I used to complain of my lady's falseness';[1] Christ's
utterance 'Into thy hands I commend my spirit' from *The Seven
Last Words* by Schütz; and the opening of Delius's *Sea Drift*,
where the sense of despair (the work ends with the words 'We
two together no more') is infused with nostalgia by the harmonization of the C sharp minor theme with a bass of E major,
creating the added sixth of longing. In Ex. 58f, the Wilbye
madrigal speaks for itself; the Bach quotations are, first, the
final utterance of Christ in the St. John Passion—'It is finished';
second, the farewell to the world of the Christian soul in Cantata
No. 82—'World, goodnight'. Ex. 58g quotes the lament of the
Princess Xenia, in Mussorgsky's *Boris Godunov*, for her dead
lover; the funeral march for Titurel, in Wagner's *Parsifal*, to
which the chorus sing 'We bear his body to-day for the last
time'; and the theme from the Passacaglia in *Peter Grimes*, which
is later connected with the passive suffering of the boy apprentice (note the spotlighted *minor second*, note of hopeless anguish,
so appropriate to this pathetically defenceless child).

Ex. 58h brings an extension of the basic term to include a
final major seventh, which adds a more bitter feeling to the
basic mood. First, a phrase from Wilbye's madrigal 'Despiteful
thus unto myself I languish, and in disdain myself from joy I
banish'; second, Seneca's friends, in Monteverdi's *L'Incoronazione di Poppea*, lament his decision to take his own life, reminding him poignantly that 'this life is too sweet to reject'; third,
the *Arioso dolente* from Beethoven's Piano Sonata in A flat,
Op. 110. Ex. 58j continues this variant with the instrumental
transformation of the words 'It is finished' in Bach's St. John
Passion (cf. Ex. 58f) for the aria following the death of Christ;

---

[1] De Lantins seems to have survived his love-lorn grief, since the poem of his
song is an acrostic which reads, 'Putain de merde'.

Micah's injunction to the Israelites to lament Samson's down-fall, in Handel's oratorio; and Elijah's despair in Mendelssohn's oratorio—'It is enough; O Lord now take away my life'. Ex. 58k gives examples of one of many other variants of the basic term: a phrase from Gibbon's madrigal 'What is our life?'—which ends with the words 'Only we die in earnest, that's no jest'; and the *lamentoso* opening of the finale of Tchaikovsky's *Pathétique* Symphony. For a further example of the basic term see Samson's despair in Handel's oratorio (Ex. 51); see also Exs. 31f and 65d; for examples of how this term may be relieved of its basic meaning by a lively or a lilting tempo, see Exs. 44a and 45.

The essential feeling of the descending minor 5–3–1 progression is of a passive falling away from the joy of life, in various degrees, the ultimate one being to reject life altogether in favour of death. Wherefore it seems clear, as many have already felt, that the opening theme of Schubert's A minor String Quartet must be taken as a gentle expression of passive sorrow, of the kind that led to the death-wish of *Die Winterreise* (5–3–1 minor, *pianissimo, allegro ma non troppo* 4/4, smooth rhythm, *legato*, played by the 'expressive' violin over a restless accompaniment, the bass part reiterating a drone of a fifth, in ominous drum-like rhythm.)

ARCHED 5–3–(2)–1 (MINOR)

To rise from the lower dominant over the tonic to the minor third, and fall back to the tonic with or without the intervening second, conveys the feeling of a passionate outburst of painful

Ex. 59 *(a)*

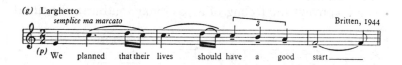

emotion, which does not protest further, but falls back into acceptance—a flow and ebb of grief. Being neither complete protest nor complete acceptance, it has an effect of restless sorrow.

Ex. 59a shows Dowland 'semper dolens' (to quote his own pun): the ayre tells of the cripple that suffered 'full many, many years' before he was healed by Christ, and ends with the words 'No David, Job, nor cripple in more grief, Christ grant me patience, patience, and my hope's relief'. The Bach is the aria

'Flow, my tears, in floods of weeping' from the St. John Passion. The two further Bach examples in Ex. 59b are the grief-stricken aria 'Have mercy, Lord, on me', from the St. Matthew Passion, and the first vocal phrase from Cantata No. 82, where the Christian soul declares that he is weary of the restless sorrow of this world, and longs for the peace of the next. All three Bach quotations have extremely restless accompaniments. Ex. 59c consists of the two Lachrymosa themes from the Requiems of Mozart and Verdi: in the latter, the slow flowing rhythm removes any 'courageous' effect that the opening 5–1–3 might have in this extended version of the arched 5–3–1.

Schubert was very attached to this phrase, as Ex. 59d shows: first, the melody of the song 'Auf dem Wasser zu singen', which ends with the reflection that life flows away like the waters of a river; second, the closing phrase of the song 'Gute Nacht' in *Die Winterreise*, in which the jilted lover oscillates between despair, wounded pride and continuing love for the faithless girl, eventually writing his name on her door before setting out on his journey, to let her know 'that I have thought of you'; and the opening of the song 'Erstarrung' from the same cycle (in a torment of grief, he 'searches vainly in the snow' for the tracks where he and his beloved used to wander in the springtime). Ex. 59e is one of Violetta's arias in the last act of Verdi's *La Traviata*: ill, and near to death, and restless because she is hoping against hope that her lover will return to her, she bids 'farewell to the past, to the fair smiling dreams', and concludes her aria with 'everything mortal ends in the tomb' (to a variant of the descending 5–3–1 progression).

In Ex. 59f, we see Wagner using the phrase in *The Ring*, for the motive attached to the renunciation of love, the step which must be taken by anyone wishing to forge the ring of absolute power from the Rhinegold: the melody goes straight to the emotional (psychological) point, expressing unhappiness—the fundamental unhappiness of those whose love of power leads them to lose all feeling of love. Mahler, as so often, shows the influence of Schubert, in two phrases from his 'Songs of a Wayfaring Lad': in the first, the rejected lover says that his love's wedding day will be the unhappiest day of his life; in the second, he says goodbye to 'all that he ever loved', before setting out, like Schubert's lover, on a journey in search of death. The

Britten quotation (Ex. 59g) shows Ellen, in *Peter Grimes*, meeting the accusations of the villagers that her sympathy for Grimes has helped to bring about the apprentice's death, with a tensely sorrowful plea of good intentions (ending on the anguished minor sixth).

We are led from the above to suppose that the second theme in the first movement of Mozart's G minor String Quintet must be expressive of restless grief, as has frequently been stated: arched 5–3–2–1, repeated, *piano, allegro* 4/4, dotted rhythm, played by the violin over a texture of throbbing quavers (tonic minor triad); after which the theme enlarges on its basic mood, by a passionate leap of a minor ninth from the lower dominant to the minor sixth, note of anguish, and a return down the 'despairing' 5–4–3–2–1).

1–(2)–3–(2)–1 (MINOR)

To base a theme on the tonic, only moving out as far as the minor third, and returning immediately, is to 'look on the darker side of things' in a context of immobility, neither rising up to protest, nor falling back to accept. Composers have frequently used this progression to express brooding, an obsession with gloomy feelings, a trapped fear, or a sense of inescapable doom, especially when it is repeated over and over.

Ex. 60 *(a)*

The Josquin madrigal in Ex. 60a is 'Parfons regrets'—'Come away, sorrow, and kill my heart, that it may drown itself in woe and weeping'; the Purcell is the sombre opening of his anthem on Psalm 52 ('Hear my prayer, O Lord, and let my crying come unto Thee'); the Debussy is his setting of that grief-obsessed Verlaine poem 'Tears fall in my heart, as rain falls on the town'. In Ex. 60b, we have a phrase from the Dies Irae of Mozart's Requiem Mass—fear of the inescapable Day of Judgment; Don Giovanni suddenly transfixed by fear as the flames of hell flicker about him; and the demons calling to the terrified and praying Marguerite, in the church scene from Gounod's *Faust*. Ex. 60c shows three *bassi ostinati*: that of Chopin's Funeral March; the one that persists for fifty bars while the 'destructive forces' gather power in Nielsen's Fifth Symphony; and the one in Stravinsky's *Oedipus Rex* which supports the chorus as they implore Oedipus to save Thebes from the plague of which it is dying (their melodic line also moves between 1 and 3 for eighteen bars). The Stravinsky in Ex. 60d is from the beginning of the Mourning Chorus for Tom's death, near the end of *The Rake's Progress*; the first Walton (from *Belshazzar's Feast*) is the Israelites' warning to Babylon of its inevitable destruction; the second their obsessive cry of revengeful satisfaction that the destruction is accomplished (moving on to a major chord). Ex. 60e shows the confined struggle, in Britten's *The Rape of Lucretia*, of the actual rape itself (with its symbolism of the horn trying to close the gap between the tonic and minor third); and the wailing of the 'Doleful Creatures' in Vaughan Williams's *Pilgrim's Progress*.

This latter forms a nice bridge from 1–3–1 to 1–2–3–2–1, using both in conjunction—and to other variants. Ex. 60f consists of two quotations from the Blessed Virgin's Cradle Song by Byrd, in which she is pictured dwelling on the thought of the slaughter of the innocents, which threatens her own child; the beginning of a madrigal by Morley—'In dews of roses, Lycoris thus sat weeping' (the obsessive repetition takes here the familiar form of continuous 'imitation'); and the opening of a Gibbons madrigal which speaks for itself. In Ex. 60g, we have the bass of the opening of the Confutatis Maledictis in Mozart's Requiem Mass (fear of inescapable damnation again); the ending of the first phrase of the theme of Chopin's Funeral March (it has remained on the tonic up to this point); and the opening theme of the first movement of the Sonata in which the Funeral March occurs (Chopin said nothing about this theme at all, but surely we need not talk of 'pure music' now). The 'pop' number is from the Maurice Chevalier film *Ma Pomme*; it is the dirge-like 'Song of the Tramps of Paris'. Ex. 6oh brings us the opening of that death-obsessed song 'Der Wegweiser' in *Die Winterreise*; Violetta's agitated, fearful, obsessive plea to her lover's father who has come to ask her to break off their affair—'You don't know what love I have for him'; and the last song of Mahler's 'wayfaring lad'—'the two blue eyes of his faithless sweetheart' have sent him out into the world on his journey to death. (See also Exs. 26, *passim*, 27c and h, 28a and c, and 58d).

It may be advisable at this point to remind the reader that the enormous difference between the various uses of a basic term are accounted for by the vitalizing agents. We are hardly likely to take Morley's shepherd Lycoris (*piano*, lively tempo, lilting rhythm, two sopranos echoing one another) as seriously as Mozart's Don Giovanni (*forte*, *allegro*, tense, hammering, thrusting rhythm, trombones and strings); but the basic sense of fixation to a painful emotion is common to both. And it is also common to the closing bars of the first movement of Schubert's Unfinished Symphony (1–2–3–1, minor, repeated, *mezzo-forte* dying away to *pianissimo*, *allegro moderato*, 3/4, swaying rhythm, first on top of the rich texture, on violins and violas, then in the bass, on cellos and basses); and to the opening theme of Rachmaninov's Third Piano Concerto.

(5)–6–5 (MAJOR)

The major sixth is often used as a melodic stepping-stone in an ascent from the dominant to the tonic, in which case its expressive identity is merged into an overall pattern with the 'optimistic' major seventh; but its most individual expressive function is its relationship to the dominant in connexion with the major triad beneath. This relationship takes various forms, some of which are shown below.

Ex. 61a shows three cases in which the major sixth is harmonized as the major third of the subdominant chord, and the effect is of a simple assertion of joy, moving up from one major

Ex. 61 *(a)*

third to another, harmonically speaking, and back again. The first is the 'fa-la-la' refrain from Weelkes's madrigal 'To shorten winter's sadness, see where the nymphs with gladness . . .' (the quotation is a composite top line made up of overlapping parts, and the harmonic counterpoint beneath it is too complex rhythmically to be made clear on one stave); the second and third need no comment.

Ex 61b demonstrates the simple alternation of 6 and 5 either unaccompanied, or in the triadic context; the effect is similar to the previous case, but there is not so much an assertion of joy as a joyous vibration. The Beethoven is the short, breathless lead-up to the final jubilant outburst of the finale of the Choral Symphony; the Britten is the music of the church bells on the bright Sunday morning in *The Turn of the Screw*; the Stravinsky is the cheerful, jogging tune of the soldier's violin in *The Soldier's Tale* (the A minor triad scarcely disturbs the G major triadic basis).

In Ex. 61c, we see the sixth functioning as a short anacrusis leading on to the fifth, unaccompanied, or in a triadic context; the effect is practically the same again, that of a joyous vibration, with the faintest touch of longing. The Bach is the opening of the aria 'See, Jesus stretches out his hand towards us' in the St. Matthew Passion. The Mozart is the persistent figure which runs through the scene in which Don Giovanni suggests to Leporello that they should go and console the lady in distress—Donna Elvira: the figure underlines the sense of amusement inherent in the situation. The Schubert is another quotation from 'Der Lindenbaum'—the joy brought to the love-lorn wanderer's heart by the favourite linden-tree.

Ex. 61d shows the effect of leaning on to the sixth, slowly, and falling back again: a sense of joyful serenity, with a slight element of longing, or pleading: the Sanctus from Fauré's Requiem, and the Kyrie in *The Dream of Gerontius*—the loving prayer of the dying man's friends.

The remainder of the examples show the commonest form of the (5)–6–5 progression, concerned with the *appoggiatura* 6–5, producing the effect of a burst of pleasurable longing. Ex. 61e presents Michal's admiring longing for David, in Handel's *Saul*; Don Giovanni's luring call to Donna Elvira (cf. Ex. 61c, which immediately precedes this); and from *La Traviata*, Violetta's last delirious cry 'O joy', when at the moment of her death she feels that she is returning to life (dominant ninth harmony of longing). In Ex. 61f, we have Marguerite's cry of 'He loves me', in Gounod's *Faust* (dominant ninth again); the love-theme from Tchaikovsky's Overture *Romeo and Juliet*; and the opening of Debussy's song *En sourdine*, which tells of two lovers 'mingling their hearts and souls in the evening air'. Ex. 61g quotes the ending of one of Britten's Michelangelo Sonnets, in which the lover expresses his utter dependence on the beloved, comparing his beneficent effect to that of the sun; a recurrent phrase from the *Air de Danse* in Stravinsky's ballet *Orpheus*, expressing Orpheus' longing for the dead Eurydice; and the well-known dance-tune 'Cheek to Cheek' by Irving Berlin, the words of which express an intense attraction towards dancing with the beloved. (See also Exs. 29 and 31, *passim*.)

(5)–6–5 (MINOR)

The chief and almost only expressive function of the minor sixth is to act as an *appoggiatura* on to the dominant, giving the effect of a burst of anguish. This is the most widely used of all terms of musical language: one can hardly find a page of 'grief' music by any tonal composer of any period without encountering it several times.

The quotations in Ex. 62a are the opening of a fourteenth-century Belgian *chanson* 'Slave to grief'; the opening of Josquin's *Déploration sur la mort de Ockeghem* (the tenor part uses the plainsong Requiem theme, but converts its rise and fall of a tone to that of a semitone, 5–6–5 in D minor); the lullaby refrain from the aforementioned sorrowful Virgin's Cradle Song by Byrd (3–2 in D minor as 6–5 in A); and, from Schütz's *Resurrection*, the setting of the words 'Mary stood before the grave and wept'. Ex. 62b shows two Mozart examples: the demons threatening Don Giovanni with the words 'any punishment is all too little for your sins' (we hear this statement through the Don's anguished feelings); and the setting of 'how great will be the trembling, when the Judge shall come' in the Requiem Mass. The Beethoven is from *Fidelio*—the introduction to the scene where Florestan lies suffering in the dungeon. In Ex. 62c, the friends of Gerontius, in Elgar's oratorio, hearing him cry out in fear of death and damnation, change their serene prayer of 'Kyrie' (cf. Ex. 61d) to a more urgent and anguished plea for divine aid (note also the quicker tempo and louder dynamics). The Walton is from his setting of 'By the waters of Babylon' in *Belshazzar's Feast*; the Britten from *The Rape of Lucretia*—the morning after the rape, Lucretia cannot bear to look at the flowers brought to her by her servants; the Stravinsky from *The Rake's Progress*—Tom, in the madhouse at the end of the opera, sings remorsefully to Anne 'In a foolish dream, in a gloomy labyrinth, I hunted shadows, disdaining thy true love'.

Ex. 62d quotes the opening of a Morley madrigal; a recurrent phrase from the aria 'Atonement and repentance break the sinful heart in twain' in Bach's St. Matthew Passion; and a phrase from another sorrowful aria in that work—'For love my Saviour will die'. In Ex. 62e, we see Donna Anna's perturbation on discovering the dead body of her father, in Mozart's *Don Giovanni* (the whole scene is permeated with the minor 6–5 *appoggiatura*); a persistent phrase from the last page of Verdi's *La Traviata* (it bursts straight in as a contradiction of Violetta's major 6–5 to the words 'O joy'—cf. Ex. 61e); and the weeping phrase of the timorous Vestal Virgins in Berlioz's *The Trojans*, against which Cassandra addresses them scornfully 'You who tremble', coming down sternly and fatefully on to the minor third. Ex. 62f shows how Wagner made a *leitmotiv* out of the figure, in *The Ring*, in opposition to the joyous major 6–5 of the Rhinegold motive (cf. Ex. 31c): first, Mime howling while he is bullied by Alberich; second, the Servitude motive of the Nibelungs groaning under Alberich's yoke; third, the final, bitter, mournful, 'hating' form of the motive, when it attaches to the evil and self-confessedly unhappy figure of Hagen, in *Götterdämmerung*.

In Ex. 62g, Mussorgsky is also shown deriving an instrumental term from a vocal one: the wailing of the Simpleton in *Boris Godunov* is taken up as an ostinato for his lament over the future fate of Russia. The extract from the Dies Irae of Verdi's Requiem needs no comment; the other Verdi quotation is Othello's agonized cry to Iago 'You have bound me to the cross!' Ex. 62h shows a characteristically subtle use of the term by Debussy for the closing page of *Pelléas*: the mingled serenity and pathos of Mélisande's death is conveyed by a *major* triad with a *minor* 6–5 *appoggiatura*. The Bartók is from the *Cantata Profana*: the eldest of the nine sons, who are turned by a spell into deer, cries out to his father not to shoot them. The Britten is from *Peter Grimes*, from the final pathetic scene where Grimes, at the end of his tether, stumbles about in the darkness in a frenzy, while the far-off sound of his name being shouted by the pursuing villagers is accompanied by the equally distant, and dismal wail of a fog-horn (tuba, off-stage, minor 6–5).

The Britten quotation in Ex. 62j is the opening of his Donne Sonnet 'O might these sighs and tears return again into my breast and eyes'; the Schoenberg occurs in *A Survivor from Warsaw*, at the point where the narrator says 'you had been separated from your children, from your wife, your parents, you don't know what happened to them. . . '. The Stravinsky, from *The Rake's Progress*, shows the sense of anguished despair to be obtained from deploying the minor 6–5 as an interval of a falling minor ninth (note that the phrase opens with arched 5–3–1, minor, on an F sharp minor triad—the minor 6–5 in C sharp minor is retrospective). The final quotation is from the popular Russian song about the 'Black Eyes' by which the lover has been misled and through which 'the joys of life have vanished for ever'. (See also Exs. 27j; 30 and 31, *passim*; 35b, 41a and f, 48, 49 and 50.)

Having identified this term of musical language, are we not in a position to understand the moods of the opening pages of Mozart's Fortieth and Vaughan Williams's Fourth Symphony? The latter, it is true, gives the impression of beginning with minor 2–1 rather than minor 6–5, but the terms are partly interchangeable, the former being a darker version of the latter (see Ex. 35b).

1–2–3–2 (MINOR)

This term is actually a fusion of the gloomy relationship between the tonic and minor third, and (harmonizing the third as a minor sixth of the dominant) the emotional effect of the minor 6–5 progression. It has been employed rarely, but these are three outstanding examples which give it the status of a basic term in musical language.

The fact that Beethoven and Tchaikovsky hit on the same phrase to open works which they entitled 'Pathétique', and that Purcell also used the same progression to open Dido's Lament 'When I am laid in earth', in his opera, puts the expressive function of the term in a clear light. To make the restricted movement from the tonic to the 'dark' minor third, and fall back by a harmonic 6–5 *appoggiatura* at a slow tempo, is naturally to express a sense of brooding grief swelling out briefly into a burst of anguish and dying away again; when the phrase is played quickly, and repeated, as in Tchaikovsky's *allegro*, the brooding feeling is replaced by one of agitated obsession. A similar kind of term, substituting for 1–2 the ascending 1–3–5 of protest plus the ascending 5–1–3 of courage, forms the basis of the opening theme of the finale of Mozart's Fortieth Symphony (see Ex. 87f).

1–(2)–(3)–(4)–5–6–5 (MAJOR)

The ascending major 1–3–5 progression, with the 5–6–5 phrase dovetailed on, is another of the most widely-used terms of musical language; it is almost always employed to express

the innocence and purity of angels and children, or some natural phenomenon which possesses the same qualities in the eyes of men. That this should be so is hardly surprising, when we consider that the phrase confines itself entirely to the joyful elements of the scale, and being an ascending one, it is consequently an affirmation of maximum joy. It is, in fact, expressive of an absolute happiness that can never be fully experienced in civilized human life but only by savages, children, animals or birds, or saints or imaginary blessed beings. In expressing the normal emotions of life, man has to undermine the joy of the major system by means of the pathetic 4–3 and 8–7 suspensions, or by chromatic tensions, and at least half the time looks on the darker side with the minor system: 1–3–5–6–5 in the major system is set aside for states of pure blessedness.

Ex. 64a and b show the simplest form of the term—1–5–6–5. In Ex. 64a, the first quotation shows the derivation from plainchant ('A boy is born to us'); the second is an adaptation of the plainchant tune by Morales for a Christmas motet; the third, the opening of Byrd's madrigal on the innocence of youthful love—('When younglings first on Cupid set their eyes . . . they ween he can work them no annoy'). Ex. 64b consists of the opening of Wilbye's madrigal 'As fair as morn' (the connexion between the freshness of morning and innocence is obvious); the chorale which rides with divine purity over the tumultuous human grief of the opening chorus of Bach's St. Matthew Passion—'O Lamb of God, guiltless'; and the children's nursery-tune known the world over (in this country as 'Baa-baa black sheep'). (See also Ex. 97).

With Ex. 64c, we turn to the 1–3–5–6–5 version, with another plainchant derivation—from the Gradual of the Holy Innocents ('The snare is broken, we are delivered'); a well-known Czech carol (one of the innumerable Christmas carols which open with this phrase); and the song of a thirteenth-century troubadour about the nightingale (another 'innocent' and 'fresh' natural creature). In his chapter on medieval song, in Vol. 2 of *The New Oxford History of Music*, J. A. Westrup draws attention to the widespread use of this figure in the songs of the troubadours, trouvères, minnesingers, and mastersingers, and in the Italian *laudi spirituali*: I have taken the nightingale song and the 'Laqueus' plainchant theme from his article. Ex. 64d brings some variants of the basic pattern: the German chorale 'How brightly shines the morning star'; the opening of Bach's cantata 'Hold in remembrance Jesus Christ'; the Cum Sancto Spiritu (With the Holy Ghost') from his Mass in B minor; and the Osanna (the song of the Cherubim and Seraphim) from Mozart's Mass in C minor.

Ex. 64e quotes a theme from Mendelssohn's *Elijah* which needs no comment; and the opening of Wagner's *Parsifal*—the theme of the Holy Grail (the sixth does not fall back to the dominant here, since the theme continues with the phrase connected with the spear that pierced Christ on the Cross, modulating into C minor with the minor 6–5 term and a fall to the minor third—when the opera opens, purity is stained with sin and suffering). The Humperdinck is, of course, the prayer of the children in his opera *Hansel and Gretel*—'When I go to bed at night, fourteen angels stand around me'. In Ex. 64f, the Busoni fragments are from the Easter Chorus in *Doktor Faust*; the Vaughan Williams is the opening of the final chorus of *The Pilgrim's Progress*, sung by voices from the Celestial City. Ex. 64g shows the variant 1–3–4–5–6–5 in another carol; in the theme from Vaughan Williams's *Job*, to which young men and women on earth, after Satan's defeat, play instruments and decorate the altars; and in the theme sung by the Heavenly Beings to Christian, in *The Pilgrim's Progress*, when they tend his wounds after the fight with Apollyon—' So shalt thou enter in the gates of the Celestial City'.

In Ex. 64h, we have the complete form 1–2–3–4–5–6–5: once more the plainchant derivation, in a French 'Alleluia'; the Pastoral Symphony in Handel's *Messiah*; and the lark in Haydn's *Creation*. Ex. 64j shows two further variants: the theme to which the Angel sings to Gerontius of his salvation, in Elgar's oratorio; and the words of Ellen, in *Peter Grimes*, greeting the peace of the bright Sunday morning after the human and elemental turmoil of the storm—in company, significantly, with the innocent boy apprentice.

In 1948, Anthony Alpers gave a radio talk in the Christmas edition of the BBC's Music Magazine, drawing attention to the derivation of many Christmas carols from this term; he reminded his listeners that the fourteenth-century German mystic, Henry Suso, who composed the tune of 'In Dulci Jubilo', said it had been sung to him by the angels, and that the melody was so joyful that he had been drawn into dancing with his heavenly visitors. Alpers made the amusing suggestion that this tune was the 'song the angels sang' at the first Christmas; and indeed, one is inclined to believe that if the angels did appear to the shepherds at the first Christmas, the opening strains of their song may well have been 1–(3)–5–6–5. Alpers also pointed out that the opening violin theme of the finale of Vaughan Williams's Fifth Symphony must naturally be regarded in this light, an opinion with which we are by now disposed to agree.

1–(2)–(3)–(4)–5–6–5 (MINOR)

The minor version of the foregoing term, confining itself to the two basic 'grievous' notes of the scale in a triadic context, clearly expresses a powerful assertion of fundamental unhappiness—the 'protest' of 1–3–5 being extended into the 'anguish' of 5–6–5.

Exs. 65a and b show the simple form 1–5–6–5. Ex. 65a quotes a twelfth-century troubadour song 'He who counsels me to have done with loving does not know how he arouses me, nor what are my grievous sighs'; the opening line of Ockeghem's *chanson* 'Misfortune afflicts me'; and the beginning of Byrd's anthem 'O Lord my God, let flesh and blood thy servant not subdue'. In Ex. 65b, we have the opening of the chorale 'In deepest need I cry to thee'; and from the St. John Passion of Schütz, the setting of the words 'Then they crucified him'. Ex. 65c shows the form 1–3–5–6–5, from the opening of Josquin's motet 'Thou who didst veil thy face and suffer poverty, O Sun of Justice, have mercy on us.' Ex. 65d brings the form 1–3–4–5–6–5: the opening of the Kyrie in a Service by Byrd; and the opening of a madrigal by Giaches Wert (note that 'O unhappy parting' is set to the despairing minor 5–4–3–2–1.

In Ex. 65e, we have Seneca's words in Monteverdi's *L'Incoronazione di Poppea*, as he comes to the point of taking his own life, 'Friends, friends, the hour has come'. Seneca is an equivocal case: he declares that he goes to his death with joy, but he is after all the Stoic philosopher, facing the final misfortune with unbowed head; the stoic emotions function in a tragic context, for which the simple joy of the major system would be inappropriate. In Ex. 65e is also the phrase with which Aida

greets Radames as she enters the tomb to die with him, in Verdi's opera.

Ex. 65f quotes two uses of a folk-song common to many countries—the minor version of 'Baa-baa, black sheep' (Ex. 64b) —the original words, in both major and minor cases, being impossible to trace. It is not surprising that the Jewish race, with its tragic past, should have chosen a stern variant of the theme for the Israeli National Anthem (note that the minor sixth is harmonized firmly as the minor third of the subdominant minor chord.) Smetana used a Czech version of the tune as the main theme of his tone-poem portraying the river Vltava, the first part of the cycle *Ma Vlast*, which evokes the heroic-tragic past of his native land. Although to some extent the theme is infused with a legendary-heroic character, the general effect is not in any way tragic in feeling (rather genial in fact), owing to the buoyant rhythm, the flowing semiquaver accompaniment tone-painting the river, and particularly the transformation of 6–5 into 4–3 in the relative major, any suspicion of 4–3 pathos being removed by harmonizing 4 firmly as the tonic of the subdominant major chord of the new key.

For two superb uses of this term in its basic sense, see Ex. 52a and b, and for a 'pop' version, Ex. 27j.

Aaron Copland has drawn attention to an isolated example of the effect of this term (conflated with the minor 5–4–3–2–1) in a piece of 'pure' music: the subject of Bach's E flat minor fugue in Book I of the 'Forty-eight'. He says 'To analyse why this theme, consisting only of a few notes, should be so expressive, is impossible'—yet he goes on to try and analyse it: 'Something in the way the theme rises bravely from 1 to 5, rises again from 1 to 4, only to fall back slowly on 1—something also about the shortened rhythmic sense of the second part of the phrase— creates an extraordinary feeling of quiet but profound resignation'.[1] Copland's analysis is, of course, hampered by a lack of consideration of the tonal tensions. First, he does not mention that this all happens in the minor scale: the effect of the same procedure in the major scale would be quite different. Secondly, he does not mention the minor sixth. Thirdly, he does not mention the basic terms 1–5–6–5 or 5–4–3–2–1. Nevertheless, it is clear that he has felt the emotion in the theme exactly.

[1] Aaron Copland, *What to Listen For in Music*, Chap. 2.

The effect of the whole theme is explained as follows. The minor system, soft dynamic, and slow tempo set a quiet, serious mood; and 1–5–6–5, a subdued assertion of anguish, merges into 5–4–3–2–1, a subdued expression of resigned despair. Thus the final effect, which Copland has felt but been unable to account for, is one of 'quiet but profound resignation'. His pinpointing of the other expressive elements—of the fall from 5 to 1 and the subsequent rise only up as far as 4 (within the overall shape 5–4–3–2–1) and of the rhythmic contraction—shows the endless subtleties of expression to be gained from the inflection of a basic term.

8–7–6–5 (MAJOR)

To fall from the tonic to the dominant, taking in the optimistic major seventh and sixth, is to express an incoming emotion of joy, an acceptance or welcoming of comfort, consolation, or fulfilment.[1] The term is clearly a near-synonym of the major 5–4–3–2–1, with which it often combines into a descending major scale, in the way that the ascending triadic figures 1–3–5 and 5–1–3 combine and intermingle. However, when it is used separately, the fact that it ends on the dominant gives it a more open, continuing feeling towards the future, compared with 5–3–1, which suggests finality.

In Ex. 66a we see three composers using the term, like 5–4–3–2–1, to invoke the Deity as a bringer of consolation or other blessings, together with an operatic excerpt. First, an early setting of the words 'O Lord God, Lamb of God'; second, a phrase from Dunstable's *Veni sancte spiritus* (the words here are 'Come, bestower of gifts'); the third and fourth quotations are complementary to their 5–(4)–3–2–1 counterparts (see Exs. 57a and c, where the general contexts are explained). Bach made much use of this term, Ex. 66b giving two cases; the aria 'See, Jesus stretches his hand towards us' in the St. Matthew Passion; and the aria 'Sweet consolation, my Jesus comes' in Cantata No. 151. Mozart is represented in Ex. 66c by Idomeneo's song of relief at the end of the opera—'Peace returns to my heart; as in the season of flowers the trees blossom, so age now flowers in me'; and the Christe Eleison from his Mass in C minor (which follows a Kyrie Eleison based on the minor 1–3–5

[1] See note on p. 167

Ex. 66 *(a)*

progression). The Verdi is from the aria in the last act of *La Traviata*, in which Alfredo tries to console Violetta by saying that they will leave Paris, the scene of all their unhappiness, and live peacefully in the country; the Wagner is the theme of Faith in *Parsifal*, which reveals its true significance at the end of the opera, portraying the descent of the Dove (the Holy Ghost) during the final scene of redemption. Ex. 66d quotes the theme which brings temporary consolation amid the despair of the finale of Tchaikovsky's *Pathétique* Symphony (it is marked 'soothingly and with devotion'); the opening of the love-duet in Debussy's *Pelléas*, in which the lovers welcome the long-awaited relief of being able to avow their passion; and

Bianca's complementary phrase to that of Lucia in the linen-folding scene in Britten's *The Rape of Lucretia* (see Ex. 57e for theme and general context). See also Ex. 5 (Dowland).

All the above quotations are slowish in tempo; we now turn to quicker, more animated examples. Ex. 66e shows again Bach's fondness for the term, in the aria 'At last, at last, I am free from my yoke' in Cantata No. 56, and the Domine Deus ('Domine *Fili*') from the B minor Mass. The Mozart is from another of Belmonte's arias in *The Seraglio*, in which he is anticipating the relief of seeing Constanze again after long separation; the Stravinsky from the opening aria of *The Rake's Progress*, in which Anne is enjoying the beauty of spring, and receiving assurance from the thought that 'Love reigns o'er his own'.

Ex. 66f brings louder and weightier versions: the phrase 'Et in terra pax' from the *Gloria in modum tubae* (in the style of the trumpet) by Dufay; the last line of the chorale 'A stronghold sure' which voices the all-embracing sense of fulfilment in the words 'There is nothing on earth like Him' to 8–7–6–5 plus 5–4–3–2–1; and the heartfelt song of thanksgiving for the relief of the rain, in Mendelssohn's *Elijah*. (See also Ex. 6, Handel.)

The remaining examples reveal that this term is employable, in the same sense, as a bass. In Ex. 66g, we see it at work peacefully, in Wilbye's madrigal 'Draw on, sweet night, best friend unto those cares . . .'; actively, in the Easter Hymn which brings temporarily its inherent solace to the tormented Faust, in Berlioz's cantata; and peacefully again, as Anne, in Stravinsky's *The Rake's Progress*, sings her unhappy, demented lover to sleep. In, Ex. 66h, it acts firmly as the ground bass for the final duet of Monteverdi's *L'Incoronazione di Poppea*, in which Nero and Poppea, all their worries over, welcome the opportunity to enjoy their love; majestically, in the Sanctus in Bach's B minor Mass; and actively again, in the angel's chorus 'Glory to God' in Handel's *Messiah* (the fulfilment of the long-awaited 'good tidings of great joy').

8–7–6–5 (MINOR)

To fall from the tonic to the dominant, taking in the 'mournful' minor seventh and 'anguished' minor sixth, is clearly to express an incoming painful emotion, an acceptance of, or yielding to grief; passive suffering; and the despair connected with death. As with the major form, it is a near-synonym of 5–4–3–2–1, and often merges with it; but again, when it is used on its own, it has an open, continuing feeling (never-ending despair) whereas 5–4–3–2–1 suggests finality (death itself). The three quotations in Ex. 67a are: the opening of Ockeghem's *chanson* 'Except only the expectation of death, no hope remains in my weary heart'; a phrase from Obrecht's 'By the waters of Babylon'—'If I forget thee, O Jerusalem, let my right hand forget her cunning'; and Weerbecke's setting of the Tenebrae—'There was darkness over all the land as they crucified Christ of Judea'. Ex. 67b shows the opening of Josquin's chanson 'Come away, sorrow, and kill my heart, that it may drown itself in woe and weeping'; and the first line of Dowland's famous 'Lachrymae' (note the dovetailing of 8–7–6–5 with the variant of the arched 5–3–1). In Ex. 67c, we have two cases of the fusing of 8–7–6–5 and 5–(4)–3–(2)–1 into a single expressive unit: Pamina's aria in *The Magic Flute*, 'Ah, I feel it; the joy of love has vanished for ever'; and the opening of Verdi's Requiem. The Tchaikovsky is the minor transformation of the

'consoling' theme in the finale of his *Pathétique* Symphony (see Ex. 66d) on its second and last appearance, when it falls down and down the minor scale to die out on double-basses. Ex. 67d is an elaboration of 8–7–6–5—the final theme of *La Bohème*, to which Rudolph sobs out his grief at Mimi's death: this too dovetails into 5–4–3–2–1. Mélisande's death evoked a more rarified version of the phrase from Debussy, and so did Orpheus's grief from Stravinsky (Ex. 67e): the stage direction in the latter case is 'Orpheus weeps for Euridyce; he stands motionless, with his back to the audience'. See also Exs. 5, 30a, 32d, 41a, 41g (with flattened fifth).

The superb passage from Weelkes's madrigal 'Ay me, my wonted joys forsake me, and deep despair doth overtake me', demonstrates how 8–7–6–5, by contrapuntal imitation, will function as a bass (notice 5–4–3–2–1 as an inner part). The remaining examples are of such basses.

Ex. 67g brings us the equivocal Seneca again, from *L'Incoronazione di Poppea*: 'Death is but a brief anguish' he sings, but his philosophy is that death is the end of everything. Blow and Purcell, setting the same poem of lamentation for Queen Mary's death, at approximately the same time, both wove 8–7–6–5 into their otherwise different basses. Ex. 67h shows the bass of the 'Way of the Cross' aria in Bach's St. Matthew Passion; of the opening remarks of the Statue, coming to claim Don Giovanni for hell, in Mozart's opera; and of the dirge to which Lucretia walks to meet her husband in Britten's opera, in despair at the shattering of their love by the rape. (See also Ex. 46b).

THE DESCENDING CHROMATIC SCALE

To complete our account of the sixteen simplest basic terms of musical language, it is necessary to mention the descending chromatic scale, which is essentially the minor 8–7–6–5 with the intervening semitones filled in, plus or minus the minor 5–4–3–2–1, treated likewise. The effect of filling in the gaps is to make the 'despairing' descent more weary, and to increase the element of pain by every possible chromatic tension. Examples are too long to quote, so a list will be given.

As a melodic line, descending chromatics appear in the following: Giuseppe Caimo's lamenting madrigal of 1564,

'Piangete valli abbandonate' ('Weep, ye forsaken valleys')—
8 down to 5, answered by 5 down to 2; Gesualdo's madrigal
of 1611 'Moro, lasso' ('I die, weary of my grief')—free chromatics, E sharp, E, D sharp, D, in D minor; Purcell's Lament
for the Death of Queen Mary, on the word 'moerore' (to lament)
—8 down to 5; Mozart's *Don Giovanni*, accompanying the deaths
of both Don Giovanni and the Commendatore (both 8 down
to 5); and Schubert's song 'Der Wegweiser', where the winter-
journeyer sings of the signpost pointing out a journey 'from
which no-one ever came back' (free chromatics, F, E, E flat, D,
D flat, C, in a G minor context). The procedure is used for the
dying utterances of Dido, in Berlioz's *The Trojans* (8 down to 2),
Valentine, in Gounod's *Faust* (5 down to 1), and Gerontius in
Elgar's oratorio (5 down to 2).

As an inner part, a descending chromatic scale from the
minor seventh down to the major second ends the Chorus of
Mourning for the death of Tom, in Stravinsky's *The Rake's
Progress*.

As a bass, the descending chromatic scale is used for the
death of Dido, in Purcell's opera, and the Crucifixus of Bach's
B minor Mass (both 8 down to 5); during the scene of Mélisande's death, in Debussy's opera (4 down to minor 6); and in
the opening chorus of Stravinsky's *Oedipus Rex*, to the words
'Thebes is dying' (5 down to 1).

Such general agreement would suggest that this slow, gradual,
painful sinking expresses the feeling of life ebbing away
altogether.

There are, of course, many other terms of musical language
which we have not considered. For example the phrase in the
major system, beginning on various notes, which rises three
steps, repeats and accents the last, and falls a fifth, sixth or
seventh; which, if we are to accept the instinct of composers,
expresses a feeling of passionate love. Consider Christ's words
in Bach's St. Matthew Passion 'I shall not drink of this cup
until that day when I drink it again with you in my Father's
Kingdom': at the words 'until that day', the melody takes the
pattern 1–2–3–3–lower 6. Or Zerlina in *Don Giovanni*, who uses
exactly the same phrase, on the same notes, but to a quick,
light rhythm befitting her skittish nature, as she presses Masetto's
hand to her heart, singing 'Feel it beating; feel it beating', in

the aria 'Vedrai carino'. Or the drawn-out theme in Wagner's *Tristan* (the second theme of the Prelude) connected with the glance of the wounded Tristan into Isolde's eyes, which began the fatal attachment (6–7–8–8–2); or the unmistakably erotic tune of the slow movement of Tchaikovsky's Fifth Symphony, which includes the phrases 3–4–5–5–lower 6, 2–3–4–4–lower 5. There is also the 'lullaby' phrase which moves between the major third and the dominant: Wilbye's 'Draw on sweet night' (Ex. 66g); the lulling accompaniment of Bach's 'Komm süsser Trost' (Ex. 66b); Schubert's well-known Cradle Song, his song 'Des Baches Wiegenlied' in *Die schöne Müllerin*, his song 'Liebesbotschaft', and his song 'Im Dorfe' in *Die Winterreise*, in which the wanderer envies the villagers sleeping in their beds on that cold night; Brahms's Cradle Song; Tarquin's words as he stands by the sleeping Lucretia's bedside in Britten's opera—'To wake her with a kiss would put Tarquinius asleep awhile'; and the lullaby Anne sings to Tom in Stravinsky's *The Rake's Progress* (Ex. 66g).

But the sixteen terms dealt with above are undoubtedly the really basic ones, and are sufficient for our immediate purpose— an examination of the more far-reaching aspects of the language of music.

NOTE:—On pp. 106, 130, and 159, the expressive effect of a melodic descent in the major, and particularly of the descending major basic terms 5–4–3–2–1 and 8–7–6–5, is described as 'an incoming feeling of joy' and 'an acceptance of comfort, relief, reassurance, or fulfilment'. This is only half the story, since out of these expressive qualities another equally important one arises—a sense of confidence—which becomes more particularly noticeable as the volume becomes louder and the phrasing more staccato or accented. This is, of course a different kind of confidence from that expressed by ascending major music: it is the sweeping confidence that takes for granted that all difficulties are over, as opposed to the active, assertive confidence that goes out to overcome whatever difficulties there may be.

4

THE PROCESS
OF MUSICAL COMMUNICATION

Having isolated the elements of musical expression, and identified the basic terms of musical vocabulary, we have to some extent prepared the way for an attack on the main problem—how a large-scale musical work functions expressively as a whole. But before we can turn our attention to this, a number of important questions remain to be answered. How, precisely, does music communicate the composer's feeling to the listener? Granted that the same phrases are used over and over again to 'express' the same emotions, how are they made to 'convey' composers' own personal experience of these emotions, and of various shades of these emotions? To phrase it another way, how is a musical phrase made to bear a particular 'content'? What *is* content, in reality? How does it get into the music? And how does it get out of it again, and into the listener? Only by answering these questions can we come to understand exactly in what sense music is expressive, what sort of things it can express, and how far we can hope to give a sense of them in words.

The most convenient way of tackling the whole problem is to analyse the process of musical communication all the way along the chain, from the moment the work begins to stir inside the composer's mind to the moment it makes its impact upon the listener. Perhaps the knowledge we have gained of the elements of musical expression and the basic terms of musical vocabulary offers us a chance of understanding at last just how this chain works.

To begin at the beginning: how does a musical work originate in the composer's mind? Normally as a *conception*. This can arise in four main ways. (1) From a *literary text* which the composer feels an urge to set to music (masses, anthems, songs, some operas and oratorios). (2) From a '*literary*' *idea* which the composer feels an urge to use either as a basis for a vocal and instrumental composition (some operas and oratorios) or as a programme for a purely instrumental work (symphonic poems, and programme-symphonies like Berlioz's *Symphonie Fantastique*). (3) From an *ideal or concept* which the composer feels drawn to use as the basis of a purely instrumental work without a specific programme (Beethoven's *Eroica* Symphony, or Carl Nielsen's *Inextinguishable*). (4) From a '*purely musical*' *impulse*—the desire, say, to write 'a great symphony' (Schubert's Ninth).

What motivates a conception? Why does a composer suddenly feel an impulse to write a work founded on a certain text, programme, idea, or musical genre? Something more than a passing whim, surely: it must be that he has something to say, whether he knows it nor not. In other words, a certain complex of emotions must have been seeking an outlet, a means of expression, of communication to others; a state of affairs of which the composer may have been quite aware, or only half aware, or completely unaware. The moment of conception is the moment in which the nature of the complex of emotions becomes entirely clear to his conscious mind—except in the case of a 'purely musical' impulse: here the emotional stimulus of the conception often remains almost entirely unconscious right through the whole process of composition, and beyond it, since it is finding expression in the inexplicit language of music, which is emotionally unintelligible to the conscious minds of its most powerful exponents.

And what is meant by a conception? Usually a vague sense of the nature, mood, and shape of the work to be composed, with the separate parts and the actual material as yet unrealized, or only partly realized. Examples are Beethoven's conception of a great symphony in honour of Napoleon which resulted in the *Eroica*, and Wagner's decision to make Siegfried and the Nibelung myth the subject of a new type of opera—music-drama—which materialized in *The Ring*.

What is the next stage in the act of musical creation? The event known as *inspiration*—the sudden materialization of a musical idea in the composer's mind. It has been called the 'next' stage, though it may in fact precede or accompany the conception. An example of the former is the *Hebrides* Overture of Mendelssohn. Writing home during his Scottish tour, he said: 'In order to make you understand how extraordinarily the Hebrides affected me, the following came into my head there'[1]; and he noted down the opening theme of the work in his letter. The inspiration came first, then; but the conception (that of a 'seascape' overture) must have followed close. Conception and inspiration can be simultaneous: when Schubert read Goethe's poem 'The Erl King' and sat straight down and set it to music then and there, he must have experienced the conception (a tone-painting of a gallop through a stormy night) and the inspiration (the drumming accompaniment and expressive vocal line) more or less as a single mental event. But frequently, inspiration takes its time in following the initial conception. William Byrd and Hugo Wolf pondered over words, the latter sometimes waiting for years for inspiration to arrive; Wagner brooded deep and long over mythology; Haydn, in his later years, prayed; Beethoven wrestled; César Franck played other men's music; Stravinsky sits at the piano and probes. Ultimately, however, what eventually turns up, whether quickly or slowly, whether 'pure' or in connexion with words and ideas, is musical inspiration.

And what is this 'inspiration'? Something which, in Mendelssohn's words, 'comes into our heads'—and apparently quite inexplicably. In Aaron Copland's words: 'The composer starts with his theme; and the theme is a gift from heaven. He doesn't know where it comes from—has no control over it. It comes almost like automatic writing'.[2] William Byrd has described exactly how it happens, in the preface to the 1610 edition of his *Gradualia*, in connexion with the setting of religious words: 'As I have learned by experience, there is a secret hidden power in the texts themselves; so that to one who ponders on things divine and turns them over carefully and seriously in his mind, in some way, I cannot tell how, the aptest numbers occur, as if of their own accord. . . .'[3]

---

[1] Mendelssohn, letter to his family, 7 August 1829.
[2] Aaron Copland, *What to Listen For in Music*, Chap. 3.
[3] '*Porro, illis ipsis sententiis (ut experiendo didici) adeo abstrusa atque recondita vis inest; ut divina cogitanti, diligenterque ac serio pervolutandi, nescio quonam modo, aptissimi quique numeri, quasi sponte accurrant sua. . . .*'

But inspiration does not come from nowhere: nothing can come out of nothing. Music as we know it could not be created at all but for the existence of a long tradition of past music; and every composer draws continually on his experience of this tradition—which cannot be anywhere else, for him, but in his own *unconscious mind*. In the composer's unconscious is stored all the music he has ever heard, studied, or written himself; some of it, to use the Freudian term, is 'pre-conscious', i.e. more or less accessible to the conscious faculty of memory, but most of it is forgotten, or half-forgotten. And it is from this storehouse that inspiration must come: any new musical idea which suddenly 'comes into the composer's head' must be created in some way or other out of his experience of the music of his predecessors and contemporaries (and of his own music), which belongs to the vast mass of life-experience retained in his unconscious. In other words, what we call 'inspiration' must be *an unconscious creative re-shaping of already existing materials in the tradition*.

This unconscious process has always been regarded as an ultimate mystery, but our identification of the basic terms of musical language, in Chapter 3, offers us a chance of coming to grips with the problem at last. For in the music examples in that chapter, we have a mass of detailed evidence to support the hypothesis that inspiration is an unconscious re-shaping of already existing material: all the 'inspirations' assembled there have quite obviously arisen out of the various composers' experience of the music of their predecessors. Our hypothesis is, in fact, already confirmed in one particular field—that of *melody*—and we may use this fact as a starting-point for our investigation of the problem of inspiration. No doubt the unconscious process of re-shaping must also occur in the fields of harmony and rhythm; but let us ignore these for the moment, and concentrate entirely on the melodic element, since we have the evidence at our disposal, and since melody, as we have tried to show, is the fundamental basis of musical language. We can begin from this undeniable fact: that the 'basic term' type of inspiration, as profusely exemplified in Chapter 3, is clearly a matter of reproducing certain well-worn melodic *formulae* in new guises.

At first sight, this would seem to be a bewildering state of affairs. Many of the inspirations in the music examples of Chapter 3 are of the highest order; yet how can there be anything 'inspired' about a process which merely reproduces, in slightly different form, something which has already been used many times before? How are we to reconcile this constant reliance on the same melodic material with the indisputable fact of the creative vitality of 'inspiration'? Before we can solve this problem, we must first answer the preliminary question (posed at the beginning of Chapter 3 but left unanswered there): how is it that composers do return again and again to the same few scraps of melody?

There can be only three possible explanations of the fact that a handful of melodic phrases have been used over and over again: plagiarism, unconscious 'cribbing', and coincidence. The first of these may be ruled out straightaway since, apart from isolated examples like Handel and Bononcini, composers have not been guilty of intentionally stealing other men's themes as a basis for their own works; and in any case, we are concerned only with unintentional, unconscious resemblances.

Unconscious cribbing seems a fairly obvious explanation in certain cases, where the 'inspiration' is clearly a reproduction of another composer's idea in easily recognizable form: here 'inspiration' functions simply as the sudden return to consciousness of an actual theme by another composer, once heard, since forgotten or half-forgotten, and now no longer recognized when it reappears. How easily this can happen was experienced by Manuel de Falla. The opening theme of *Nights in the Gardens of Spain*, according to the biography by Pahissa, 'came to Falla spontaneously, without his having any idea that it might have originated in his subconscious,[1] yet one day, he met Amadeo Vives, who told him that, oddly enough, he had written a *zarzuela* which began in exactly the same way. This coincidence troubled Falla until the explanation suddenly came to him— he and Vives lived on two different floors of the same house in the Calle Serrano in Madrid. On the pavement below, an aged blind violinist had every day come and played these notes on a badly tuned violin. Constant repetition had fixed the notes in

[1] A strange remark: where *can* such spontaneous inspirations originate, if not in the composer's unconscious?

their minds so that, without realizing it, they had both written them as their own'.[1]

Similarly Wagner, rehearsing Act 3 of *The Mastersingers* one day, and arriving at Hans Sachs's words 'Mein Freund, in holder Jugendzeit', suddenly realized, and pointed out with a smile, that the melody was straight out of Nicolai's *The Merry Wives of Windsor*. And others have noticed that in *The Ring*, the Rhinemaidens' motive appears to be from Mendelssohn's *Melusine* Overture, the theme accompanying Sieglinde's dream from Liszt's *Faust* Symphony, and the Nibelung motive from Schubert's 'Death and the Maiden' Quartet—but here we run up against an obstacle. Is the last of these three examples in fact a case of 'unconscious cribbing'? We are all too apt to jump to conclusions in these matters. It is not certain that Wagner ever heard any of Schubert's chamber music; this may be just as much a coincidence as is the resemblance between the tragic themes of *Parsifal* and Verdi's *Otello* (Ex. 52).

When it comes to it, we shall find that any attempt to make a wholesale attribution of musical resemblances to unconscious cribbing will take us on to shaky ground, even when the composer points it out himself. Returning to the melody in *The Mastersingers* which Wagner recognized as belonging to *The Merry Wives of Windsor*, what is it in reality but one further variation of the sequence of falling fourths (major 6–3–5–2–4) which pervades the whole opera in different forms, and which originally appears in the Overture, the first part of the work to be composed, in a form quite unlike Nicolai's tune? Again, the Rhinemaidens' motive, when it first enters in *The Rhinegold*, acts as a derivative of the opening motive of the whole work, which is quite different from the *Melusine* melody. There can be no simple explanation of examples like these. In any case, unconscious cribbing can hardly be the explanation of the many resemblances shown in Chapter 3.

The answer to our problem, then, can only be *coincidence*—which would seem to be no answer at all, unless we are prepared to believe that the world is ruled by blind chance. Yet it is in fact the correct and perfectly satisfying answer, if we despoil the word of its acquired connotation of chance, and understand it in its simple generic sense of a 'happening together' or a

[1] Jaime Pahissa: *Manuel de Falla, his Life and Works.*

'happening in the same way'. For it is clear from the examples in Chapter 3 that, in tonal music, things just do happen over and over again in the same way, melodically—but for a very good reason. There are only twelve notes in the scale; and a tonal composer intent on expressing a certain emotion is limited to fewer; and there is not an infinite number of shapes into which he can weave the few notes at his disposal—in fact they will often fall quite naturally into those familiar patterns which we have called the basic terms of musical vocabulary. Given the structure of the scale, with its tonic and dominant, and that of the triad, with its third, these patterns were inevitable from the beginning: they might be described as *propensities* to group certain tonal tensions together in certain ways, which crystallized into *habitual propensities*, and were handed down unconsciously as elements of the musical heritage of Western Europe. Some of them, such as the 'wailing' minor 6–5, and the 'innocent' pentatonic (major) 1–3–5–6–5, must date back into pre-history; others, such as those involving the augmented fourth or the chromatic scale, are obviously of later date, and the process of their growth into habitual propensities could no doubt be accurately plotted by painstaking research into the history of expressive idioms in music.

It does not seem fanciful to suppose that, in the tonal composer's unconscious, a state of affairs exists which can be described metaphorically in the following way.[1] (1) Memories of the innumerable expressive uses of each of the *tonal tensions* must attach themselves together in groups, by the association of ideas (or, rather, by the association of feelings); and each group of this kind must be attached to a kindred group of memories of sense-experiences, life-experiences, and literary and artistic experiences, also by the association of feelings. (2) These composite groups must contain within them certain sub-groups, each attached to a specific melodic use of the tonal tension concerned, i.e. to one of the *basic terms* of musical vocabulary: for example, of the vast number of associations connected with the

---

[1] One says 'metaphorically' because, as Freud admitted, one imagines a kind of topography, in discussing unconscious mental events, which doubtless bears no relation to the (so far undiscovered) physical reality. This latter must be akin to the intricate layout of the electronic brain, though naturally of infinitely greater complexity; in the meantime, one realizes that, although it is necessary to talk of a basic term as though it were a kind of spatial pattern, it is nothing more tangible than a kind of habitual propensity.

major sixth, many will be attached to the major 6–5, or 8–7–6–5, or 1–3–5–6–5, or to other patterns involving the major sixth, no doubt, not identified in this book. (3) Memories of the expressive uses of certain *keys* must also attach themselves together, by the association of feelings, and these groups must also attract memories of life- and art-experiences, thereby forming the well-known associations in composers' minds between certain keys and certain moods. Owing to individual idiosyncrasies difficult to analyze, these associations tend to vary from composer to composer, but there is a large measure of agreement (owing to the historical development of key-signatures, instruments, etc.): the 'tragic' C minor, for example, the 'common light of day' C major, the 'brilliant' D major, and the 'luxurious' D flat major. Naturally, in view of this, the various basic terms will be attracted with greater or less intensity to the different key-areas.

Returning now to the question of inspiration, and looking back to the music examples of Chapter 3, we can see that 'inspiration' can often mean 'the breaking through into consciousness of a particular basic term, in a certain form, from a certain key-area'. This is obviously what happened to William Byrd when the inspiration came to him for some of the motets in his *Gradualia*. If we turn to the openings of *Gaudeamus Omnes* (Let us all rejoice—No. 29), or *Plorans Plorabit* (Weeping, mine eyes shall weep—No. 28), or *Beati Mundo Core* (Blest are the pure in heart—No. 32), we shall find it amusing to imagine the austere composer 'pondering' on the texts, 'turning them over carefully and seriously in his mind', until 'the aptest numbers occurred as if of their own accord'—as re-shapings of the basic terms 1–2–3–4–5 (in the traditionally 'simple' key of F major), 1–3–4–5 (in the 'melancholy' key of G minor), and 1–5–6–5 (again in the 'simple' F major). We should not be too amused, though, since without undergoing the experience of 'inspiration' we can do nothing with these dead patterns, whereas by doing so Byrd has turned them into living themes.

How does the process actually work? Let us try and imagine how inspiration of this kind would function in the case of a tonal composer who had conceived an opera on the subject of Hamlet. The opening scene (assuming it to be the same as

Shakespeare's), with its combination of night, bitter cold, an armed guard, disquiet, and a foreboding of tragedy, would inevitably call forth inspiration from the key-area in his unconscious closely connected with such gloomy associations— undoubtedly a minor one, and if the composer were in the Mozart-Beethoven-Wagner succession, it could easily be C minor. In this area, the tonal tensions connected with tragic feelings (minor third) or with anguish (minor sixth) would be stimulated to rise to consciousness, already integrated into one of the basic terms—perhaps the 'heroic' rising 5–1–3, or the 'anguished' 6–5, or the 'brooding' 1–3–1, or perhaps a conflation of two or more, according as the composer *felt* the scene (and the result would no doubt be deployed in march rhythms, *piano*, in mysterious tone-colours and textures). Later, the ghost might well arouse the augmented fourth; and at the very end of the opera, Hamlet's dying speech might easily call up the descending chromatic scale (slow tempo, inevitably, and soft dynamic).

But in itself, all this is not enough. The inspiration may be of the highest or lowest order. If our imaginary composer is a tyro (or a genius on an off day), the basic terms will make their appearance as inspirations of the feeblest kind; if he is a great composer in the throes of true creation, they will materialize as the powerful inspirations out of which masterpieces are made. What determines the *quality* of an inspiration of this type? It can only be the vitality of the 'particular form' in which the basic term comes to the surface: in the unconscious of the genuinely creative composer, the breath of life is blown into it in some way.

And what is it that blows this breath of life into a basic term? It can only be that mysterious, unconscious power, the *creative imagination*, which, in the words of Coleridge, 'instantly out of the chaos of elements or shattered fragments of memory, puts together some form to fit it. . . .' And how does this creative imagination exert its influence on the stock melodic material at its disposal? If we look at any of the examples in Chapter 3, one fact stands out unmistakably: the well-worn pattern of two or more notes has been stamped afresh with a new creator's personality almost entirely by being given *a particular rhythmic articulation at a given tempo*. Volume, tone-colour, and texture may have played their parts in making the term the composer's own, but it is by being infused with an individual rhythmic life that it has really been created anew. So we may say that *in inspirations made out of basic terms, the creative imagination must function mainly in the rhythmic sphere.*[1]

Before proceeding to analyse the rhythmic functioning of the creative imagination, it would be as well to make clear that this is only one of its aspects. We shall see later that when the inspiration does not involve a basic term, the creative imagination must function in the melodic field; it also functions in the fields of harmony and form, of course, and to a lesser degree in those of tone-colour and texture. We have begun with the rhythmic aspect simply because this approach to the problem has been forced on us: in our investigation of musical language, we have been necessarily concentrating on fundamentals—pitch and tonal tension; these have led us to the basic melodic terms of musical language; and now, encountering the plain fact that the use of these simple melodic patterns entails no creative activity in the field of pitch at all, we suddenly find ourselves face to face with the creative imagination in what is perhaps its most primitive and dynamic capacity—that of a creator of rhythms.

THE CREATIVE IMAGINATION AS RHYTHM

To demonstrate how the creative imagination functions in the rhythmic field, let us take a concrete example: the opening of the Gloria of Beethoven's *Missa Solemnis*. Although Beethoven left nothing on record concerning his original conception of the whole work, we may safely assume that he foresaw himself expressing in the Gloria all that he felt of jubilant praise towards the Deity—which was an extraordinary amount, as we know from his incoherent, inarticulate scraps of writing on the subject of a Supreme Being.

The inspiration which eventually came to him for the purpose was a basic term: the major 1–2–3–4–5, rising from the D major key-area of his unconscious (see Ex. 53g), This key-area would

---

[1] In the three above-mentioned motets by Byrd, the essentially rhythmic nature of the creative imagination, in such cases, is completely isolated: in each instance, the volume is only implicit (there are no dynamic markings), and the tone-colour and texture are the basic, habitual, inescapable 'black-and-white' of the poly-phonic period—the human voice and the *a cappella* choir.

be inevitably associated with 'glory' there, due amongst other things to memories of Bach's B minor Mass, with its D major Gloria, Credo, and Sanctus, and of the oratorios of Handel, for which Beethoven declared his unbounded admiration on more than one occasion. D major was the habitual trumpet-and-drum 'glory' key of these and lesser predecessors (owing to the special efficiency of the D trumpet); and the brilliant tone-colour of the trumpet and the *fortissimo* dynamic must have come to Beethoven linked with the D major 1–2–3–4–5. In fact, we can with some certainty suppose that the inspiration materialized as 'the imagined sound of the major 1–2–3–4–5 played loudly on the D trumpet' (with or without the accompanying texture).

But this particular kind of inspiration, as described in the phrase in inverted commas above, had occurred many times before to many composers, notably to Handel in *Messiah* as a means of expressing his joy in contemplating the 'glorious' moment when 'The trumpet shall sound'. Yet, in the form in which it opens the Gloria of the *Missa Solemnis*, it is pure Beethoven, Beethoven at his very greatest: the music has a fierce white-hot vitality of a kind never known before or since. Of course, there is more to the Gloria than this short theme, but already, in this theme alone, the genius of the music is manifest: if we were hearing it for the first time on a gramophone record, and the needle were lifted in the middle of the third bar, we should already have recognized supreme greatness in it. To what else can this be due but the fact that 'the imagined sound of the major 1–2–3–4–5 played loudly on the D trumpet', rising to Beethoven's consciousness as inspiration, came already infused by the creative imagination with an electrifying rhythmic impulse—that swift breathless thrust in fast triple time, driving through the five notes of the basic term from a barely established foothold on the tonic straight up to the dominant—which raised the loudly-trumpeted basic term's potential for expressing triumphant joy to an unprecedented pitch of intensity, forcing into it that specific feeling of exultant super-vitality peculiar to Beethoven? (The 'flashing' texture, consisting of racing octaves on full orchestra minus trombones with the strings *tremolando*, whether or not part of the original inspiration, naturally contributes much to the final effect; but the pure essence of the inspiration is in the initial three bars of the first trumpet part.

In trying to analyse this inspiration, we are of course breaking down an indissoluble melodic-rhythmic unity, which must
have materialized as a single mental experience. And we must
continue to do so a little longer, for the very purpose of showing
that it *is* an indissoluble unity. Just as the basic term 1–2–3–4–5
owes all its vitality in this particular context to its particular
rhythmic vitalization, so does the rhythmic impulse owe all its
expressive effect to the particular basic term it is vitalizing. If
the melodic pattern, uninfused with rhythmic life, is nothing
more than a potentiality for expressing a general type of
emotion (assertive joy) in various specific ways, the rhythmic
impulse, divorced from the melodic term, is nothing more than
a potentiality for enabling any basic term to express its general
type of emotion in a specific way (an *urgent* way). Thus, if we
imagine it attached to a different term, say the 'despairing'
minor 5–3–2–1, played softly by the cello, in a string quartet
texture, it enables that term to realize its expressive potentiality
as a specific expression of urgent despair, subdued (soft dynamic)
and intimate (string quartet texture) in tone, but essentially
passionate (cello tone-colour):

Ex. 68

(It might be as well to make here what is perhaps an obvious
point: the *tempo* is an integral part of a rhythmic impulse's
expressive potentiality. If we alter the tempo of the one under
consideration, its character is changed entirely: it can become
quite a different potentiality—one for enabling a melodic pattern to realize its general emotive power in, say, a dignified, or
a graceful way:

Ex. 69

As can be seen, the rhythm itself, independent of *tempo*, is
nothing more than an ebb and flow of rhythmic tension. Obviously, everything depends on the speed at which this ebb

and flow occur: the term 'rhythmic impulse' can only have any meaning if we include under it a *tempo* as well as a particular combination of note-values.)

And now we come to the most important point of all: the expressive effect of a given rhythmic impulse subsists not merely in its vitalization of a particular basic term, but *in the specific way in which it vitalizes it.* This can be demonstrated by detaching the rhythmic impulse of the Gloria theme and re-attaching it to the same basic term in different ways:

Ex. 70

As can be seen, a given rhythmic impulse has a number of different 'potencies' in relation to a given basic term, some more fruitful than others.[1] In the above two examples, the urgency is still there, but the particular degree of urgency is not. The thrill of Beethoven's theme resides in the special *kind* of thrust which the rhythmic impulse gives to the major 1–2–3–4–5, by placing it across the bar-line with a powerful accentuation of the joyful major third. Handel had already done the same thing at least twice, in 'The trumpet shall sound' (at a slower tempo), and in 'For he is like a refiner's fire' (in the more 'controlled' common time):

Ex. 71

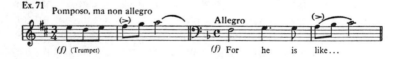

In other words, in inspirations of this type, we have really nothing as simple as a vitalization of a basic term by a rhythmic impulse. The process could be better described as the *fertiliza-*

[1] If this procedure of separating and re-fusing rhythmic impulse and basic melodic term seems to be rather factitious, a glance at Ex. 80x and 80B (first two bars) will reassure the reader. There, we can see Beethoven actually 'testing out' two different 'potencies' of a single rhythmic impulse in relation to a basic term (or rather a conflation of two—the rising minor 5–1–3 and the minor 1–3–1); and it is clear that only by actualizing the second and most fruitful (Ex. 80B) could he transform his emotion of dark grief satisfactorily into musical form— the opening phrase of the *Eroica* Funeral March.

tion of a basic term by a rhythmic impulse, in which melodic and rhythmic tensions fuse inextricably to interact in the most fruitful way for the realization of the composer's expressive purpose.

And here we penetrate to the very heart of musical creation. For in this kind of inspiration, the rhythmic impulse can be nothing other than *a form of physical energy* into which the 'current' of the composer's emotion is converted by the act of the creative imagination (just as, without the intervention of that faculty, it might be converted into a vocal utterance or a physical movement); and thus the fertilization of the basic term by this rhythmic impulse, in a specific way, again by the act of the creative imagination, is nothing other than the transformation of the 'current' of the composer's emotion into *a form of musical energy, consisting of interacting melodic and rhythmic tensions*—or, in other words, into a vital melodic-rhythmic phrase. Thus we can see that, in cases like this at least, the moment of inspiration—the moment in which the musical work begins its actual life—is the moment in which the creative imagination transforms the 'current' of the composer's emotion into musical form and transmits this form to consciousness: and this form is not a dead pattern on paper, but a pattern of live musical sounds; and not a pattern of 'pure' musical sounds, but a pattern of pulsating sound-waves whose tensions correspond in intensity to the emotion which originated the whole process. This is, we may say, how the content gets into music; or at least, into this kind of music.

Four questions arise here. How do rhythmic impulses originate? Are there in fact such things as newly-created rhythmic impulses? Are there basic rhythmic impulses, just as there are basic melodic terms? If so, could it not often be by a cross-fertilization of two specimens, one from each type, that an inspiration is produced?

That there are definitely certain basic rhythmic impulses is obvious, and can be confirmed by a glance at the following examples: Handel's 'Lift up your heads' (Ex. 6); Morley's 'Miraculous Love's wounding' (Ex. 55b) and 'Clorinda false' (Ex. 56a); Wagner's 'Annunciation of Death' motive (Ex. 56d); and Chopin's Funeral March (Ex. 60g). In each of these, the rhythmic impulse is —|—◡|— at a slow or steady tempo, and

the effect is that the basic term discharges its emotional potential in a certain solemn, dignified way. However, since musical
time, with its almost infinite number of rhythmic possibilities,
is so much more fluid a medium than musical pitch, with its
scale of only twelve notes, a classification of rhythmic impulses
is beyond the scope of this book: it suffices to say that such things
as basic rhythmic impulses do exist, and that inspiration can
obviously be the result of a cross-fertilization between a basic
rhythmic impulse and a basic melodic term. Here the act of the
creative imagination must consist entirely in the bringing
together of rhythmic impulse and basic term, and in the
actualization of the strongest 'potency' of the former in relation
to the latter.

   With regard to the question whether there really are such
things as newly-created rhythmic impulses, we are already all
the time assuming an affirmative answer, but in fact it is very
difficult to give an answer at all. The difficulty lies in the task
of establishing a lack of precedents for a given rhythmic impulse;
all one can prove is that one has just not encountered any.
However, since no precedent for the rhythmic impulse of the
Gloria theme comes to mind (such as might replace the
specially-concocted Ex. 68), we may assume that it was newly
created for Beethoven's special purpose—the transformation of
an emotional current of especially high tension. What we can
establish with certainty is that the particular combination of
note-values, irrespective of speed, was not entirely new, as is
shown by the Mozart quotation in Ex. 69. (The fact that
Beethoven's inspiration achieved a masterstroke in lengthening
the combination by one bar, and making the strong beat of that
bar a climactic one overshadowing the normal climax on the
strong beat of bar 2, need not worry us any more than the
extension of a basic melodic term by another climactic note—
see Ex. 56j). Nor was the particular kind of fusion between
melodic and rhythmic elements (the cross-accentuation of the
major third) an entirely new one, as is shown by the two Handel
quotations in Ex. 71. This is not to suggest that the Gloria
theme was an unconscious cross between Exs. 69 and 71, but
merely that such elements were part of Beethoven's tradition,
and could have reached his unconscious from all sorts of sources,
and interpenetrated there to produce a new melodic-rhythmic

pattern.[1] It would be quite impossible to demonstrate that such a process had occurred, of course, even if all the sources were at our disposal, owing to the fluid nature of musical rhythms and melodies. But even assuming that such an interpenetration did take place in Beethoven's unconscious—a blending of already existing rhythmic elements connected and unconnected with the major 1–2–3–4–5—it is obvious that the result was given an ultra-rapid thrust unknown to the original elements. And herein lies the essence of the creative act, for, as we have seen, a rhythmic impulse comprises a certain succession of note-values *at a certain tempo*. The high-tension 'current' of Beethoven's emotion, we may say, had to be converted into a high-tension rhythmic energy.

And here we come face to face with an ultimate mystery—how exactly the creative imagination produces vital and significant new rhythms out of the elements of old ones. Although the composer's rhythmic sense is undoubtedly connected with the whole rhythm of nature (through his senses, bloodstream, and glands), with the speed and rhythm of the life he leads, and with the rhythm and cadence of his native tongue (not only in obvious cases like Mussorgsky and Janácek), it remains inaccessible to our understanding—until, perhaps, the musicians, physiologists, and psychologists of the future explain its functioning for us.

Before leaving Beethoven's inspiration for his Gloria theme, let us take one more look at it, and attribute its electrifying effect quite simply to the particular sound-tensions whose interactions make it what it is: the basic term of triumphant joy, the major 1–2–3–4–5; the most vivid of tone-colours, the trumpet; the loudest volume, *fortissimo*; a dynamic new rhythm at the fastest possible speed at which it can register, *allegro vivace*; the most intensifying texture possible, a duplication of the theme in *fortissimo* orchestral octaves.

[1] This process would be somewhat analogous to that which gives birth to much poetic inspiration—a process demonstrated by John Livingston Lowes in *The Road to Xanadu*. Some of the ideas in the present analysis of musical inspiration arose out of a study of Lowes's book.

THE CREATIVE IMAGINATION AS MELODY

The foregoing is an analysis of the type of inspiration which involves a basic term, but in many inspirations no basic term is involved at all. Turning back to Byrd's *Gradualia*, we find that No. 8 (*Virgo Dei Genetrix*), No. 21 (*Gaude Maria*), and No. 30 (*Timete Dominum*) all open with themes which cannot be related to any of the basic terms established in this book, nor do they give the impression of being related to basic terms as yet unidentified, for they do not call to mind a single theme, or scrap of theme, by another composer. We must assume that there is such a thing as melodic creation, and try to explain how the creative imagination functions in inspirations of this kind.

Just as we managed to isolate its functioning in the rhythmic sphere by examining a 'basic term' type of inspiration, i.e., one in which no creative power had been exerted in the melodic field at all, so we may hope to isolate its activity in the melodic field by choosing an example in which the rhythmic element (and the harmonic, if any) is clearly reproduced from the stock of familiar, traditional material. An apt one is the opening theme of Beethoven's Pastoral Symphony:

Ex. 72

Here the harmonic element, whether part of the original inspiration or not, is well-worn (tonic and dominant), and the rhythmic element is hardly new: the first two bars reproduce a rhythm already used by Bach in the A flat fugue in Book 2 of the 'Forty-Eight', and doubtless by other composers. The melodic element, however, is entirely individual. The best way of describing the functioning of the inspiration is as follows. Beethoven's emotion ('happy feelings on getting out into the country') naturally stimulated the joyful tonal tensions (major third and sixth) in the F major (traditionally pastoral) key-area in his unconscious; and they broke through into consciousness, not integrated into one of the basic terms, but into an entirely new melodic pattern. In other words, the strongly individual nature of the composer's emotion lay not in a particular state of animation, as in the Gloria, but in a kaleidoscopic alternation of incoming and outgoing feelings of joy; and hence the current of it was converted, by the act of the creative imagination, not into a rhythmic but into a *melodic form of physical energy* corresponding to that swift emotional ebb and flow (quick alternations of rising and falling pitch). The state of animation was quite normal, and in consequence the new melodic term was fertilized by a familiar jog-trot rhythmic impulse with a special kind of potency towards it. Thus again, the current of the composer's emotion was converted into a form of musical energy consisting of interacting melodic and rhythmic tensions—otherwise a vital melodic-rhythmic phrase.

In the attempt to explain the 'coincidence' whereby composers have returned again and again to the basic terms, it was said that there is not an infinite number of patterns into which a tonal composer can weave the few notes available for the expression of a particular emotion. This is no doubt true, but it is evident that there must be a very large number, when one considers the quantity of fine melodies which are independent of the basic terms. The expressive quality of every such melody can, of course, be referred right back to the tonal tensions themselves, and the general effects of rising and falling pitch. In the Pastoral Symphony theme we may note that the first phrase is a rising one of assertive joy, moving from the major third, by means of a step and a jump, up to the major sixth; and this latter note has momentarily its effect of 'joyous vibration' in its function as an anacrusis to the heavily-accented dominant which initiates the second phrase. The new phrase is a falling one, almost identical with the major 5–4–3–2–1 and having practically the same feeling of joy received and welcomed. Another rising phrase of assertive joy follows, with the joyous major 5–1–2–3 split across the phrasing (in conjunction with the previous phrase we have a kind of conflation of 5–4–3–2–1 and 5–1–2–3); and the melody finally falls back and comes to a stop with a brief three-note 'welcoming' phrase. From the overall point of view, the pitch fluctuations of this beautiful theme admirably convey the sense of those little waves of outgoing and incoming joy which we experience when we have 'happy feelings on getting out into the country'. The liveliness of these feelings is manifest in the jaunty rhythm; the gentleness of them in the *piano* dynamic; the 'country' nature of them, it may not be superfluous to add, in the harmonic element—the simple 'lazy' pastoral drone bass of a bare fifth falling indolently to an open octave on the dominant.

If we ask how such original themes come into being, we may again offer the tentative explanation, as in the case of rhythm, that they arise out of a fusion of half-forgotten fragments lying in the unconscious; and again we realize that it is next to impossible to prove that this is so. Do half-forgotten themes in fact fragment and interpenetrate in the unconscious? Common experience would suggest that they do. We all know how a scrap of half-remembered tune can float about in the background of the mind, tantalizing us by 'getting on the brain' and refusing to disclose its title or context; and how, when we try to remember its continuation, it suddenly dovetails itself into part of another theme of similar character. This process could easily work entirely unconsciously to produce 'inspiration'. The once-popular comic song 'Yes, we have no bananas (we have no bananas to-day)' was confidently assumed by a friend of the present writer to be the product of a process of this kind, for he derived amusement from singing it to the following words:

Ex. 73

Hal - le - lu - jah! (ba - na-nas),   Oh, bring back my bon-nie to   me!

This sort of thing, however, is hardly the work of the creative imagination, even on the lowest level, for this power surely does not reassemble the 'shattered fragments of memory' by stringing them together in easily recognizable form, but by fusing them inextricably into genuinely 'new' creations. And here we meet again that apparently insuperable obstacle—the fluidity of musical material. If the melodic inspirations of the great composers do consist of fragments of other melodies, blended into new creations, it seems most unlikely that it could be proved, even by the most unremitting study and research, for the simple reason that notes do not retain their identity from context to context: each of the original fragments would take on a new musical sense in relation to the others. And since, as we have noticed, rhythmic and melodic elements interpenetrate, the task is made even more difficult.

With regard to the opening theme of the Pastoral Symphony, when we look at the Bach fugue-subject from which it may possibly have taken its rhythm, we notice certain striking resemblances, especially if we bring Bach's theme as near to Beethoven's as possible, by giving it the same key, tempo, dynamics, phrasing, and barring:

Could it be that, in Beethoven's unconscious, Bach's theme interpenetrated with another, or with several others, which would account for the changes it has undergone? We are on dangerous ground. Musical semi-resemblances are too often a matter of contention, even amongst musicians; it is hardly ever possible to get general agreement as to the derivation of one theme from another, even in a single work. It seems that our hypothesis is not provable: if the supposed process does occur, the very act of fusion must obliterate the traces. Nevertheless, since there is a distinct probability that melodic inventions do originate in this way, intensive research into the problem is obviously desirable.

But even if the hypothesis were to be proved, we should still come up against the ultimate mystery again—how the creative imagination actually produces vital 'new' melodic terms out of the fragments of old ones.

THE CREATIVE IMAGINATION AS HARMONY

For our example of the functioning of the creative imagination in the harmonic field, let us take that celebrated case of harmonic innovation, the opening of the *Tristan* Prelude, since there is nothing melodically or rhythmically individual about it at all.

Wagner's conception of *Tristan and Isolde* was, in his own words, that of 'a tale of endless yearning, longing, the bliss and wretchedness of love; world, power, fame, honour, chivalry, loyalty, and friendship all blown away like an insubstantial

dream; one thing alone left living—longing, longing unquenchable, a yearning, a hunger, a languishing forever renewing
itself; one sole redemption—death, surcease, a sleep without
awakening'. The Prelude he conceived as 'one long succession
of linked phrases' in which 'that insatiable longing swells forth
from the first timidest avowal to sweetest protraction. . . .'[1] It is
clear that the emotion which motivated this conception must
have been a very powerful one, and it is not surprising that it
gave rise to an inspiration of such a revolutionary nature that
it bewildered and alienated many on a first hearing:

Here, the melodic element is not in the least individual: the
opening three notes, before anything else happens, are that
well-worn basic term, the arched minor 5–3–2–1, in D minor,
disappointed of its natural conclusion on the tonic; and the four
rising chromatic notes on the oboe, in A minor, are a common
'yearning' feature of Mozart's style. In fact, we can find them
in the Andante of his String Quartet in E flat, K.428, in the
exact form in which Wagner used them; and this quotation will
also reveal that the rhythmic element of the *Tristan* inspiration
is not new either:

Strangely enough, by thus putting the music into the same key
as the *Tristan* Prelude, we can see clearly that the essential core
of the latter's harmonic element is not new either; yet it was
precisely in the harmonic field that Wagner's creative imagination exerted itself—so powerfully indeed that whenever the
harmony of Ex. 75 turned up again in post-Wagnerian music

[1] Wagner, programme-note for performance of the Prelude in Paris, 25 January
1860 (quoted in Ernest Newman, *Wagner Nights*, p. 219).

(as it often did) it immediately evoked the cry of 'Tristan!' Where, then, lies the decisive creative act? Clearly in the vital sharp fourth (D sharp), in the sounding of it in conjunction with the major seventh (G sharp) and the minor sixth (F natural), and in placing the result in a new and revolutionary tonal context, which will become clear as we proceed. (It is not intended to suggest that Wagner consciously or unconsciously 'gingered up' this passage from Mozart: such a progression was very much part of his tradition, and may have reached his unconscious from the work of composers like Spohr and Liszt.)[1]

The best way of describing the functioning of this particular inspiration is as follows. Wagner's conception of the work, given above, must have stimulated certain of the most expressive tonal tensions to materialize from the D minor/A minor key-area of his unconscious: these were, naturally enough, the 'tragic' minor third, the 'anguished' minor sixth, the 'hopeless' minor second, the 'mournful' minor seventh, the 'pathetically longing' fourth, and (most significantly) the 'violently longing' major seventh. As we might expect, the 'joyful' major third and sixth were not called upon, nor was the *tonic*—a most extraordinary omission, but only a natural outcome of the original emotion, the infinite longing that can find no satisfaction. (The dominant—context of flux—was naturally drawn on, of course.) The creative imagination integrated the above six tonal tensions into a new harmonic complex of unprecedented intensity, dovetailing into it a pair of familiar melodic progressions (one already connected with the type of harmony) and animating the whole complex by means of a familiar rhythmic impulse (also connected with the type of melodic-harmonic progression). In this instance, the 'high tension' of the composer's emotion did not reside specifically in a particular state of animation nor in a particular sequence of outgoing and incoming emotion, and so its current was not converted into new patterns of rhythmic or melodic tensions; what it did reside in was the phenomenal psychic intensity of the feeling, and it was thus naturally transformed into a vital new pattern of harmonic tensions (absorbing

[1] See the opening of Beethoven's *Sonata Pathétique* as the probable unconscious source: three slow, isolated phrases ending in *appoggiature*, the last half-repeated; melody of bar 5 (cf. Prelude, bars 18–19); melody and harmony of bars 7–8 (cf. Ex. 75: almost complete identity at the *end* of the Prelude—in C minor). Cf. also Adagio, bars 5–6, with Prelude, bars 25–8.

certain well-worn melodic tensions) corresponding to that psychic intensity. (In actual fact, there *was* something unusual about the state of animation—the abnormally low level of physical vitality; and consequently there was something new about the rhythmic impulse—its extreme slowness; but this creative act in the rhythmic sphere was submerged entirely in the extraordinary harmonic innovation, and in its own special potency towards the harmonic-melodic complex). Once again, the current of the composer's emotion was transformed into a form of *musical energy*, this time consisting of interacting melodic, harmonic, and rhythmic tensions—otherwise a vital melodic-harmonic-rhythmic phrase.

The expressive power of an essentially harmonic inspiration, like that of an essentially melodic one, can be related back to the tonal tensions themselves, and to the general effects of rising and falling pitch—naturally so, since the tonal tensions move the hearer in the same way whether they are used successively or simultaneously, the only difference being that in the latter case they can enhance one another's effect by their sympathy or repulsion (hence the 'psychic depth' of harmony).

How exactly does the *Tristan* progression function expressively? As we have said, the key of the first three notes is D minor, and we have an upward (outgoing, passionate) leap from the lower dominant over the tonic to the 'tragic' minor third, which is emphasized by rhythmic accent (here we begin to feel the special potency of the rhythmic impulse). The minor third falls to the second, which obviously functions as a passing-note, a neutral intermediate note; though there is a sense of the 'anguish' of the minor 3–2 suspension, which is to be revealed retrospectively as a minor 6–5 in A minor. At this point, the melodic line has had most of the effect of the arched minor 5–3–2–1 of 'restless sorrow' (see Ex. 59); indeed, with a lesser romantic composer, or even with Wagner himself in his earlier days, it would probably have materialized as the complete term, in some such way as the following:

Ex. 77

This routine piece of romantic expression conveys well enough a sense of restless sorrow (arched minor 5–3–2–1), and of anguish (minor sixth in harmony) shot through with sad longing (2–1 and 8–7 suspensions in minor key), but not of 'endless yearning'. If we flatten the E natural at the beginning of the second bar, the feeling of hopeless anguish characteristic of the minor second enters in, but we still have no feeling of 'endless yearning'. No attempt had ever been made to express this peculiarly romantic emotion in music before, and so audiences were conditioned by tradition unconsciously to expect some such purely sorrowful D minor continuation as Ex. 77 (especially at the beginning of a work); and it was against the background of their expectation that the famous *Tristan* chord, introducing the unfamiliar emotion for the first time in music by 'reaching out' harmonically in a way hitherto unknown, achieved its revolutionary effect. For us it has inevitably lost its freshness, but some trace of the original shock can be recaptured by playing Ex. 77 twice, followed by Ex. 75.

What happens when the *Tristan* chord enters? The E of the melody, the normal second of D minor, falls to E flat (D sharp), the 'hopeless' minor second; and this note is harmonized as though it were a new *tonic minor*, by the melancholy secondary seventh chord on its supertonic (F), a chord which derives its gloom from the presence of the anguished minor sixth, C flat (B natural). So far, so intensely sad; but the eventual resolution of the chord reveals it retrospectively as a complex of tensions *on the sharp side of the dominant key of A*: the F in the bass is the anguished minor sixth of that key; the D sharp is the 'violently longing' major seventh of its dominant, E; the G sharp is the 'violently longing' major seventh of A itself; and the B is the dominant of the dominant, having a stiffening, binding effect. So that the chord is compounded, as indeed it sounds to be, of anguish and violent longing in conflict, and of mystery, too, for its character is tonally ambiguous; its effect is emphasized by rhythmic accent (the rhythmic impulse's 'potency' at work again).

When the chord resolves, what happens? The violently longing G sharp, major seventh of A, is resolved upwards (onwards, outwards) to its tonic, which can provide no satisfaction since it is functioning merely as an unaccented passing-note; the melody moves on upwards chromatically (outwards, yearningly) on to the hopeless minor second, B flat (A sharp), which is accented by rhythmic means (the potency of the rhythmic impulse again) and harmonic means (it functions as a dissonant accented passing-note); this note resolves upwards (still outwards) on to the major second, B natural, whose natural longing is left unsatisfied, a desire open towards the future, as the upper note of a dominant seventh chord of A. Of the previous chord, the minor sixth (F) has carried out its normal, anguished resolution on to the dominant (E); the strong dominant of the dominant (B) has fallen to its major third (G sharp), which is not at all joyful, since it functions also as the longing major seventh of A: and the violently longing major seventh of the dominant (D sharp) has fallen semitonally (sadly) to its mournful minor seventh (D), which also functions as the pathetically longing fourth of A. So that this final chord is compounded, as it sounds to be, of pathos and longing combined.

This analysis of the expressive effect of each separate note can be confirmed by playing the progression over and over at the piano and concentrating on each note in turn. During a performance, or course, we cannot, and do not want to, listen like this with the analysing ear of the intellect: we are simply moved by the general effect (in which, however, every one of these details plays its indispensable part). This general effect is: (a) passionate leap from lower dominant up to minor third; (b) pathetic minor 3–2 suspension; (c) intensely poignant, mysterious chord, felt at first as a melancholy chord in 'depressed' key of the minor second, but revealed retrospectively as chord of anguish and violent longing completely overshooting the nearest legitimate object of desire (the dominant key), and falling back wearily towards it, exhausting its tension by (d) a 'resolution' on to the pathetic longing of the dominant seventh chord *in* the new dominant key, which is by implication the dominant minor (we have attained the nearest object of desire, but have found no kind of satisfaction in it); (e) there is no resolution, but instead the phrase is repeated twice, higher each time, and still without resolution on to any tonic. In each case, we are left with the major second, expressing its 'longing in a context of finality'—but there is no finality. Any better way of conveying 'endless yearning' and 'a languishing forever renewing itself' has yet to be discovered.[1]

To complete the picture, we should note that volume, tone-colour, and texture all play their parts. The opening melodic leap begins *pianissimo* (determined by the emotion behind the conception—'the first timidest avowal') and is on the 'expressive' unaccompanied cellos, which swell out on the sustained note in a rhetorical *crescendo*. The tense *Tristan* chord enters at the climax of the cello *crescendo*, and is emphasized not only by rhythmic accent and the change from melody to harmony, but by louder volume, the change from string to woodwind texture, and the bitter tang of the actual woodwind sonority, caused by the scoring. Finally, the sense of partial release conveyed by the 'resolution' on to the final unresolved chord is enhanced by a *diminuendo*.

The process whereby the creative imagination breeds new harmonic inspirations is clear enough, if we glance at Exs. 75 and 76: it vitalizes the well-worn harmonies of tradition by changing and adding notes, and by placing chords in new contexts; by fertilizing them with rhythmic impulses possessed of a special potency towards them; and by letting them fertilize familiar melodic terms. But exactly how this is achieved is another of our ultimate mysteries—though the objection might be made that there is no mystery here at all: melodic and rhythmic inspirations may come unbidden and ready-made from the unconscious, but harmonic inspiration can be (and often is) quarried out by the composer consciously at the keyboard. Melody and rhythm are primitive, elemental, natural impulses; but harmony has been a consciously-willed, complex invention of Western European man—there is always something intellectually calculated about it.

This is an illusion caused by the fact that harmony is the youngest of the three primary means of musical expression, and still bears clear traces of the intellectual work put into its creation. Everything had to be created once, including melody

---

[1] As is well-known, Schopenhauer's philosophy of the Will partly conditioned the conception of *Tristan*, and the Prelude is clearly an unconscious expression of the emotional reality at the heart of Schopenhauer's central concept: the idea that life is a chain of unfulfilled desire, owing to the fact that desire, each time that it is satisfied by the attainment of what one has been longing for, moves on immediately to attach itself to a new 'unattainable'.

and the basic terms, and rhythm and the basic rhythmic impulses; but whereas these have become unconscious habits in the long course of time, the organization of the harmonic element of a composition still demands a conscious effort from most composers. But harmony has been used entirely instinctively by the great improvisers, such as Mozart and Beethoven; and it seems that both Debussy and Delius were able to sit at a piano and pour out a creative flood of 'inspired' harmony. In any case, if a composer does have to search out his harmonic material painfully at the keyboard, he is hardly indulging in an intellectual activity: he is groping. For what? Something that will prove satisfying. To what? To his particular expressive need, which is a matter of feeling, of emotion, of the unconscious. We do not know how the inspiration for the opening phrase of *Tristan* came to Wagner; but even if he stumbled on it at the piano, as has been suggested, after laborious trial and error (in much the same way as Stravinsky discovers his own highly emotive harmonies to-day), it was still left for his creative imagination to select, from the random offerings of his groping fingers, the sound that he had already vaguely imagined as being apt for the expression of the insatiable longing of romantic love. He was really doing no more than Beethoven often did when he wrestled with his melodic-rhythmic inspirations, 'trying them out' in different forms as sketches on music-paper. In such cases, the flash of inspiration will function as the flash of recognition.

Whether it acts in the melodic, rhythmic, or harmonic fields, the creative imagination remains an unanalysable force, in its power to produce new shapes out of old for the embodiment of new emotions.

In order to isolate the three primary ways in which the creative imagination functions, it has been necessary to choose examples in which the act of creation affected only (or mainly) a single element; but there are several other possibilities which we may mention without analysing in detail.

It is of course always possible for the creative imagination to act in all three spheres at once—as in many of the inspirations of an 'original' like Berlioz: this might explain such a composer's lack of universal appeal, for most listeners like to feel some traditional, habitual element in a work, something to take for granted, as it were. Or it may function mainly in two spheres: in harmony and rhythm, in such a work as Stravinsky's *Rite of Spring*; or in melody and harmony, as in much of Delius's music; or in melody and rhythm, as in some of Bartók's music. And of course there are many cases in which it does not function in any of the spheres separately, but only as a blender of well-worn melodic, harmonic, and rhythmic patterns into new entities— which for all that are no less 'inspired' than those compounded entirely of new elements. For instance, no invention of new melodic, harmonic, or rhythmic elements is discernible in the opening inspiration of Handel's 'Ombra mai fu' (Ex. 66a): the whole effect is created out of a familiar basic term (the major 8–7–6–5), a familiar rhythmic pattern, and familiar harmony. But these are integrated in a fresh way to produce a new and superb unity, whose characteristically Handelian beauty and expressive power is not to be related to any of its separate components, but entirely to their fruitful interaction. Inspirations of this kind naturally have the effect of being simple, fundamental, 'inevitable' music.

Sometimes, there would seem to be nothing new at all, as for example in Verdi's inspiration for Othello's anguish: as we have seen, this passage, quite unbeknown to him, coincided in practically every respect with Wagner's inspiration for Parsifal's anguish (see Ex. 52). The melodic, harmonic, and rhythmic elements are almost identical, are not in any way new, and are integrated in almost exactly the same way. Yet there is a world of difference in the feeling: how can this be?

First of all, the two composers' creative imaginations did act slightly differently in the rhythmic sphere: whereas Wagner's drew out the basic term in syncopated 'timeless' rhythm, thus filling it with a heavy universalized grief befitting the religious subject, Verdi's presented the term in simple, basic, incisive rhythm, thus making it convey the raw emotion of pure human anguish, appropriate in a purely human tragedy. A slight harmonic diversity, too, made a great difference: Verdi's creative imagination used the bare 'tragic' minor triad, and accentuated the anguish of the minor sixth in the basic term by bringing it into direct harmonic collision with that triad, giving it the effect of a stab of pain; Wagner's used the romantically gloomy minor-triad-plus-major-sixth, and accentuated the anguish of the minor sixth in the basic term less violently by letting it contradict the major sixth in the harmony melodically, in conjunction with consonant submediant major harmony, thus giving it the effect of a more 'spiritual' kind of grief. Tone-colour also helped to differentiate the two inspirations: Wagner's mellow, eloquent, romantic horn places us at one move from the actuality of purely human grief, whereas Verdi's hard, bitter, plangent combination of cor anglais and bassoon gives us the naked reality. These subtle dissimilarities between two nearly identical complexes of sound-tensions are sufficient to explain the extraordinary difference we feel between the symbolic German romanticism of Wagner and the realistic Italian romanticism of Verdi. The very key-areas in which the two inspirations arose are significant: Verdi's materialized in the 'bare', 'naked' key of A minor, Wagner's in the 'richly sorrow-ful' key of A flat minor (the difference is, of course, entirely one of the two composers' psychologies, of no expressive value to the listener, unless he happens to have perfect pitch and a 'key-psychology' of his own).

Just as important is the way in which the two composers made use of their inspirations. Verdi's is introduced quite simply on two crucial occasions—when Othello looks down at the sleeping Desdemona, and again when he looks down at her dead body with the full realization of what he has done. It sub-sists entirely in its own right, superbly expressive of the simple, basic, human anguish; it is not sung on either occasion, and plays no other part in the work. Wagner's inspiration, however, is a development of the opening theme of the whole opera (the minor version, the second phrase of the Prelude), though it is none the less a new inspiration for all that. It is repeated twice immediately, and on the second repetition moves straight on to the second phrase of the complete theme; and in this, the tenor voice, which has already been singing the minor 6–5 of the basic term, follows the horn, rising to a 'superhuman' pitch of anguish on a top A flat, a note which makes a powerfully moving key-switch by functioning as the minor sixth of C minor and taking the music into that key. This explains. incidentally, why Wagner did not accentuate the anguish of the minor sixth in the basic term as violently as Verdi: his full expression of anguish (packed with the characteristically Wagnerian rhetoric) was yet to come. The whole difference of procedure in the two cases is a natural outcome of the emotional natures of the two composers: the complex, ramifying Wagner; the simple, straightforward Verdi.

But here we find the creative imagination functioning as form—which it obviously must do, if a work is to have any value. This is the last but not least of its functions, as may be deduced from the fact that some works use for their starting-point, not an inspiration, but a tag—an already-existing melodic-rhythmic entity taken over without modification; in such cases, it is in what becomes of the tag, and what follows from it, that the creative imagination can be seen at work. Even more conclusive is the fact that many a fine polyphonic movement (such as the Gratias Agimus of Bach's B minor Mass) is built entirely out of such a tag: here the creative imagination must function entirely in the sphere of form, as an organizer of an overall shape. But our examination of the large-scale functioning of musical language must be postponed a little longer, until we have considered the other links in the chain of musical communication: the way in which the so-called 'content' is transmitted to the listener, and the way in which he responds to it.

When we hear the living sound of the opening bars of the Gloria of the *Missa Solemnis*, or of the Pastoral Symphony, or of the Prelude to *Tristan*, we feel ourselves moved emotionally; and we assume that we are making a direct response to the emotion the composer wished to express, in the same way that we respond directly to the emotion conveyed to us by Shakespeare through the explicit medium of words, in the opening lines of, say, *Twelfth Night*. We feel that the 'content' of the music is being transmitted to us 'out of' the notes. But it is high time to take a closer look at this slippery word 'content'.

The problem of musical expression has been largely shelved in this century, owing to the violent reaction against the romantic aesthetic, the establishment of a dogma of the essential 'purity' of music, and the consequent worship of form and technique. Yet most intelligent writing about music, except the severely technical, betrays an awareness, or at least a suspicion that, as Mahler said, 'what is most important in music is not in the notes'—meaning, of course, notes considered as purely aural and intellectual experiences, as abstract concepts, as technical counters. This thing that is 'most important' is usually described as 'content', and on the rare occasions when the problem of musical expression does get discussed, much is made of the antithesis between 'content' and 'form'. And since nowadays there is a strong tendency to regard music as 'pure form', we have come to imagine 'content' as something 'apart' from 'the music'—as something 'extra-musical'; and hence, to the believers in pure form, it seems to be a spurious, non-musical thing, to be repudiated severely. *The music is what matters,* is the usual way of putting it.

But this is to make 'the music' mean merely 'the notes, considered as purely aural and intellectual experiences, as abstract concepts, as technical counters', or at most 'the form, in its widest sense, down to the smallest formal details'; whereas, if music has 'content'—and we have tried to show that it has—then 'the music' must have a more inclusive meaning: 'the music in all its aspects' and hence 'the form-plus-content that the music is'. To regard 'content' as 'extra-musical' is to commit the analytical sin of breaking down an indissoluble unity into its component parts without putting them together again. The procedure of breaking down is forced on us by the peculiarly analytical nature of verbal language; but to try and assess the value of the parts, in their separate condition, without attempting to understand their function within the unity, is to be guilty of muddled thinking.

Let us look once more at Beethoven's inspiration for his Gloria theme. We have already broken this down technically into seven parts for the purposes of analysis—a key, a basic melodic term, a sequence of note-values, a tempo, a tone-colour, a dynamic and a texture; but it is obvious that none of these parts has any genuine existence apart from the unity which comprises all of them. They are like the separate parts of a watch, which are useless apart from their mechanical interaction *in* the watch.

Looking at the watch for a moment, let us admit that there is another 'part' of it—its ability to tell the time—which is not a mechanical part, but something more intangible: the interpretation which we put upon the working of its mechanism. If the hands are both pointing vertically upwards, we know that it is twelve o'clock: 'twelve o'clock' is not a part of the watch in the mechanical sense, but it is surely the thing that is 'most important' about it? Likewise, in a piece of music, apart from the technical elements, we have to admit that there is another 'part' of it—its ability to move us—which is not a technical part, but something more elusive: the interpretation which we put upon the interaction of the technical elements. If the first, third, fifth, sixth, and eighth notes of the twelve-note scale are sounded (i.e. if we hear the major 1–2–3–4–5) loudly and quickly, we feel a sense of joyful exhilaration: 'joyful exhilaration' is not part of the music in the technical sense, but it is surely the thing that is 'most important' about it—what we call the 'content'?

'Content' is, as we have tried to show, an integral part of the music, in reality: it is the 'current' of the composer's emotion, of which the 'notes' are the musical transformation. In what sense can it be said to have any existence apart from the music— to be 'extra-musical'? In the usual phrase, the 'form' (in the case of the Gloria theme, the opening three bars of the first trumpet part) contains the 'content': but in fact we can no more extract this 'content' than we can extract the volume, or the tempo, or the basic term, or any other of the technical elements. We can, just as in the case of the technical elements, give it a name—'exultant super-vitality' was the one chosen— but this name is not the 'content', nor even a precise description of it (as *ff* is a precise description of the volume, for example): it is only a group of imprecise verbal symbols assembled in the hope of conveying to the reader an idea of the feeling one experiences, when listening to the actual sound the music makes, of being lifted out of one's seat, emotionally speaking. In other words, the 'content' is inseparable from the music, except as an emotional experience derived from listening to the music. If we use the word to signify 'the emotion contained in the music', we must keep clear in our minds that the emotion is contained, not as a necklace in a box, to be taken out and examined, but as an electric current in a wire: if we touch the wire we shall get a shock, but there is no way whatsoever of making contact with the current without making contact with the wire.

Or, returning to our idea of music as a 'transformation' of the 'current' of the composer's emotion into another form of energy (in the way that a bodily movement is), a better analogy would be that of a tape-recording. Let us imagine that a famous actor has died, leaving behind him a private tape-recording of a radio-production of *King Lear*, in which he gave an outstanding performance in the title-role, and that there is no other recording of the performance in existence. We say that his performance is 'on' the tape: actually, it is in certain patterns of magnetization on the tape, physical transformations of certain electrical impulses, which in their turn were electrical transformations of the original vocal sounds the actor made. In a sense, the performance *consists* of these patterns, *is* these patterns, since if we destroy them by wiping or destroying the tape, the performance will no longer exist. In another sense, the performance is *not* these patterns: by 'the performance' we mean 'the original vocal sounds the actor made' whereas the patterns are only a physical form capable of being transformed, by being played, into (something very closely resembling) the original vocal sounds. Properly speaking then, the performance is *in* these patterns. But it cannot be got *out* of them, except as an aural experience, gained by playing the tape. Once we do this, however, we complete the last links on the chain of communication: the patterns are transformed back into electrical impulses, which are transformed back into sounds which we hear. A philosopher may have solipsistic doubts as to whether there is any 'real' identity between the original vocal sounds and the mechanically reproduced ones, but for all practical purposes, we shall regard the final link in the chain as 'listening to X's performance of *King Lear*'.

Our analogy is that, in an expressive musical work, the relationship between the 'content' and the 'music' is of the same indissoluble kind as that between the performance of X as *King Lear* and the patterns on the tape-recording of that performance. Turning to a score of Beethoven's Gloria, let us imagine that, owing to some terrible calamity, it is the only one left in existence, that all parts have been destroyed, and that no one can remember a note of it. Where is the 'content' of the opening theme? In the score, or more precisely, in certain patterns of print on the score, physical transformations of certain musical sounds (imagined ones—the composer's 'inspiration') which in their turn were transformations of the original emotional experience. In a sense, the 'content' *consists* of these patterns, *is* these patterns, since if we destroy them, by defacing or destroying the score, the 'content' will no longer exist. In another sense, the 'content' is *not* these patterns: by 'the content' we mean 'the original emotional experience', but the patterns are only a physical form capable of being transformed, by being played and heard, into (something in some way resembling) the original emotional experience. Properly speaking then, the 'content' is *in* these patterns. But it cannot be got *out* of them except as an emotional experience gained by playing and hearing the sounds (actually, or in the aural imagination). Once we do this, however, we complete the last links in the chain: the patterns are transformed back into musical sounds which are transformed 'back' (by some mysterious process in the listener) into emotions which we feel. In this case, it needs no solipsist to question whether there is any kind of identity at all between the emotion felt by Beethoven and that 'reproduced' in the listener; but even so, in practice, we shall regard the final link in the chain as 'experiencing the emotional content of Beethoven's Gloria'.[1]

It is obvious that we cannot experience 'the content' in any other way than this, and that it has no existence apart from our experience of it in this way. To show how the notion of an actual, somehow self-subsistent 'content', apart from the music, is apt to creep in, we may quote from an article entitled 'Music and the Human Personality' by Rollo H. Myers in *The Score* of March 1957. The article, sensibly deploring the present-day 'de-humanized' attitude towards music, contains the following passage: 'With Beethoven, it seems to me, the musical matter and the musical thought are moving, as it were, on two different planes, whereas with Stravinsky, one feels that matter and thought . . . are one and indivisible. . . . The transcendental essence of Beethoven's conception emerges from the sounds heard and detaches itself from the actual material like a statue arising from its pedestal. In the music of Stravinsky, on the

---

[1] There is no intention of pushing this analogy as far as to make any *value*-comparisons: patterns in a score are intelligible in a way that patterns on a tape are not; the sound of music, considered purely as such, has an aesthetic significance, whereas electrical impulses have no intrinsic significance at all. The analogy has been used to elucidate certain points only, and can be taken no further without becoming false.

other hand, it is useless to seek for a meaning, an idea, or any transcendental concept elsewhere than in the musical substance itself; here the fusion between form and content is complete . . .'

Such an antithesis cannot have any meaning, as we have tried to show. One sees what the writer is getting at: the fact that Beethoven and Stravinsky express themselves in very different ways—the one with the directness and gusto of a Shakespeare, the other with the obliquity and circumspection of a T. S. Eliot (though the existence of *The Rite of Spring* and the last quartets of Beethoven makes such a distinction pretty meaningless); but in both cases, the expression *is* the music, and quite inseparable from it. In the work of any composer, 'form' and 'content' are not separate, nor even fused, but ultimately two aspects of a single entity: 'form' is, in fact, as the word implies, the form-into-which-the-composer's-emotion-has-been-converted, and 'content' is a word to indicate the fact that this form can be converted 'back' into some kind of equivalent of that emotion. In fact, the 'pure music' theorists are right up to a point: there is only one thing and that is the form—only they will not admit that the form can be regarded in two lights. It cannot be denied that there is such a thing as form, pure and simple, since it can be analysed as pure structure, either while it is sounding or in its dead state as patterns on paper—much as the patterns of magnetization on a tape can be magnified and analysed as structures.[1] But we cannot say that there is any such thing as 'content' considered as a separate entity: it is nothing more than the form's potentiality for turning back into what it once was— emotional experience. When we say that the 'content 'of the Gloria theme is a feeling of 'exultant super-vitality', we merely mean that Beethoven once experienced an emotion which can be loosely characterized by those words, and his creative imagination converted the 'current' of that emotion into those particular sounds, the aural experience of which the listener converts into an emotion which may also be loosely characterized by the same words. There is no such thing as a 'content' floating about divorced from the sounds, except in the brains of those who are no longer listening to the music. Perhaps it is

---

[1] Again, no *value*-comparison is intended: printed musical patterns have a meaningful visual relationship to the 'content' quite different from that which the magnetization-patterns have to the sounds recorded on a tape.

impossible for some people not to *think* about 'heroism' as a concept during a performance of the *Eroica* Symphony (just as others may find it impossible not to have *visual images* of barbaric rituals while listening to *The Rite of Spring*; but once we do begin to apply a name (or a visual image) to the emotion awakened by the music during a performance, and to use it as a counter in a private thought-process (or dream-fantasy), we are on the way to losing contact with the music, and in consequence with its *actual* 'content'. Whether we are listening to the Gloria of Beethoven's *Missa Solemnis*, or to the Laudate Dominum of Stravinsky's *Symphony of Psalms*, the feeling of joyful praise which the music awakens in us (a vastly different one in each case) we experience as the direct impact of the actual sound, through our ears, on some transforming faculty inside us.

In consequence, any attempt to abstract the 'content' of a piece of music, for purposes of discussion and evaluation, is doomed to failure, for one is only describing the emotional experience into which one's transforming faculty has converted the music; and even then, the only means one has of conveying this intensely individual experience, which music can do with such extraordinary precision, is words—words like 'exultant', 'super', and 'vitality' which, though they have very definite and definable intellectual meanings, are too indiscriminate and all-embracing as descriptions of emotion to be able to deal with subtleties, shades, and nuances. Such attempts are only worth making if the words are used purely as general pointers to help towards an understanding of the music as a unity—emotion-in-musical-form—and not as a means of getting a 'meaning', or 'message', or 'concept' from it. Thus, it is quite possible that discussion of Beethoven's (and our own) conception of a Supreme Being may help towards an understanding of the *Missa Solemnis* (just as discussion of Stravinsky's—and our own—conception of Catholicism may help towards an understanding of *The Symphony of Psalms*)—by enabling us to get an idea of the original conception of the work, and hence to understand what kind of emotions gave rise to it, and hence to clear up perhaps certain puzzling aspects of style, form, and expression, and hence to remove certain obstacles which may impede our eventual conversion of the form into emotional experience. It is also possible that, by describing our own emotional experience of a piece of music to a friend, in the imprecise terms of verbal language, we may be able to put him in the right receptive mood to absorb the 'content' of the music in his own way, though he had been unable to 'understand' the work before. But during a performance, the unconscious process of conversion should be allowed to go on unhindered by intellectual preoccupations: any 'concept' in the listener's mind can only be an intellectual abstraction deriving, not from the music itself, but from private thought-associations connected with the kind of emotions aroused in him by the music, and possibly with memories of his reading and discussion about the composer as a human personality. He will be no closer to the music than that, whereas he ought to be responding purely to the music as emotion-in-musical-form. This may be a counsel of perfection, but at least, if 'concepts' do arise in our minds and get in the way of our emotional experience of the music, we should blame our own psychology and not the composer, who cannot convey 'concepts' to us even if he wants to, by the very nature of the language of music.

It remains to examine the process whereby the musical form is converted 'back' into emotional experience.

Let us first of all completely ignore the problematical part played by the performer. For our purposes, the problem has quite a simple solution: if the performer is unmusical, the chain of communication is broken or impaired; if he is genuinely musical, it is undamaged. We will imagine the ideal case of a great artist, who is able to identify himself entirely with the composer's emotion, and transmit it to us practically unmodified in a performance such as the composer himself imagined. The music sounds; the listener listens; what happens?

First, we must divide our listeners into two groups—the musical and the unmusical. These words must not be taken to imply respectively 'the professional musician' and 'the layman': they mean simply those (professionals or laymen) who can respond naturally to music with their feelings, and those (professionals or laymen) who cannot. With the unmusical, whether they are practically illiterate and tone-deaf or highly cultured and thoroughly grounded in the technicalities of music, we can have nothing to do: the incapacity to transform music into feel-

ing is as clear evidence of unmusicality in a professor of music as
it is in a navvy, even though the professor may have performed
miracles of musicology or technical analysis, and even have a
long list of opus numbers to his credit. In music, as in many
another activity, it is possible to reach the highest level of technical proficiency without having any real feeling for the art
at all.[1]

Turning to the truly musical, we can now introduce our
distinction between professional and layman with some meaning; though the distinction is a superficial, not a fundamental
one. The difference is that the professional, besides apprehending the music emotionally, can analyse the form with his
intellect, and can admire its formal beauty with his aesthetic
sense (strange to say, these three processes can go on simultaneously); whereas the layman, unable to lay hold on the
fluid, intangible sounds with his intellect, can only apprehend
the music as emotion (and vaguely as formal beauty, no doubt,
in an unconscious way). So that, after a performance, the professional can discuss the technical aspects of the music with one
person, and its formal beauty with another, using a technical
vocabulary to describe the various elements; but the layman,
even though he may have more than an inkling of these things,
is more or less tongue-tied for lack of technical knowledge. But
when we come down to the fundamental musical experience—
the transformation of the sound into emotion—the professional
is as tongue-tied as the layman. Suppose that a professional and
a layman-friend have both been deeply moved by a piece of
music, and have come to an agreement that the emotion it
expresses is one which can be loosely characterized by the
words 'a melancholy longing'; and suppose that a third party
(an unmusical person, or a musical one with a blind spot for
this particular piece) declares that it expresses nothing at all, or
perhaps only a vague feeling of tranquillity: does not the professional find himself as much at a loss for a reply as the layman?

[1] A small point should not be overlooked here: everybody is unmusical at
times—i.e. when he is listening to a work for which he has a 'blind spot'—and he
should not delude himself into thinking that his criticisms of the form have any
meaning, since they are divorced from any emotional experience of the music.
Too often we read 'musical criticism' which is mere abuse of a form by someone
who cannot feel what the form is a form *of*. Musicality—i.e. a sympathetic emotional response to a work—is a *sine qua non* of valuable criticism; and when our
musicality deserts us for a moment, revealing a blind spot, we should remain silent.

His technical vocabulary is quite useless on this plane: any reference to the minor key of the music, say, will be immediately countered with the truthful statement that some minor music is not at all melancholy.

The point of our example is not that there can be no certainty as to the emotion expressed by a piece of music: this whole book is an attempt to prove exactly the opposite by enlarging the technical vocabulary to take in terms for the expressive elements of music. What our example does show is that the fundamental musical experience—the transformation of music into emotion—is the result of an entirely *unconscious* process, since, all through the centuries, the professional, with all his technical knowledge, has been no more able to explain his emotional experience of music than the layman. And even now, if we are at last in a position to give technical names to the basic terms that have been used unconsciously for so long—say, the 'rising minor 5–1–3' with its connotation of bravery, courage, heroism—the process of transformation will still remain unconscious; for quite obviously it will still be only by *feeling* the emotion in the music that we can experience it, not by identifying its musical form and giving it a technical name.

What exactly is meant by 'feeling the emotion in the music', or more precisely, 'transforming the heard sound of the music into emotional experience'? How does this process actually work? We must suppose that, in the unconscious of the musical listener, professional or layman, a state of affairs exists, musically speaking, similar to that which exists in the unconscious of the composer. In other words, there will be similar groups of memories of the expressive uses of the various tonal tensions, attached to non-musical experiences of a similar nature; and the same subdivision into groups of memories of the various melodic uses of these tensions, i.e. of the basic terms. In the professional alone, of course, will there be any key-areas, derived from the actual practical performance of music or from score-reading; but, as we have said, key is largely a matter of individual psychology, not a fundamental element of musical expression, and we may ignore it here, as a side-issue.

Returning to the Gloria of the *Missa Solemnis*, what happens in the listener's unconscious when he hears the opening bars? Something very similar, surely, to what happened in Beethoven's own unconscious when he himself first *heard* the imagined sound which was his inspiration. We must remember that, when the inspiration materialized, Beethoven was the first *listener* to it: he had to assess its quality and its suitability to the expressive purpose; and he could only do this by 'playing it over' in his aural imagination, and exercising some unconscious faculty of recognition to apprehend its significance. If his intellect was already considering what could be 'done with it', he must have been excited emotionally to hear it arise—the sound of the joyful 1–2–3–4–5 *fortissimo* on the D trumpet, played with a speed and rhythmic impetus hitherto unknown (though of course he would not have analysed his experience like this but only reacted to it unconsciously): the emotional excitement was of course the one that gave rise to it, though it must have been swelled by the excitement of the recognition that it was the exact transformation of the original emotion.

Lest this be thought idle speculation, let us again call upon that clear-minded non-romantic Aaron Copland, as a witness: 'Now the composer has an idea. He wants to know what he has. He examines the musical line for its purely formal beauty. He likes to see the way it rises and falls, as if it were a drawn line, instead of a musical one. . . . But he also wants to know the emotional significance of his theme. If all music has expressive value, then the composer must become conscious of the expressive values of his theme. He may be unable to put it into so many words, but he feels it! He instinctively knows whether he has a gay or a sad theme, a noble or a diabolic one. Sometimes he may be mystified himself as to its exact quality. But sooner or later he will probably instinctively decide what the emotional nature of his theme is, because that's the thing he is about to work with'.[1] (The emphasis on the word 'instinctively' is worth noting.)

How does this recognition of the emotional character of an inspiration work? To return to Beethoven's Gloria theme, it presumably functioned as an instantaneous unconscious relating of it to all his memories of other uses of the major 1–2–3–4–5 (including the two in Ex. 71), whereby its phenomenal power, as the most vital form of that joyous term ever conceived, was isolated. The process is another of our ultimate mysteries, no

---

[1] Aaron Copland, *What to Listen For in Music*, Chap. 3.

doubt, but the main point is clear: just as Beethoven knew the sound to be the musical transformation of his feeling of 'exultant super-vitality', by the act of some unconscious cognitive faculty relating it to all his stored-up memories of other uses of the term, so do we feel it to be the musical transformation of *a* feeling of 'exultant super-vitality', akin to any such feeling we have ourselves, by the act of this same unconscious cognitive faculty, relating it to all *our* stored-up memories of other uses of the term.

But this is only one aspect of the experience—the 'knowing' or 'recognizing', the ability to respond at all; how is the music actually transformed into feeling? It can only be by stimulating our emotional faculties themselves. Just as Beethoven's feeling of joy, reaching a high pitch of excitement, must have powerfully stimulated the memories of musical elements attached to it, until one day it was suddenly converted by the creative imagination into a form of musical energy produced by the interaction of tensions from all these elements—so, when that form of musical energy is let loose on us by a performance of the actual sounds, it must powerfully stimulate *our* memories of similar musical elements; and through them must violently arouse the feelings attached to them, and the emotional faculty whence these arise, which must in the very nature of things be the emotion of joy. It must be in some such way as this that we transform music 'back' into emotion.

One final and most important question remains: how closely does this emotion into which we transform the music resemble the original emotion of Beethoven of which the music is a transformation? There can be only one answer to this: about as closely as the emotions of one human being can ever resemble those of another—and how closely that is can never be proved. We can never know exactly how another person feels: presumably the species and genus of feeling are the same, the individual specimen different. Beethoven experienced a feeling of 'joy'; we experience a feeling of 'joy'. But he experienced a feeling of 'exultant super-vital joy'; and we experience a feeling of 'exultant super-vital joy' in so far as we have such a feeling in us. But he experienced a 'Beethovenianly exultant super-vital joy', and we can only feel 'our own exultant super-vital joy' which will inevitably be different from Beethoven's, and quite likely much less intense. This need hardly worry us, for we can only experience anything in this world in terms of our own temperaments. We do not expect to feel *exactly* how Keats felt when we read the *Ode to a Nightingale*; in fact we are likely to be farther away from the original feelings when we read poetry than we are when we listen to music, owing to the practically infinite possibilities of verbal ambiguity as compared with the direct emotional impact of music. Yet we feel that Keats has communicated a very particular complex of emotions to us through the medium of words, and just so may we feel that Beethoven has communicated (perhaps less ambiguously) a very particular feeling to us through the medium of music.

Actually, the process of musical communication is fundamentally a very simple one, which only appears complicated because of its complicated apparatus. There is nothing more involved about it than there is in any form of emotional expression—say, a physical movement or a vocal utterance. Beethoven, to give vent to his sense of joy in 'the glory of God', might have jumped for joy, or shouted for joy (with his violent temperament, he probably did both, many times), and thus communicated his sense of joy to a few people living in Vienna at that time. Being a composer, he was not content merely to transform his powerful emotional energy into such ephemeral forms of physical energy, but felt the need to convert it into a permanent, stored-up, transportable, and reproducible form of energy —a musical shout for joy, as it were, that all the world might hear, and still hear over and over again after he was dead and gone: the living sound of the major 1–2–3–4–5 blasted out on the D trumpet, in a certain fiercely impetuous rhythm which made it convey what he wanted it to convey. Had he been a trumpeter, he could have immediately, directly, physically achieved this transformation of energy by picking up a D trumpet and emitting his musical shout for joy then and there, for the delectation of anyone who happened to be passing (just as the jazz trumpeter of our time, pouring out his improvisations, is all the time engaged in the immediate, direct, physical transformation of his own emotional energy into forms of musical energy). But in order to ensure that his shout would be always heard, he had to go to the labour of 'dehydrating' his form of musical energy, writing down certain hieroglyphics on music-paper: these have been reproduced ten-thousandfold since he did so, and have by now acquired the kind of 'aura' that attaches to a 'score' of a piece of 'classical music', but they only ever were and only ever will be a command from Beethoven to blow his eternal shout for joy, together with a set of instructions, addressed to those proficient in such technical matters, exactly how to do so. The 'score' is simply Beethoven's message down the years: 'pick up a D trumpet and play these notes at this dynamic level, in this rhythm, at this speed, and everyone within hearing will know how I felt' (so do we nowadays put on a gramophone record of some dead-and-gone jazz trumpeter and know how *he* felt). Thus Beethoven still shouts for joy, and we still listen to him; but since the shout is a musical one, we do not merely have a vague impression that he felt joyful (as those who only heard his vocal shoutings did)—we feel, to the best of our capacity, just how vitally and intensely joyful he felt, and we are renewed and inspirited by our direct emotional contact with his indomitable being. As Neville Cardus has admirably said: 'The body and brain of Beethoven, as so much physiology, have rotted away long since; what we hear in the concert room is not a symphony with an Opus number—not a Thing-in-Itself, not just an important link in a chain of musical evolution; it is Beethoven's spirit, and also (just as important) it is his juice and his humours.'

Beethoven himself may as well have the final word on the problem of musical communication. He summed up the whole thing in a nutshell in the words he wrote on the manuscript of the *Missa Solemnis*: 'Von Herzen—möge es wieder—zu Herzen gehn!'—'From the heart—may it go back—to the heart!'

5

THE LARGE-SCALE FUNCTIONING
OF MUSICAL LANGUAGE

Everything that has gone before must have aroused in the reader's mind the question: 'What happens when we move off the plane of *minutiae*?' The initial theme of a movement may begin with a basic term, so that bit of it expresses that particular emotion—granted; but how does it go on after that? And what happens when this theme is developed, brought into contact with other themes, and 'worked out' in conjunction with them? Single phrases may be very expressive in themselves, but they have to be built up into an overall structure; and surely this building-up must proceed by the laws of purely musical logic, heedless of expressive considerations? *Can* a musical structure function continuously as expression, in reality? Is it not rather a purely musical pattern woven out of fragments of expressive material? And does not this account for what Hindemith calls the 'delirious, almost insane manner of appearance' of the emotions expressed in a piece of music?

In answer to these questions, we may reply with a sentence from Chapter I of this book: 'Music is no more incapable of being emotionally intelligible because it is bound by the laws of musical construction than poetry is because it is bound by the laws of verbal grammatical construction'. The artist who has something to communicate through the medium of his chosen language—be it speech or music—must be the master of that language, not its servant. We should laugh at a literary critic who maintained that verbal language had a logic of its own which made it incapable of coherent emotional expression; then let us laugh at the musical theorists who say the same of musical language—for it is they who have said so, and not (with one or two very recent exceptions) the composers. The whole misconception stems from some strange delusion that because music cannot organize its expressive terms into those logical sequences of intellectual meaning peculiar to verbal syntax, it is debarred from any kind of coherent expression whatsoever: any idea that there might be an entirely different but equally coherent kind of organization of expressive terms, peculiar to musical syntax—i.e. that our so-called 'purely musical logic' might be just as much an *expressive* logic as is 'purely verbal logic'—seems far from the thoughts of most modern theorists.

In fact, however, this is just what it is. The 'laws' of musical construction which are supposed to preclude coherent emotional expression are used, by the great composers, for the very purpose of achieving such coherent emotional expression. Consider the shattering and completely unambiguous emotional effect which Tchaikovsky achieved in the finale of his *Pathétique* Symphony by adhering to a simple and well-worn formal procedure: (A) first subject—'despairing' 5–4–3–2–1 in basic context of tonic minor, *forte*, eventually alleviated by (B) second subject— 'consoling' 8–7–6–5 in the subsidiary (interlude) context of relative major, *pianissimo* swelling to *forte*, eventually swept aside by (A) return to first subject—again 'despairing' 5–4–3–2–1 in basic context of tonic minor, *forte*, swelling to *fortissimo*, leading to (B) second subject again, which this time, however, is the 'despairing' 8–7–6–5 in the basic context of tonic minor, *fortissimo* dying away to *pianissimo*. Here, at the second (B), an orthodox adherence to an iron 'law' of classical sonata-form— that the second subject must be recapitulated in the tonic key— plus the exercizing of the choice whether that tonic shall be major or minor, is the actual means whereby Tchaikovsky has achieved the final and clinching expression of emotional catastrophe.

Such an example shows clearly that music has its own method of coherent emotional expression, quite different from that of speech-language. This method is nothing more mysterious than the presentation of some general but clearly-defined attitude towards existence by the disposition of various terms of emotional expression in a significant order. *And musical form is simply the means of achieving that order.* The finale of Tchaikovsky's *Pathétique* Symphony is of course an instance of the simplest kind—a case of romantic rhetoric; but it is not thereby a false example. However complex and allusive the form of an expressive musical work may be, it is still simply the means whereby the composer has expressed an emotional attitude towards existence by imposing a meaningful order on expressive terms; and it is the continual failure to recognize this fact that is responsible for our generally ambiguous and fruitless approach to music—which can be summed up as 'form is form, and expression is expression, and never the twain shall meet'. Consider the normally intelligent commentary, so often encountered in musical biographies and concert-programmes, on a sonata-movement of an expressive masterpiece. The writer has obviously apprehended the basic emotions of the music through his innate musicality, since he has labelled the themes with emotional adjectives—say, 'the heroic first subject' and 'the sorrowful second theme'; but the moment that he has encountered the 'transition section' with its 'busy passage-work', and the 'development' with its 'fragmentation and re-integration of the main material', he has moved on to another plane altogether. It seems as if he must feel that expression gives way entirely to 'pure form' at these points, for we are suddenly faced with arid technical description such as 'in a short transition section a four-note rhythmic figure deriving from the second bar of the first subject is worked up in imitation, reaching a powerful climax in the key of the submediant'. After which we may well be switched back suddenly to the expressive plane: 'then follows the sorrowful second theme'.

Such writing is quite useless, not only because the layman cannot understand it and the professional does not need it, but for the more fundamental reason that the expressive significance of the 'transition section' (i.e., the emotion conveyed by this working-up of a fragment of the first subject) is not stated, and thus the ultimate point of the passage is ignored. Having stated that the composer began with a 'heroic' theme, the writer has neglected to tell us what happened to it, *considered as a heroic theme*; why should we care, then, whether it is heroic or not, if it suddenly becomes nothing more than a technical gambit? Of course, the actual sound of any such passage is instinctively apprehended as emotion by all genuinely musical listeners—a category which may well include the commentator himself, who is merely defeated by the problem of trying to get it all into words; nevertheless, the fact remains that in all our writing and thinking about music, we do most unfortunately tend to preserve the fallacy that musical form cannot function continuously as expression, whereas in fact the two things are only two aspects of another of our indissoluble unities. Looking at the finale of Tchaikovsky's *Pathétique* Symphony, we have an unmistakable example of the creative imagination transforming the composer's emotion into musical expression by functioning in the sphere of form, a process which was touched on in the previous chapter.

Emotion . . . creative imagination . . . the reader will be getting restive. Are musical compositions entirely the products of inspired somnambulism? Does the intellect play no part at all? What of the sheer hard work that goes into the art of composing? When a composer comes to the task of building up his overall structure, does not his *technique* take over?

No one would wish to deny that a composer, however richly endowed with creative imagination, must possess a first-rate technique if he is to achieve satisfying forms, or that the acquiring and applying of such a technique are intellectual activities involving an enormous amount of hard work. But the question is, where exactly in the process of composition does the creative imagination leave off and the technique take over? The answer is, surprisingly enough, nowhere—as we realize when we look a little more closely at the question. It implies that first of all the creative imagination, working in the unconscious, provides an inspiration of some kind—say, a short melodic-rhythmic phrase; and that after that, the technique, applied by the conscious mind, begins the task of building up a form—a large-scale pattern into which the inspiration is integrated. But this widespread conception of the process of musical creation is naïve in the extreme. There is no such simple 'first of all' and 'after that': technique is present at the very beginning, and the creative imagination keeps on working to the very end. The two move together hand in glove all the time, and are indeed nothing other than two different functions of the same faculty.

If this seems an obscure saying, let us ask ourselves: 'What *is* technique, in reality?' It is simply the knowledge necessary for the building up of forms, or rather the ability to use that knowledge. But we have already encountered the 'building up of forms', on a small scale, in the inspirations produced by the creative imagination. In analysing the 'Gloria', 'Pastoral', and 'Tristan' inspirations, we established that each of them is nothing other than a very intricate, if minute form; it is, as we said, the 'form into which the current of the composer's emotion has been transformed'—a highly organized complex of inter-acting tonal and rhythmic tensions. In other words, the creative imagination itself, working on the smallest scale, is a shaper of forms. Wherefore we must admit that it too can draw on 'the knowledge necessary for the building up of forms' and must possess 'the ability to use this knowledge'; naturally so, since this knowledge and ability are part of the composer's experi-ence of the musical tradition, and must therefore be stored in his unconscious (pre-conscious) mind. Are we then to say that the creative imagination is an unconscious technique? That would be absurd, since by 'technique' we mean specifically a conscious faculty. What we can say, and what gives the answer to the whole problem, is this: in the mind of the composer is stored 'the knowledge necessary for the building up of forms', and when 'the ability to use this knowledge' manifests itself instantaneously as an unconscious process (i.e. as 'inspiration'), we call it the 'creative imagination'; but when it manifests itself comparatively slowly and laboriously as a conscious pro-cess (i.e., as 'building up a form'), we call it 'technique'.

But it will be objected that there is all the difference in the world between putting a few notes together and putting whole themes and groups and sections together. Surely the 'ability' in each case is a very different one? The creative imagination can-not produce large-scale works as complete entities by an instan-taneous unconscious process, but only very small-scale forms, which are not forms in the generally accepted sense at all. Like-wise, technique is not really concerned with shaping *minutiae* such as those produced by the inspiration, but with organizing complete movements and works. Wherefore, for all practical purposes, even if we grant that the two powers are different functions of the same faculty, surely the unconscious one (the creative imagination) does give way to the conscious one (tech-nique) at a very early stage, and it is the latter that really does all the work?

Such a clear dividing-line is impossible to fix. For instance, it would seem undeniable that the first stage—the moment of inspiration—is entirely unconscious: that this is the special province of the creative imagination. But then we have to remember the strange case of Beethoven, with whom an 'inspiration' was often a most unsatisfactory affair: his creative imagination frequently did not 'hit on' the complex of tonal and rhythmic tensions which was the exact form of the emotion he wished to express; and so he was forced to apply his technique, consciously 'trying out' the inspiration in different forms (as sketches on music-paper) until the right one was discovered. So that here we find technique already at work, at the earliest stage, on the smallest scale, in the realm usually regarded as sacred to the creative imagination. But what *is* technique here but a continuation of the work of the creative imagination by other means? The creative imagination 'knew what it wanted', we might say —the correct musical form of the original emotion; only it had to delegate the task of working out the details to the technique. Or, to phrase it more correctly, Beethoven's 'ability to use the knowledge necessary for building up forms' did not always function smoothly, spontaneously and unconsciously, at the early, small-scale stage, as the normal composer's does: a conscious effort was needed to make it work properly. Nevertheless, this conscious effort was not different in aim from the unconscious one: it merely continued its work and eventually fulfilled its intention—the building up of the right musical form of the composer's emotion. Now the true nature of that emotion was known only to the unconscious; the various attempts of the technique to discover the right form had to be 'vetted' by the unconscious faculty of cognition mentioned in the previous chapter, and one of them—the right one—accepted. Consequently, we may say that technique (the conscious functioning of the composer's 'ability') is ultimately at the service of, and answerable to the creative imagination (the unconscious functioning of the composer's 'ability'); and naturally so, since it is the unconscious that 'knows what it wants'.

And it is clear that this is true, not only on the small scale, but on the great. For the point at which the creative act becomes an attempt by consciousness to fulfil the intention of the unconscious merely occurred one stage earlier with Beethoven than with most other composers (and several stages earlier than with such a composer as Schubert, who would often pour out a whole song as 'inspiration'). The process whereby Beethoven actually realized a vital melodic-rhythmic phrase out of a vague 'inspiration' is a microcosm of the process whereby all composers realize a complete work out of a vague 'conception'. Just as, with Beethoven, the individual inspiration—the 'rough idea' or 'conception' of a melodic-rhythmic phrase—was produced by the creative imagination in the unconscious as an adumbration of the expression of a single emotion, and was ultimately realized, through the conscious application of technique, as the correct transformation of that emotion into a small-scale musical form; so the original conception of a whole work is produced by the creative imagination in the unconscious as an adumbration of the expression of a whole complex of emotions, and is ultimately realized, through the conscious application of technique, as the correct transformation of that complex of emotions into a large-scale musical form. The only difference is in the vast scale on which the technique has to work in the latter case, which naturally calls for a correspondingly larger amount of conscious intellectual effort; but, just as with Beethoven's inspirations, the technique is always at the service of the creative imagination, and ultimately answerable to it—i.e., to the intention behind the original conception.

So we can see that technique, on whatever scale it is used, is a continuation of the work of the creative imagination by other means, and that this work is the creation of forms, whether large or small, whether parts or wholes; and these forms are not 'abstract' forms, but 'forms-into-which-the-composer's-emotion-is-transformed'. Wherefore we should always remember that 'form' means 'form of expression' and 'technique' means 'technique of creating forms of expression'. Except in 'architectural' polyphonic works built out of inexpressive material, technique cannot be considered apart from the emotions it is used to express: it cannot be used in an expressive vacuum except to produce *pastiche*, experiment, or those useful student exercises which help the budding composer to add to his store of 'knowledge necessary for the building up of forms'. If technique were ever to be used to develop expressive material without any expressive purpose, the result could only be a haphazard jumble of emotions which would convey nothing coherent to the listener. For example, if a composer were to open a symphony of serious intent with a powerfully heroic first subject and then immediately develop it in a flippantly joyful way, we should just not 'follow', however intellectually intelligible the working of the technique might be. (In fact, composers of any standing are never guilty of this type of expressive *non-sequitur*, even though they are working entirely unconsciously— i.e. writing 'pure' music—unless their intention is purely satirical.)

Again, when in the composition of an expressive work the technique continues to act independently of the demands of the expression, owing to a failure of 'inspiration', the result is a sudden intrusion of empty, meaningless, dead music. For instance, when Schubert, composing the finale of his Ninth Symphony, reached the point where his second subject was due to begin, he at first wrote a few bars of *fugato*; but, dissatisfied, he 'thought again', crossed them out, and substituted the big pulsating four-beat tune which stands in the score to-day. It cannot have been purely an intellectual dissatisfaction that made him delete the (technically satisfactory) *fugato*—it must have *felt* all wrong to his unconscious faculty of cognition. It must have been alien to the original conception: whatever he was unconsciously expressing (and we cannot go into that here) demanded a pulsating rhythm from beginning to end of the movement. For a moment, his sheer impulse to go on creating, working at high pressure, must have outrun his creative imagination, and continued to function as technique, independently of the expressive intention; then suddenly the creative imagination must have 'caught up', taken over (unconsciously) the four-beat pulsations of the rhythmic approach to the preceding cadence, and turned them into a pulsating melody for his technique to work out in detail. Had Schubert left the *fugato* in, and continued on the basis of that, his finale, however he had managed to end it, would have been ruined, and we could have pointed sadly to the *fugato* as the spot where it broke down— where the technique suddenly began to work all on its own without regard to the expressive need.

Actually, anyone who has ever composed, on whatever level, knows that terrible moment when the brain goes on spinning notes from which the breath of life has been withdrawn, and however hard it tries, gets more and more bogged down in meaninglessness. Few are lucky enough to confess it to themselves as quickly as Schubert, and even fewer to find immediate salvation in the sudden resuscitation of the creative imagination. Unless this faculty continues to function throughout an entire composition, keeping the broad outline of the conception in view, and acting decisively as inspiration at crucial moments, the work will be still-born, however brilliant the composer's technique may be at making do with essentially uncreative material. Schubert (like Mozart) was one of the lucky ones, whose creative imagination rarely deserted him, and whose technique was often practically inseparable from it, for it apparently functioned much of the time in the same smooth, swift, somnambulistic way.

Summing up, we may say that the creative act in music is a unity—the transformation of a complex of emotions into musical form—normally manifesting itself as a continuous process divisible in to stages which overlap, as follows. (1) A complex of emotions within the composer's unconscious presses for an outlet—for expression, communication to others, in musical form. (2) The composer's 'ability to use his stored-up knowledge for the building up of forms' functions unconsciously, adumbrating a general overall pattern which the form will take: this we call 'the creative imagination providing a conception'. (3) The 'ability' functions again unconsciously, actually transforming the current of the basic emotion of the complex into a small-scale musical form: this we call 'the creative imagination providing inspiration'. (4) The 'ability' functions consciously, spinning the 'inspiration' into larger forms, which are continually scrutinized by the unconscious faculty of cognition, and accepted, modified, or rejected, according as they fulfil, or fail to fulfil, the demands of the original conception: this we call 'the technique building up the overall form under the control of the creative imagination'. (5) During the building up of the overall form, the 'ability' still manifests itself unconsciously all the time, transforming the other emotions of the complex into other small-scale musical forms, and these are also spun into larger forms by the 'ability' working consciously: this we call 'the creative imagination continually providing further inspirations for the technique to work on'. (6) The work stands complete as the accurate transformation of the composer's complex of emotions (content) into musical form (form) by the composer's 'ability' functioning unconsciously (creative imagination) as a transformer of single emotions into small-scale forms (inspirations), and consciously (technique) as a builder of small-scale forms into a large one (form); acting in its latter capacity (technique) as a realizer of the potentialities (conception) envisaged in its former capacity (creative imagination).

Having established that form, on a large scale no less than on a small, is simply expression, and that technique on any scale is simply the means of achieving this expression, we can at last leave the plane of *minutiae* and move on from the single phrase to the extended theme. This need not detain us long: a theme is obviously only an extension of a single phrase, and will function expressively as a series of phrases. These may be either basic terms or independent creations, or a mixture of the two; whatever they are, their expressive effect can easily be analysed, either by reference to the basic terms, or back to the tonal tensions and the rise and fall in pitch. It will suffice to give a single example of the very simplest type: that of a theme which is a rhythmic fertilization of a 'basic sentence', as we might say, in the way that a phrase is a rhythmic fertilization of a basic term. Let us look first at the bare pattern itself, a dead thing, uninfused by the power of the creative imagination:

A bad composer might give it some such rhythmic 'life' as this:

But see opposite what Mozart, Beethoven, and Dvorak made out of it. (For ease of comparison, the Mozart is written out at the actual pitch at which the tenor sings it—it is of course notated an octave higher nowadays, though Mozart wrote it at pitch on the tenor clef—and the original 4/4 barring has been cut into bars of 2/4. Also the Dvorák has been transposed up a semitone from B minor to C minor, and the notation transferred from the bass to the treble clef.)

221

It can be seen at once that the three themes are all rhythmic fertilizations of the basic pattern in Ex. 78; and that they are all obviously 'inspirations' (i.e. they must have been conceived by the creative imagination as complete entities). We are lucky to have Beethoven's sketches for the magnificent theme of the *Eroica* Funeral March: Mozart's and Dvořák's inspirations may have materialized fully-fledged, but Beethoven, as so often, was obliged to apply his technique to complete the unfinished work of his creative imagination, and we can watch it in action. We see him groping among the ever-fruitful roots of musical language, striving to fulfil the intentions of the creative imagination: the fourth bar, in Ex. 80x, takes the same form as Mozart's,[1] and could easily have occurred first in the same form as Dvořák's; but Beethoven searched for (and found) the pathetic 3–2 suspension treated as an anguished 6–5 on the dominant, which, out of the many purely technical possibilities, was the right one for transforming his emotion of dark grief. Also in the first two bars, we see a single rhythmic impulse testing out two different 'potencies' towards the opening melodic phrase, and eventually actualizing the stronger one—the one that dwells longest on the lower dominant (conveying the inertia of the grief) before moving up to the tonic. Bars 6 to 8 of Ex. 80y show how the simple 5–4–3–2–1 lies at the root of the final and more ornate ending to the theme, and this enables us to equate the corresponding phrases in the Mozart and Dvořák examples with the same basic pattern; nor need we now be worried by the fact that Mozart's first bar has 1–5 instead of 5–1.

Naturally the three entirely different ways in which the 'basic sentence' has been rhythmically fertilized, and characterized by volume, tone-colour and texture, are referable to the three entirely diverse aspects of a basic emotion which it has been used to express. The Mozart example is from the opening of *The Magic Flute*: Tamino, the hero (not a very brave one!), is running for his life, pursued by a serpent—hence the *allegro* tempo, the loud volume (implicit, though not marked), the voice rising by means of falling phrases thrown out in breathless rhythm, the shout on the top A flat (minor sixth, note of anguish), and the falling 5–3–1–(7) and 5–(2)–3–1 of despair to the words '(Help me) *or I am lost!*'—which he fears he will be. Hence also

---

[1] Ex. 80A and Ex. 80x tempt one to think in terms of unconscious cribbing.

the fact that the opening term of the sentence is not realized as the rising 5–1–3 of courage, so much as the rising 1–3–5 of grief asserted, of which we have indeed used it as an example in Chapter 3 (Ex. 55d). In Beethoven's Funeral March, the tempo is naturally dead slow, the volume as soft as possible, the rhythm dragging yet firmly pointed in heroic fashion. The actual theme, as so often in Beethoven's music (and not in the Mozart and Dvořák themes), is made up of the basic elements of musical language in their fundamental simplicity: first a conflation of the heroic 5–1–3 and the brooding 1–3–1; then the falling 5–4–3–2–1 of despair and the pathetic 3–2 suspension treated as an anguished 6–5 on the dominant; a rising (protesting) phrase culminating on the minor sixth of anguish, emphasized by a *sforzando*; and finally another descent down the (ornamented) 5–4–3–2–1 of despair. If we add that the theme, on repetition, modulates to the relative major, E flat, and yields to the consoling or comforting major 8–7–6–5; and that the Trio opens with the latent triumph of the C major 1–3–5, hushed (*piano*) and serene (*adagio assai*), which swells in volume to burst out as real triumph in quicker rhythm (semiquaver triplets) on trumpets, going over into the fundamental affirmation 5–1 in a major context; we may see that Beethoven's peculiar greatness resides in his truly basic use of musical language.

Mozart and Beethoven vitalized the thematic pattern, in their different ways, for a context of 'hero', 'tragedy', 'grief', 'anguish', and 'despair'. But what of the Dvořák—the opening theme of the finale of his Cello Concerto, which is 'pure' music? We must notice two things: whereas Mozart's rhythm is breathless and agitated, and Beethoven's solemn and dragging, Dvořák's is firm, bold, and thrusting; moreover, Dvořák has removed much of the grief and anguish from the melodic pattern by accenting 2 instead of 3 at the beginning, accenting 2 again firmly at the halfway stage, and accenting 7 instead of 6 at the climax of the third phrase.[1] A Czech writer has described

---

[1] In the final, definitive version. Dvořák apparently left no sketches of the theme, but in his original draft of the whole work, there is one significant difference at this point: the second half of the sixth bar appears as 6 (quaver) 5–4 (semiquavers), so that the climax accent *is* on 6. Technically adequate, but too gloomy for such a bold theme; to play this version, and then the final one, is to realize that 7–6 is a magnificent sweeping gesture, crowning the whole theme with a feeling of care-free indomitability. (For knowledge of this 'first thought' of Dvořák's, I am indebted to Dr. John Clapham, who kindly made a copy of the original version of the theme for me, from the MS. in Prague.)

this theme as 'strongly marked and coloured with national rhythm': it derives, in fact, like so many of Dvořák's themes, from Czech folk-music, and is perhaps a little influenced by the Negro melodies which so delighted him when he was in America (where he wrote this work). We have to remember that the Czechs were engaged in a heroic struggle against foreign domination (and that Dvořák recognized that the Negroes, too, were not their own masters). Consequently, in much of his music, like Smetana, he drew on the legendary-heroic, nationalist elements in his country's traditional music; and in this music, as in much other Central and Eastern European folk-music, lively rhythms expressive of unquenchable vitality fight against (and often subdue) the painful melodic elements of the minor system expressive of suffering and hardship. Play the Dvořák theme slowly, and the sadness of the tonal tensions becomes immediately apparent; play it up to tempo, and the effect is of a fierce, robust, heroic sweeping aside of trouble. There is no intention of saying that Dvořák had any concrete idea in mind when he was inspired to write this tune, but simply that when he composed, he did so as a whole man; that one most important aspect of this man was an oppressed Czech, a patriot, one of the 'folk', a man of vigour and courage; and that this splendid, inspiriting theme must have materialized from the area of his unconscious containing musical and non-musical elements such as these. It is, in fact, simply a 'heroic' theme, but an assertively, positively, actively heroic one.

So much for the extended theme as an expressive unit. Its functioning is hardly more complex than that of the single phrase: it merely expresses two or three kindred emotional elements mingled together, instead of a single one.

But what happens when the theme is over? We have given a hint of an answer to this question when considering the *Eroica* Funeral March; but that is, after all, essentially a sectional movement in which each section is simply and straightforwardly melodic, a movement which proceeds mainly by the continual provision of the 'basic term' type of inspiration by the creative imagination. What happens, for example, in an opening *allegro* movement, when the theme goes over into some kind of 'transition section', on which the technique has obviously worked hard to achieve exactly the desired form of expression? What happens in the first movement of the *Eroica* Symphony, for example?

Anyone can see clearly by looking at Beethoven's sketches for the movement, which are unfortunately too lengthy to reproduce here. The principle is exactly the same as in the building up of the theme of the Funeral March: the continuous flow of the music is set down over and over again; each time it is a little nearer (in details occasionally a little farther from) the desired form; and each time it gets a little longer. And the important thing is that it figures as a single line of melody, exchanging the bass for the treble clef according as the true melodic line is in one or the other part. Sometimes the melody is right and the rhythm wrong; sometimes the rhythm is right and the melody wrong; occasionally there is only a harmonic indication without any melody or rhythm at all.

A study of these sketches makes it quite clear that the technique is only doing on a large scale what the creative imagination (or the technique itself in Beethoven's case) does on a small one—building up the correct musical form of the composer's emotion. Thematic development is simply the extension of melody, and functions in exactly the same way as melody does; the organization of the tonal scheme is simply an extension of harmony, and functions in exactly the same way as harmony does; and the overall form—the fixing of the exact moment at which everything shall happen—is simply the extension of rhythm, and functions exactly as rhythm does. Just as the creative imagination, in putting together the small-scale form which is an inspiration, makes melodic, rhythmic, and harmonic tensions interact in the most fruitful way for the composer's expressive purpose—rhythmically accenting or harmonically emphasizing this or that moment of rise or fall in pitch, this or that tonal tension, so can Beethoven's technique be seen functioning, on a larger scale, in building up the massive first movement of the *Eroica* Symphony. To look at the sketches is to watch the gradual fixing of the exact rhythmic moment for each melodic and harmonic tension (each point in the thematic development and the scheme of tonal organization) to realize its full expressive power. And it is impossible not to get the impression that the technique is only impatiently labouring its way towards some definite expressive end already envisaged by the creative imagination; and that the latter is only waiting all the time to recognize and ratify each scrap of it the moment it materializes, in the same way that it did while the Funeral March theme was being groped for.

There can be only one final confirmation of our theory that music can function continuously as expression down to the last detail, and that is a detailed expressive analysis of a complete work. Unfortunately, such an ambitious undertaking is impossible, owing to the enormous number of words it would require: when we consider how many words have had to be expended on an analysis of the brief phrase which opens the Prelude to *Tristan*, it is evident that a detailed expressive analysis of a work like the *Eroica* Symphony would require a large volume to itself. What is more, it would probably defeat its own ends, by becoming a vast labyrinth of verbal descriptions in which the naked impact of the music was lost altogether. How then are we to proceed?

Fortunately, of recent years, an entirely new approach to the problem of purely formal analysis has come into being, which we can adapt to our own purpose. The methods arising out of this approach have escaped once and for all from the unwieldy old process of giving a detailed description of the various formal procedures in a work, in the order in which they actually occur (and usually omitting to explain the inner relationship between them): instead they go straight to the main point—the formal unity of a work—by showing how all its material stems ultimately from the initial theme or phrase (what we have called the original 'inspiration').[1] To give a simple example of how the new approach works, let us turn to the *Eroica* Symphony and show the most obvious instance of formal unity: the con-

---

[1] The brilliant exponent of the new approach in this country is Hans Keller, who has evolved a method of his own, which he calls Functional Analysis. He eschews words altogether: instead he 'composes' an analytical score, to be played together with the work it analyses; and this score makes clear the unity underlying the various contrasting parts—the diverse movements and different themes—by manipulating the material aurally, as it were, fragmenting it and reintegrating it in the way that the creative imagination would seem to do with the material of tradition when it provides the original inspiration. It was the sudden illumination brought by a hearing of Keller's Functional Analysis of Mozart's String Quartet in D minor, K. 421, that gave the idea for the method of analysis used in this chapter.

tinual transformation of that familiar basic term, the major (5)–1–3–5, which occurs in the opening theme, into new melodic shapes. Here are the ways in which (5)–1–3–5 appears in the Symphony:

One hopes not to be accused of simple-mindedness. It is obvious that many a work by a tonal composer of such fundamental simplicity as Beethoven will abound in the melodic use of the triad. But the fact remains that the *Eroica* is built largely on a specific form—ascending (5)–1–3–5—which is not a unifying element of, say, the Pastoral Symphony, nor the Seventh Symphony, though it does play a part in the Fifth. In any case, there are other elements at work in our example, as is shown by the amazing (surely unconscious) fusion of the main themes of the first and last movements in the finale's horn tune in Ex. 81d; and the fact that the theme of the Scherzo's Trio (only partly

quoted) is a major version of the same basic pattern as the
theme of the Funeral March, as far as ascending 5–1–3 plus
descending 5–3–1–2 (note Beethoven's sketch, incidentally, the
rhythm of which shows the intention behind the conception—
of deriving the Scherzo's Trio theme from the main theme of the
first movement).

But the real point is this. The *Eroica* owes a large part of its
formal unity to its continual transformation of the ascending
major (5)–1–3–5 announced at the outset—*which is only natural
in a 'heroic' symphony*, since the phrase is a conflation of the joyful
major 5–1–3 and the triumphantly joyful major 1–3–5, and its
minor version is a conflation of the heroic minor 5–1–3 and the
protesting minor 1–3–5. It is significant that the other great
work unified to a large extent by the forceful use of a similar
term is *The Ring*: Wagner was, as we know, consciously and
unconsciously influenced by Beethoven's emotional and musical
conception of heroism—see the basic motive of the whole work
(Ex. 25f—in the key of the Symphony) and the Sword motive
(Ex. 54e—in the key of the Funeral March's Trio) for a conflation of the major 5–1–3 and 1–3–5; and the Volsung, Valkyrie,
Annunciation of Death, and Siegfried motives (all in Ex. 56—
two of them in the key of the Funeral March itself) for minor
equivalents.

In other words a work must have formal unity because it
must have expressive unity. A theme from the *Eroica* will not
fit into the Pastoral Symphony because it does not make formal
sense there, true; but the more fundamental reason is that
themes like those of the *Eroica* simply will not 'come into the
head' of a composer intent on expressing emotions arising out
of contact with natural surroundings, because they are not
attached to those emotions in the unconscious. Likewise, the
diverse themes of the *Eroica* (and those of any other expressive
masterpiece) are bound to have a family resemblance, are
bound to have a common derivation from the original inspiration, because all the various emotions of the complex which the
work as a whole expresses are closely related to one another—
are in fact various aspects of one basic mood. In the *Eroica*, the
tragic grief and supreme triumph of the Funeral March, the
bounding joviality of the Scherzo's Trio, and the jubilant thrust
of the horn tune in the finale that brings the wheel full circle—

these are all concomitants of the basic emotion expressed in the initial theme, the emotion of joyful confidence that is at the heart of heroism.

Once more, let us call in Aaron Copland for confirmation: 'Always remember that a theme is, after all, only a succession of notes. Merely by changing the dynamics . . . one can transform the emotional feeling of the very same succession of notes. By a change of harmony, a new poignancy may be given the theme; or by a different rhythmic treatment the same notes may result in a war dance instead of a lullaby. Every composer keeps in mind the possible metamorphoses of his succession of notes. First he tries to find its essential nature, and then he tries to find what might be done with it—how that essential nature may momentarily be changed'.[1]

It now becomes quite clear how a large-scale form is built up to function continuously as expression. After the general shape has been adumbrated by the creative imagination (as a 'conception') to accommodate the expression of the original emotional complex in all its aspects, and the current of the central emotion of the complex has been converted into a small-scale musical form (an 'inspiration') also by the creative imagination —then the technique and the creative imagination, acting hand in glove, work outwards from this central point, as it were, extending the small-scale form of the inspiration in all directions to build up the large-scale form which is the realization of the original conception. The chief task of the creative imagination is this: just as it originally built up the small-scale form of the inspiration out of some familiar traditional element in the unconscious (in the case of the *Eroica*, a conflation of two familiar basic terms), so now it builds up new small-scale forms (new 'inspirations', the other main themes of the work) out of the small-scale form of the original inspiration. The chief task of the technique, working under the supervision of the creative imagination, is to develop these forms: to expand them, spotlight them, dovetail them into one another, and dispose them into significant order, thus realizing in every detail the correct musical form of the original complex of emotions which was envisaged in the conception.

---

[1] Aaron Copland, *What to Listen For in Music*, Chap. 3.

If formal and expressive unity are one and the same, it should be possible to adapt the new methods of purely formal analysis to our own purpose; since to trace all the main elements in the form back to the initial theme would be in fact to trace all the main elements of the expression back to the original inspiration.[1] Unfortunately, however, this also would be too ambitious an undertaking: a complete demonstration of the formal unity of a work is a lengthy and complex business in itself, and to attempt to combine such an analysis with an explanation of the expressive significance of every formal element would require more words than can be spared. In our *Eroica* example, we have merely glanced at the simplest and most obvious element in the formal unity; we have not shown how, for instance, the second group of the first movement or the material of the Scherzo are related to the initial theme. In cases like these, the underlying unity is an extremely subtle one, involving the use of inversion, retrograde motion, and interversion;[2] wherefore it follows that the expressive unity at such points must also be an extremely subtle one, requiring lengthy explanation. Consequently, we shall use only the essential idea of the new methods for our purpose, showing the main elements of the formal-expressive unity, without going into every subtlety, and without tracing everything back to the original inspiration. For example, we may be obliged to ignore such a subtlety as the following, from the *Eroica*, though it would be a natural and inevitable part of a purely formal analysis of the work (Ex. 82).

(Note even here, though, the expressive aspect of 'a transition section working up a three-note figure from the first subject and establishing the dominant key'. The three-note figure, in the first subject, ends on the 'defeatist' minor seventh (the C sharp is a D flat), throwing an immediate shadow across the confident

---

[1] It might be pointed out here that not all those musical analysts who are apparently only intent on demonstrating formal unity are unaware of the corollary of expressive unity. Hans Keller, for example, says that his whole method of Functional Analysis would be impossible without the recognition of extreme expressive contrasts, whose background unity—a basic mood expressed in a basic idea—he proceeds to uncover. (Oral communication.)

[2] 'Interversion' means the switching-around of the notes of a phrase into a different order, without destroying the essential unity. The idea that such a thing could be has been fiercely denied, and the whole conception has been derided as a mere tool invented to enable its users to discover resemblances which do not exist; yet a glance at the last two bars of Beethoven's sketches for the *Eroica* Funeral March (Ex. 80) shows that he took the principle for granted (D, E flat, C; E flat, D, C).

Ex. 82

start; but when the music starts to 'move off' towards the dominant key ('onwards' and 'upwards'), the three-note figure is used in a version ending on the 'highly optimistic' sharp fourth of the dominant: the very essence of defeat is thus transformed into the very essence of striving for victory—formal–and–expressive contrast-in-unity).

One day, perhaps, it may be possible to make a complete formal-and-expressive analysis of a work like the *Eroica*, but in the meantime we can make a beginning by demonstrating fundamentals and essentials. Two works will be analysed: Mozart's Fortieth Symphony and Vaughan Williams's Sixth. They have been chosen for five reasons. Firstly, because they lie outside the romantic period, and are therefore free from any suspicion that nowadays attaches to the music of that period: one is a classical work, the other a contemporary one. Secondly, because they would both appear to be 'pure' music, since we have no evidence that their composers ever imagined that they expressed anything at all. Thirdly, because in actual fact they must be expressive works, otherwise there would not have been so much argument as to what they do express. Fourthly, because they present a challenge, in the shape of a problem which has always been regarded as insoluble; to establish objectively the 'meaning' of a piece of 'pure' music. Lastly, because they both achieve their expression almost entirely through the basic terms, which makes them more susceptible to analysis.

We shall boldly assume what seems obvious to common sense: that if a composer uses expressive material, even though he is writing 'pure' music, he must consciously or unconsciously intend it to express what in fact it does express, otherwise he would not use it but would turn to material of a less expressive kind. If Bach, for example, began the slow movement of his Two-Violin Concerto in D minor with the major 8–7–6–5, he must have meant to express a feeling of joy welcomed and received as comfort or consolation; and if Beethoven used the same term to open the slow movement of his Fourth Symphony, and Brahms to open the slow movement of his First Piano Concerto, they too must have meant to express the same feeling (Brahms, the romantic, avowed as much by writing the word 'Benedictus' over the music). And in the same way, if Mozart and Vaughan Williams, in the two works to be analysed, have used certain basic terms in such a powerful way as to move the listener deeply, they must have intended the listener to be moved in the way that he *is* moved, whether they realized it or not. Our task is to discover, in each case, exactly what basic terms have been used, and exactly what complex of emotions has been expressed by them, that affects the listener so profoundly.

SYMPHONY NO 40 IN G MINOR (K.550) BY MOZART

Mozart may with truth be described as the most persistently misunderstood composer of all time: owing to his miraculous blend of intense emotion and perfect classic form, he has remained an enigmatic, ambiguous figure from his own day to ours. Although in each age he has been loved and admired in no uncertain measure, it has proved ultimately impossible to strike a balance, to see him steadily and see him whole.

His contemporaries were unable to understand him because he was so new: they complained of his bizarre effects, of his straining after unnatural emotionalism, and one writer declared him to be 'a sectary of that false system that divides the octave into twelve semitones'(!) To their ears, nurtured on the normal 'tasteful' classical style of the *galant* and *rococo* periods, Mozart's exploitation of the expressive power of music, in chromatic melodies and dissonant harmonies, appeared to be wild and perverse experiments; and the perfect (but ever-new) forms in which he controlled this turbulent material seemed to be bursting at the seams. Mozart was indeed inclined to be a 'modernist', as we have seen from his E flat String Quartet (Ex. 76) and as we can see from his Fortieth Symphony:

Ex. 83

The romantics, on the other hand, could not understand him because by their time, half a century after his death, he had become a remote composer whose music was written in an outdated style. After the Beethovenian expressive revolution, they were beginning a further 'advance' towards conceiving music entirely as the most intense expression; and as they went on giving a more and more rhetorical emphasis to the emotive tensions and patterns of musical language, Mozart's subtle employment of the same tensions and patterns in the clear-cut outlines of eighteenth-century sonata-form appeared to be a purely artificial expression of emotion. The form, realized to be perfect now that the 'modernisms' had vanished, was everything. There were, of course, works in which Mozart appeared as an unmistakable forbear of the more turbulent brand of romanticism—the D minor and C minor piano concertos, the Statue music in *Don Giovanni*, the Requiem Mass—and these were acknowledged and admired as such; but with strange exceptions. For instance, at least the first and last movements of the Fortieth Symphony belong to this category; but Schumann seems not to have felt this at all. He was criticizing the poet Schubart's idea that keys are connected with certain emotions, and particularly his equating of G minor with 'displeasure, discomfort, worrying anxiety, discontented gnawing at the bit', and commented: 'Now compare this idea with Mozart's Symphony in G minor—that floating Grecian Grace!' In fact, as true Mozartians know, the key of G minor was nearly always used by Mozart for the emotions listed by Schubart, and not least in this symphony: never did a great composer and penetrating critic more openly betray a 'blind spot' than Schumann did here. Of course, Schubart was wrong in supposing keys to have universal connexions with particular emotions; as has been mentioned, the emotional connotations of keys are entirely a matter of the psychology of the individual composer. But his choice of words looks very much as though he might well have been thinking of Mozart.

Those romantics who actually worshipped Mozart did so entirely for his supposed 'divine purity'. Tchaikovsky and Brahms acknowledged this in their different ways: amid the heavily expressive romanticism of their own music, they looked back and glamourized him as a kind of musical angel. In short, the true essence of Mozart was inaccessible to the Romantics, since his music had become 'old music'.

Our own age has retained the romantic period's conception of Mozart as a 'pure' composer, but adopted a different attitude. Whereas most romantics sensed the emotion in the music, but were more fascinated by the apparent 'purity' of the expression, many modern musicians refuse to admit the presence of any emotion in the music at all: it has now become pure sound-structure, an intellectual and aesthetic delight. We are under constant pressure, from the written and spoken word, to make only a half-response to all music—to admire the form without apprehending it as expression—and especially so in the case of Mozart: the general judgement of the twentieth century, ratified during the 1956 bi-centenary celebrations, is that his music is 'impersonal' and consists of superbly-wrought sound-patterns not connected in any way with human attitudes and feelings.

This is sad ingratitude to a man who portrayed so eloquently the joys, sorrows, hopes, fears and desires of the very human characters in his operas, and who in general lavished upon us the riches of his heart and soul (as well as his mind) in some of the most moving music ever written. If our enjoyment and understanding of his art are not to be sadly impoverished, we cannot too strongly oppose the fashionable dogma. Mozart, like all other composers, wrote his music out of his total experience; far from being impersonal, it is in fact the expression of the *richest* personality in all musical history, for he was the most universal of the great composers. If this seems a large claim to make, consider how many sides to his character there are, as revealed in his music: a Christian spirituality, like Bach; a sense of the power and the glory of life, like Handel; a sense of

fun, like Haydn; a grim, tragic power, like Beethoven; a mer-
curial wit, like Rossini; a wistful, 'innocent', child-like tender-
ness, like Schubert; a yearning intensity and demonic force,
like Wagner; an erotic sensuality like Richard Strauss; a deso-
late melancholy and acute anguish, like Mahler. This long list
can be heavily substantiated by many passages from his works.
And there is, of course, a caressing charm, a kittenish playful-
ness, like only Mozart; a suave serenity, a feline grace, like
only Mozart; an elegance, sophistication, and exquisite taste,
like only Mozart. And all these form the unity that was Mozart's
balanced personality. In fact, the only thing that Mozart's music
lacks is what the twentieth century declares it to consist of
entirely—purity. It is not pure at all, as Palestrina is pure. It is
far too human for that.

It should be clear by now that to say that a composer writes
music out of his whole experience is not to entertain crude
notions of music's dependency on life—to imagine, say, that
the melancholy of the Fortieth Symphony was the immediate
result of an influx of bills into the poverty-stricken composer's
home, or that the comparative joy of the *Jupiter* arose out of
the receipt of a large loan from a friend. An artist's emotions
are not the playthings of trivial events, being rooted in his
unconscious, where they form his basic life-attitudes; the Fortieth Symphony and the *Jupiter* are visions of the sadness and
the joy of life respectively, as experienced by Mozart—not in
his superficial, everyday reactions, but in his deep, enduring
self.

To ask what was Mozart's 'state of mind' when he conceived
and wrote the Fortieth Symphony in a fortnight or so in the
summer of 1788, three years before his death, or to dismiss such
speculations as irrelevant—both these approaches to the work
are equally meaningless. His 'state of mind' was what it always
was, a compound of many conflicting elements; and if physical
deterioration and growing penury had brought melancholy
uppermost, thereby helping to crystallize this last and finest of
his G minor protests against life's terrible sadness, these mis-
fortunes did not in the least prevent him from creating immediately afterwards the last and finest of his C major paeans for
life's inexhaustible wellspring of gladness. He knew the naked
emotional realities of life, and could express them to the full in

his music; the immediate 'state of mind' forced on the man by the contingencies of physical existence was not important to the creative artist.

We are assuming in advance that the Fortieth Symphony *is* a melancholy work, an assumption for which material proof will be forthcoming; and indeed true Mozart-lovers of the nineteenth and twentieth centuries have realized this instinctively, proving that prevailing fashions are all too often set by the uncomprehending. But it is precisely these fashions, these dogmas, that we are combating, not merely contradicting them, but attempting to prove them wrong. My own first experience of the Fortieth Symphony, like that of many other people, was as a child, knowing nothing of musical history or aesthetics, or of the many writings about the symphony, but reacting instinctively with the comment 'What a sad piece of music!' Yet so excellent a musician as the late Richard Capell declared that he could see nothing of all this supposed melancholy in the work; the opening, he said, belonged to the world of comic opera, being very like the music given to the young girl Barbarina in *Figaro*, fretting over her lost pin. We can call this a blind spot, if we wish, but what are we to reply to it?

First of all, that Barbarina is in fact, in her childish way, in a state of anguish. After all, if she is a comic figure to us, that is precisely because she takes herself so seriously (or rather, because Mozart, with his sure dramatic instinct, does). It is an old axiom of the theatre that nothing can be funny on the stage (except knockabout farce) if the supposed feelings of the actors are not represented as genuine; Barbarina has to feel truly sorry for herself, if we are to smile at her making such a fuss over nothing, and so Mozart has written some genuinely sad music for her. But more important is the fact that Barbarina's childish self-pity is appropriately rendered in a gentle 6/8, *allegretto*, in a circumscribed little tune just touching the anguished minor sixth off the beat, with a lilting accompaniment; whereas in the Fortieth Symphony, Mozart has expressed his own adult masculine anguish in a driving 2/2, *allegro molto*, in a wide-ranging broad-spanned theme that gives little stabbing accents to the minor sixth, with an accompaniment of fluttering agitation. The only genuine points of resemblance between the two pieces of music are the presence of the minor 6–5 in the melody, and the soft dynamic; but these mean nothing at all, considered apart from the rhythmic impulse.

Recently, another attempt has been made to link the opening theme of the Symphony with the world of comic opera—again with *Figaro*, and again, strangely enough, with an adolescent character: J. A. Westrup has offered the theory that it first came to Mozart as inspiration for an aria which replaced Cherubino's 'Non so più' in a production of the opera in the spring of 1788.[1] Surely this cannot be so, however well the first four phrases fit the rhythm of the words; the theme is too full of real anguish to be able to represent the semi-pleasurable erotic turmoil of the adolescent heart. Used in a comic opera, it could only function in some such way as the (much weightier) Statue music in *Don Giovanni*, i.e. pass beyond the bounds of comic opera altogether. An operatic character would have to be hard-pressed indeed to sing this broken-hearted theme: if Mozart did originally come by it in connection with Cherubino's love-lorn frenzy, he must have realized it to be a 'slip of the mind' (much as Wagner rejected the first offering of his creative imagination for the joyful pipe-tune in *Tristan*, recognizing it eventually as the theme he was unconsciously seeking —the so-called 'Love's Resolution' motive—to wind up the last act of *Siegfried*). The important thing is that the definitive aria is in E flat *major*, and has a melody appropriately filled with the pleasurably longing suspensions of the major system.

The only way to escape entirely from subjectivism, however, and to establish the true character of the Symphony, is to analyse its use of the various basic terms of musical language. But before we attempt this, two points must be made clear. (1) In that the Symphony makes use of the ascending minor 5–1–3 and 1–3–5, we shall be obliged to use the words 'heroic' and 'protest', and it must be kept in mind just what these words mean in relation to Mozart's experience. It is too often forgotten that Mozart lived until the French Revolution was under way; that he came into violent conflict with an unjust aristocratic patron; that *Figaro* and *Don Giovanni* contain a certain amount of satire on the aristocracy; that he suffered the appalling injustice that, genius as he was, he was allowed to die in penury at the age of thirty-six; and that he expressed moods of

---

[1] 'Cherubino and the G minor Symphony', in *Fanfare for Ernest Newman*.

rebellious dissatisfaction in his music which were regarded in the elegant eighteenth century as 'bad taste' or 'bad form'. Mozart's personality contained elements of 'heroism', 'rebelliousness' and 'protest', in the context of the composer's position as a servant in the eighteenth-century; let it not be imagined that our use of the words will carry the same weight as they would in an analysis of Beethoven's Fifth Symphony or *The Ring*. (2) Mozart expresses his emotional attitude in terms of eighteenth-century musical style, and within the formal scope of the classical symphony; hence, if we use such a word as 'anguish' it will not have the intensely subjective connotation that it would in an analysis of Tchaikovsky's *Pathétique* Symphony. The classical composer does not wear his heart on his sleeve, but weaves his subjective emotions into a lucid, universalized, objective statement.

Ex. 85 *(a)*

Our method of analysis will be to set side by side the various uses of the basic terms of musical vocabulary which recur throughout the symphony, at once making clear the emotional expression and demonstrating the expressive and formal unity of the work. We begin with our familiar term 1–3–1 (minor), which is, as it were, the womb of the symphony, the fundamental mood from which it derives its being—a brooding obsession with 'the darker side of things' (Ex. 85).

These might seem to be mere inessential details, but they are nothing of the sort: they are the opening and closing bars of the three G minor movements, together with the persistent accompaniment figure of the first movement and the obsessive pattern which drives the finale to its end. Fluttering in rapid quaver figures on *divisi* violas, *piano*, 1–3–1 initiates the opening movement in a mood of suppressed agitation; rocking in the bass or middle part it sets up the agitated rhythmic figure which pervades the second half of the exposition (in B flat major) and the recapitulation (in G minor); flashed out in an ornamented version, and hammered out in its simplest form as three separate notes, in both cases on the cutting tone of the violins, it ends the movement in a mood of fierce assertion (Ex. 85a). Played *staccato* in heavy rhythm, *forte*, it opens the Minuet with a feeling of stern courage in the theme (ornamented) and in the bass; piped out in ornamented form by the flute, in the same heavy rhythm, *piano*, it ends it with a feeling of pathetic resignation (Ex. 85b). Throbbing, *piano*, on strings, it launches the finale, like the first movement, in suppressed agitation; flashed out in ornamented form, *forte* on violins (cf. first movement again), it acts as closing phrase to both halves of the main theme, like an obsession; reiterated in this form over and over, *piano* and *forte*, it drives the exposition (in B flat) and the whole work (back in G minor) to their conclusion; and it recalls the fiercely assertive ending of the first movement to conclude the symphony, functioning in its basic form, 1–3–1, as three separate notes, *forte*, on violins (Ex. 85c). It is worth noting that the work opens and closes without a fifth in the chord, and both the Minuet and the finale open in the same way. Enclosing the whole symphony, and functioning as the basis of its varying moods, is this fundamental sense of obsession.

Ex. 86 (a)

Turning to the melodic elements which create the action, as it were, against the 1–3–1 background, we have first the minor sixth, and that well-worn term, the minor 6–5 (Ex. 86).

In the first movement, of course, the minor 6–5 is practically omnipresent. It initiates the opening theme in urgent, repetitive (obsessive) three-note rhythm, with a subsidiary, not a main accent on the minor sixth (Ex. 86a). Functioning as a stab of anguish, it permeates the movement, either as the three-note figure itself, or as the threefold repetition of it, or simply as 6–5. This latter persists uninterrupted as a harmonic inner part beneath the theme, as 6–5 in G minor, as the same thing also functioning as the 'hopeless' minor 2–1 on D, and as 3–2 in G minor functioning as 6–5 on D (Ex. 86a). Moreover, after the confident 'transitional' theme in B flat major, the minor sixth itself (most unusually) dominates the affirmation of the cadence in F major before the 'second subject' (Ex. 86b). The minor sixth is *the* note of this symphony, and it must be emphasized that it is omnipresent only because of the needs of both formal and expressive unity, arising out of the main theme: in all the above harmonic examples the music could be re-written without it, and still make excellent sense from the small-scale technical point of view.

The three-note thematic form of the term is the main tissue of the movement. It opens the exposition, and closes it (in B flat, functioning temporarily as the major 6–5 of 'joyous vibration', but still breaking in as the minor 6–5 in G minor). Back permanently in its true minor form, it dominates the development section, achieving the extremes of fierce agitation (*forte*, rushing counter-themes, and wild modulations), pathos (*piano*, chromatic harmonies) and acute poignancy (extreme dissonances— see Ex. 83). It opens and closes the recapitulation, and forms the entire basis of the coda (still in the minor), both as itself and as the 'hopeless' 2–1 (6–5 in C minor). The basic mood of the first movement is clearly then one of obsessive, agitated anguish, manifesting itself gently or fiercely, pathetically or clamourously, according to the dynamic level and the harmonic and tonal implications.

The minor 6–5 also permeates the *Andante*, even though the movement is in E flat *major*. We must remember here that the expressive significance of a section of a work is conditioned by its context. In a G minor symphony, second subjects in B flat, a slow movement in E flat, and a Trio in G major, are not basic, but parenthetic: the fundamental context is G minor, and what happens in these other keys is not abiding actuality, but possibility, hope, hypothesis, or at best interlude. The E flat slow movement, turning from a driving *allegro* 2/2 to a solemnly-moving *andante* 6/8, and from the minor to the major, is essentially an interlude of relief, a turning for a moment to another side of the picture—a meditative look at the 'brighter side of things'. But this basic mood is continuously and progressively undermined by various chromatic tensions, particularly the minor 6–5 of anguish, which functions here subtly (*andante*, usually *piano*) as a wistful sense of regret troubling the pleasurable tranquillity. It steals in gently at the outset in the bass of the second bar (Ex. 86b); then rises to the treble more insistently, taking the form of a drawn-out suspension (Ex. 86c). Little more is heard of it till it opens the development sternly in the bass; it returns, still in the bass, at the end of the development, growing more melancholy (Ex. 86c). This initiates a sequence of four identical phrases, each in a different key, using the minor 6–5 as it first appeared in the movement; sighing, even plangent, on the woodwind, they lead back to E flat and the recapitulation (Ex. 86d). Even now, the minor 6–5 has not been exorcized. It appears as before, in the bass, and rises to the treble, but this time it culminates in a cluster of suspensions taking the main theme into F *minor*: minor 6–5 once in E flat major; twice in F minor, in the treble and the bass (functioning also as the minor 2–1 on C); and three times as 3–2 (6–5 on C) in the inner parts (Ex. 86d). Once more in F minor, and again in E flat, and the movement is left to move more serenely to its conclusion.

In the Minuet the minor 6–5 appears sternly, in steady 3/4 tempo, *forte*. It is only one of several suspensions (3–2, 2–1, 5–4, as well as 6–5), but it is significant that it is the clinching one at the climax (Ex. 86e). In the finale the term returns to its original permeative status, ending the first phrase of the theme (3–2 in G minor harmonized as 6–5 on D) and the third (pure 6–5 in G minor) (Ex. 86f). Approached as it is by a 'protesting' ascent up the minor triad (and diminished seventh), it is pointed fiercely as a sudden burst of anguish (even with the soft dynamic, owing to the high pitch). It also reappears as the original three-note rhythm of the first movement and with a similarly obsessive repetition, to form the middle section of the theme (coupled with 3–2 as 6–5 on D—Ex. 86f). In these two forms it opens the exposition; in the first form it dominates the development, as in the first movement, reaching as fierce a pitch of intensity; and it opens the recapitulation. It does not close either the exposition, or the work, for in the end active anguish fades back whence it came, into the obsessive 1–3–1, a fierce affirmation of which ends the symphony.

Other strong unifying elements are the ascending triadic figures 1–3–5 and 5–1–3, both major and minor (Ex. 87). Once again, one hopes not to be accused of simple-mindedness: triads are ubiquitous in tonal music. But they do not usually figure in such a persistently thematic way, nor with such a persistently identical shape: ascending 5–1–3, 1–3–5 and upper 5–1–3 are interlocked in different ways into an *identical arpeggio of six notes* (ascending 5–1–3–5–1–3) in all the examples given, except for (a), which is, after all, the point of departure for the whole process. No such triadic basis can be discovered in the earlier G minor Symphony, for example, or in the C minor Piano Concerto, or in the Jupiter Symphony: in fact, there are no purely triadic themes in these works at all.

The process begins, then, as a subsidiary element in the first movement. The bold B flat transitional theme which dramatically interrupts the anguished main melody has the ascending major 1–3–5 of joyful confidence (Ex. 87a). But when it is recapitulated, in E flat, it is immediately repeated in F minor in the bass, and developed through major keys: 1–3–5 is imitated in the upper part as a joyful 5–1–3, in violently agitated rhythm, the two figures in each case combining to form our basic six-note arpeggio (Ex. 87b). The music moves back to the basic G minor, and the theme is stated a third time in this key, in simple form, with the rising 1–3–5 in its minor 'protesting' form.

The major six-note arpeggio, so briefly established, reappears as an element of joy in the *Andante* (context of interlude) stated in terms of the clipped little figure of the opening theme: it functions as part of the cadence leading to the 'consoling' second subject. The simple 1–3–5 also appears as a joyful

Ex. 87 *(a)*

element in the codetta that ends the exposition and the recapitulation (Ex. 87c).

In the Scherzo, the six-note arpeggio takes on the minor form of heroic protest, in heavy rhythm (Ex. 87d).[1] It is stated as three separate phrases, each of which falls back again defeated; the first and second by the basic 1–3–1 obsession, the third by the basic 6–5 of anguish (3–2 in G minor treated as 6–5 in D minor). The Trio (context of interlude) returns to the joyful

---

[1] A point worth noting is that the triple time of the minuet rhythm does not bring its normal feeling of relaxation, owing to the stamping cross-rhythm and the heavy accentuation of the strings' detached bowing; at least, this feeling of relaxation is deferred until the Trio.

major form, the strings opening with 1–3–5, the oboes continuing with the six-note arpeggio, the first two notes being telescoped harmonically (Ex. 87e). There is pathos in this 'joyful' Trio, deriving from its position between two statements of the striving but defeated minor Minuet, the use of 'longing' suspensions (4–3, 8–7, and others), and the fact that the rising arpeggios always fall back again, as in the Scherzo.

In the finale, the six-note arpeggio crystallizes into a leaping minor heroic version, to form the opening phrase of the main theme (Ex. 87f). As in the Scherzo, it climbs only to run into the basic 6–5 of anguish (again 3–2 in G minor treated as 6–5 in D). Answered by a balancing phrase, it is repeated higher, as a diminished seventh arpeggio, and encounters the true G minor 6–5; the balancing phrase this time takes the form of the obsessive G minor 1–3–1 figure, ornamented, which rounds off this first section, the whole theme, and eventually the whole symphony, like a refrain.

So we see the major 1–3–5 and 5–1–3 of joy, and the minor 1–3–5 and 5–1–3 of heroic protest, emerging amid the basic 6–5 anguish of the first movement; the major forms persisting subsidiarily in the Andante and the Trio of the Scherzo; the minor forms making a fight of it in the Minuet proper and the finale, only to be defeated by the minor 6–5 of anguish, and finally routed by the obsessive minor 1–3–1. This is not a 'programme' but an artistic expression of a life-attitude, built up by opposing various expressive terms in a kind of battle, certain ones being basic, persistent, and finally victorious, while others are subsidiary, intermittent, and finally defeated. Mozart could have ended his symphony in G major, and let 'joy win through' but he preferred to remain faithful to his fundamental obsession. Not that 'defeat', in this context, means spiritual downfall: the assertive, virile tempo of the 2/2 *allegro* of the first movement, and even more that of the finale, give a fiercely assertive quality both to the anguish and the dark obsession, that is a 'protest' in itself—an indictment, one might almost say.[1] It is the possibility of happiness which is defeated, i.e.

---

[1] Much of the fiercely assertive quality of the music derives from the biting dissonance and hard texture of the woodwind writing: only those who have heard the work played in a small hall, by a Mozart-size orchestra with a handful of strings, can be said to have experienced the truly violent impact of the symphony (see Ex. 83).

denied; the vital force (rhythm) remains heroically un-
diminished, persisting with full power in a world deprived of
joy (contrast the *Adagio* finale of Tchaikovsky's *Pathétique* Symphony). One need hardly say that this is only one of Mozart's
life-attitudes: the joyful E flat symphony had preceded the G
minor, and the C major 'Jupiter' was to follow, in which joy
is basic, and pathos and suffering subsidiary.

It remains to deal with the three other unifying elements.
First, 8–7–6–5 in its major and minor forms:

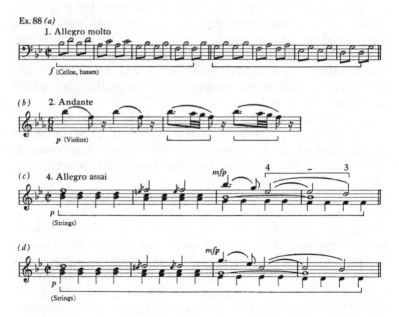

Ex. 88 *(a)*
1. Allegro molto
ƒ (Cellos, basses)

(b) 2. Andante
p (Violins)

(c) 4. Allegro assai
p
(Strings)

(d)
p
(Strings)

The major 8–7–6–5 (*forte*) enters as a bass to the confident B
flat transitional theme of the first movement, supporting the
upper 1–3–5 figures of assertive joy with a feeling of relief
welcomed (the agitated rhythm, of course, makes the general
atmosphere feverish); when the theme makes its final appearance in the recapitulation, 8–7–6–5 is transformed into its G
minor version, supporting the 1–3–5 figures of protest with a
feeling of despair (Ex. 88a). And exactly the same thing happens
in the finale: the partially joyful B flat second subject, shot
through with pathos and longing (4–3 suspension) is supported

by the major 8–7–6–5 of consolation; in the recapitulation, the second subject returns in G minor, its joy gone, and it is supported by the minor 8–7–6–5 of despair (Exs. 88c and d). The second subject of the Andante also uses the major 8–7–6–5 as comfort or consolation (Ex. 88b). The contrast of minor and major forms in the exposition and recapitulation of both first and last movements shows how the large-scale elements of form function as expression. The 'transition' and the 'second subject' enter as interludes of partial joy in the 'subsidiary' key of the relative major, B flat; but when they are recapitulated, they are absorbed into the basic key of G minor, giving up their joy to acknowledge the fundamental sense of sorrow.

Next, 5–4–3–2–1 in its major and minor forms (Ex. 89).

The minor 5–4–3–2–1 forms a hinge for the main sections of the first movement. After the first appearance of the main theme, which opposes against the anguish of its obsessive 6–5 a forward-looking modulation to the dominant and a strong affirmation of that key, the despairing minor 5–4–3–2–1 falls on melancholy bassoons back into G minor for the anguish to begin again (Ex. 89a). After the end of the exposition has established the key of B flat, the violent diminished seventh chord at the opening of the development is followed by the minor 5–4–3–2–1 on hollow-sounding woodwind, in the unexpected key of F sharp minor (a semitonal depression of the tonic), to let the anguish of the main theme begin once more in an even darker context (Ex. 89a). When the development's wildly-modulating search for some way of throwing off the minor 6–5 only ends, as it must do, by returning to the home key of that obsessive phrase—G minor, the minor 5–4–3–2–1 enters on the pathetic tone-colour of the flute, beginning with the 6–5 itself, falling by weary steps, and taking in semitonal inflections to become a descending chromatic scale: it finally touches on the hopeless minor second, and the main theme steals in to begin the tale of fundamental anguish all over again (Ex. 89b).

During the exposition, the second subject in B flat (context of interlude) consists essentially of two ornamented statements of the 'consoling' major 5–4–3–2–1—shot through with chromatic sadness (Ex. 89c); in the recapitulation this is transformed into two ornamented statements of the 'despairing' minor 5–4–3–2–1,

Ex. 89 *(a)*

in the basic context of the tonic G minor. And the second subject of the finale no less consists of two ornamented statements of the 'consoling' major 5–4–3–2–1 in the subsidiary context of the relative major, B flat, recapitulated in the basic context of the tonic G minor as two ornamented statements of the 'despairing' minor 5–4–3–2–1 (Ex. 89d and e).

The final appearance of 5–4–3–2–1 is where we should naturally expect it, at the end of the work, in the basic tonic minor context (Ex. 89f); flashed out on the violins, *forte*, in a high state of animation but with a sense of inescapable finality, it is the last fierce assertion of despair, arising out of the inevitable and final return to the obsessive 1–3–1 which has immediately preceded it.

Lastly, the descending chromatic scale, which we have already seen functioning as an intensification of the minor 5–4–3–2–1 (Ex. 89b).

Ex. 90 *(a)*

The chromatic element first insinuates itself at the end of the opening theme of the symphony, in the bass, as a descent of three notes: this is picked up to open the second subject—the establishing of B flat has brought joy, but a joy which is full of remembered sorrow (Ex. 90a). In the second subject the three-note figure is balanced by an extension of itself into a descending six-note chromatic scale, and the second time it leads down on to a seventh note, the fourth of the key of A flat (Ex. 90b).

This is the key on the minor second of G minor, and the danger is of falling hopelessly, by the 'Neapolitan' modulation or that of the German sixth, into the melancholy home key. The fourth (the D flat) becomes a pathetic, longing 4–3 suspension, while the upper part has the striving 7–8 figure, trying to pull the music back up to B flat: as it is aiming at A flat, the minor seventh of B flat, it cannot succeed, but the music returns to B flat with the aid of E natural, the 'optimistic' major seventh of the dominant F, in the bass. As a result of this happy outcome, the falling chromatic (seven-note) scale enters *inverted*, in a virile *forte*—an additional element in the formal and expressive unity which would take us too far afield to examine.

When the second subject is recapitulated, in G minor, the chromatic descent begins on the anguished minor sixth, and the second time it leads down to the fourth of the key of E flat; this time the climb back has no happy outcome, arriving logically back in the tonic G minor.

The 'sighing' effect of descending chromatics in the major system is seen again in the last phrase of the Andante's main theme (Ex. 90c): the movement is in fact full of pathetic chromatic inflexions.

In the Scherzo, the return to the obsessive 1–3–1 at the end, piped out sadly by the flute, is accompanied by a falling six-note chromatic scale on the mournful bassoon, this time an intensification of the despairing 8–7–6–5; it too, like the phrase in the first movement, goes on to a seventh note with woeful effect (Ex. 90c). It might seem coincidence that both phrases use exactly the same seven notes (G down to C sharp or D flat), but the finale clinches this unifying identity in no uncertain terms, repeating the first six notes again in both B flat and G minor contexts.

The second subject of the finale picks up the six-note chromatic scale of the second subject of the first movement (Ex. 90d); when it is recapitulated, the same notes are used in the bass, as in the Minuet, to form an intensification of the despairing 8–7–6–5, while the theme has a six-note chromatic descent beginning on D, which acts as an intensification of the despairing 5–4–3–2–1 (Ex. 90e). The whole process is repeated, the once-lovely theme becoming more and more nothing but a complete descending chromatic scale in two halves, and the theme ends with the obsessive 1–3–(2)–1. It is immediately after this that the ornamented version of 1–3–1 strikes in on the violins, and begins to impel the symphony towards its logical conclusion.

Here ends our analysis of Mozart's Fortieth Symphony—that miracle of formal-and-expressive unity. It has been a broad, general, basic one, dealing only with the main elements, and not every single one of those. For example, the fact that the opening 1–3–1 is coupled with 3–8–3, oscillating at the interval of a sixth, and thereby producing maximum agitation, and that this interval of the sixth is picked up at the end of the first phrase of the theme, as a passionate leap from the dominant up to the minor third above—we have had to ignore things like this, and what finally comes of them. And there are, of course, an infinite number of expressive details that could be examined in a book five times the size of this one: the reader may be left to look for them himself.

Before we turn to our next analysis, an important point must be considered. In dealing with the Mozart Symphony, it seemed wise to jog the reader's memory and save him referring back, by throwing in all the time the emotional nouns and adjectives by which I have attempted to convey the expressive qualities of the various tonal tensions and basic terms; and these words are, of course, quite inadequate to describe the subtle shades of emotion expressed in Mozart's (or anyone else's) music. To quote Mendelssohn once more: 'The thoughts expressed to me by a piece of music which I love are not too indefinite to put into words, but on the contrary too definite. And so I find, in every attempt to express such thoughts, that something is right but at the same time something is unsatisfying in all of them.' My analysis has had to be expressed in the ambiguous medium of words, but let it not be thought that it is intended in any way as a 'translation': it is meant to be a clue, to lead back to the music itself. The words 'anguish', 'joy', 'despair', and 'obsession' are only hazy (but, one hopes, basically accurate) symbols for the particular kind and degree of anguish, joy, despair, and obsession which Mozart expressed *precisely* in his Fortieth Symphony, and which we can only experience by listening to that work.

By 'basically accurate' one means that a million different

types of anguish can be covered by the word 'anguish', but not by the word 'joy'. Nevertheless, the subjective element is bound to enter in, and one's use of terms is partly influenced by one's own subjective reactions to music (and to life). Maybe 'anguish' will strike some readers as too strong a word for the feeling expressed by the minor 6–5, which may have a less acute effect on them. It has been used in this book as a basic word to embrace all degrees of painful grief; and when the volume is *piano*, as at the opening of the symphony, it may well seem an over-violent term to describe such a soft, sighing sorrow. Moreover, since there are no cool, clinical terms to describe emotions, but only words which themselves have an emotional effect on the reader, the persistent use of such words in the above analysis may produce an over-heated, crudely emotionalistic impression which was certainly not intended. The warning was given that Mozart nearly always speaks within the scope of eighteenth-century 'good taste', and that his emotion is contained within an objective form (even though one feels that he passes beyond these bounds at least in the development sections of the first and last movements of this symphony, with their demonically furious modulation-sequences shooting into distant keys). These considerations should be borne in mind when reading the foregoing analysis.

In view of all this, as we turn to that other controversial work —the Sixth Symphony of Vaughan Williams—the use of emotional words will be discontinued, and the musical terms will be allowed to speak for themselves, relying on the reader's memory.

SYMPHONY NO. 6 IN E MINOR, BY VAUGHAN WILLIAMS

One well remembers the excitement, in 1947, when it was announced that Vaughan Williams had completed his Sixth Symphony. It was going to be the first big British symphony to appear after the war, and there was much speculation as to what kind of work it would turn out to be. Rumour said that it was a sort of cross between the Fourth and the Fifth, being neither as violent as the one, nor as serene as the other. Nothing could have been further from the truth.

The effect on the present writer, at the first performance, was nothing short of cataclysmic: the violence of the opening and the turmoil of the whole first moment; the sinister mutterings of the slow movement, with that almost unbearable passage in which the trumpets and drums batter out an ominous rhythm, louder and louder, and will not leave off; the vociferous uproar of the Scherzo and the grotesque triviality of the Trio; and most of all, the slow finale, *pianissimo* throughout, devoid of all warmth and life, a hopeless wandering through a dead world ending literally in *niente* (Vaughan Williams's favourite word for a final fade-out of any kind)—nothingness. This at any rate was my impression while the music was being played. I remember my attention was distracted, near the end, by the unbelievable sight of a lady powdering her nose—one wondered whether it was incomprehension, imperviousness, or a defence-mechanism. The Symphony, as a work of art, more than deserved the overwhelming applause it got, but I was no more able to applaud than at the end of Tchaikovsky's *Pathétique* Symphony—less so, in fact, for this seemed to be an ultimate nihilism beyond Tchaikovsky's conceiving: every drop of blood seemed frozen in one's veins.

The strange thing about the whole affair was the composer's own note in the programme—characteristically self-effacing, as one might expect, but going over into flippant humour that seemed to accord ill with the music: 'The principal subject does not appear at the beginning', he wrote of the Scherzo; 'various instruments make bad shots at it but after a bit it settles down . . . the woodwind experiment as to how the fugue subject will sound upside down but the brass are angry and insist on playing it the right way up, so for a bit the two go on together, and to the delight of everyone including the composer the two versions fit, so that there is nothing to do now but to continue, getting more excited. . . .' A strange way of describing music that seemed to be a masterly, dead-sure delineation of chaos.

The Symphony had a most disturbing impact on quite a number of people. There was clearly more in it than mere notes, whatever the composer's deliberately incommunicative programme-note might say. Several critics related the music to the upheaval of the war—only to be severely reprimanded by the very man who had written it! And there the matter stands;

though the feeling that the Symphony has something to do with the present state of world affairs persists.

Vaughan Williams's detestation of sensational publicity, of portentous self-explanation, of the conception of music as a personal confession, was entirely admirable; and one understands that he was averse to having crude programmatic ideas attached to the Symphony, and did not want to be regarded as a prophet, or a purveyor of a 'message', but preferred to let the music speak for itself. But what does it say? Surely no one can make so profoundly disturbing a series of sounds, and expect people not to be disturbed by them? The style of his programme-note was of course inevitable: even the composer cannot put into words the feelings expressed in his music; if he could, he would have no need to write music at all. Moreover, he is not always aware exactly what feelings he has expressed, since they have arisen out of his unconscious and found expression in a language which is not explicit like that of speech. Whatever Vaughan Williams had to say, he said it in the symphony, and was prepared to abide by that: the programme-note was written merely as a guide to the form, to help listeners to understand the symphony as a coherent statement.

Wherefore let us respect his reticence, and not attempt to find emotional terms to describe the disquieting impact of this music: rather let us analyse it as an objective musical statement of certain emotional realities inherent in the life of the present age, by letting the terms of musical language speak for themselves. And since the symphony is not all on the same plane of significance, like Mozart's Fortieth, but moves from one world to another, so to speak, we shall modify the analytical method, following the development of the various terms *en bloc* from movement to movement.

The formal and expressive unity of this phenomenally concentrated work subsists mainly in the persistent use, transformation, and interpenetration of four of the basic terms of musical language: the minor 1–3–1; the opposition of major and minor thirds; the minor 2–1 progression (with conflicts between keys separated by that interval); and the interval of the augmented fourth (with conflicts between keys separated by that interval). There seems no reason to suppose that these terms have a special significance for Vaughan Williams, different from that which they have for all other composers (see Exs. 27 and 28, 35, 41, and 60).

The first movement is largely dominated by the minor 1–3–1, with the opposition between major and minor thirds prominent, and the minor second playing an important part; all three are telescoped into the opening bar:

It should be noted first that the key is E *minor*, conflicting with F *minor*, the key on the *minor second*. The fact that these are the keys of Tchaikovsky's violent fourth and fifth symphonies is not at all irrelevant, when we remember that Tchaikovsky's Fourth actually has a similar kind of opening (see Ex. 28a) and that the Fifth is much concerned with the minor 1–3–1 (see Ex. 26h). The tempo is the virile and forceful *allegro* 4/4; the volume *fortissimo*, the texture *tutti*; the first three notes (1–2–3 in the scale of F minor) are accented and held back (*allargando*): there is the maximum of rhetorical emphasis here. The spotlighted *minor third* (A flat) is held, and with the entry of a heavy brass chord of E minor, it is transformed into G sharp, the *major third* of E, and drawn down by the semitonal tension between it and the *minor third* of E (G natural) *to that minor third*, which falls back to the tonic, E. So that we have 1–2–3 (F minor)–3–1 (E minor), or in other words the minor 1–(2)–3–1 with a new kind of emphasis: the minor third is revealed as a major third in a darker context (the key a semitone lower), and falls by the major-minor opposition to the minor third of this darker context, and thence back to the new tonic, which is a semitone lower than the one it started from. It is significant that this identical progression occurs in Vaughan Williams's opera *The Pilgrim's Progress*, when Christian, in jail, sings 'My God, my God, why hast thou forsaken me? . . . All they that see me laugh me to scorn'. Since music cannot express intellectual ideas, it would be childish to try and relate the words of the operatic passage to the opening of the symphony; as ever, it is the basic emotion which is all-important. In the opera, the progression is presented *andante*, 3/2, *piano*, *legato*; in the symphony, *allegro*, 4/4, *fortissimo*, accented. The emotional effect is extremely disturbing, to say the least; but we will not give it a name.[1]

The effect is intensified by a headlong fall (a 'rushing down' is the composer's description) of semiquavers, which are cross-accented as triplets, taking over from the initial quaver triplets —and each consists of the same three notes: 3 (major)–3

---

[1] Compare the exactly opposite procedure in the 'aspiring' opening of the *Sinfonia Antartica*, where the *major* third is revealed as a *minor* third in a *brighter* context (the key a semitone *higher*), and rises *to its major third*: the words appended to this movement are Shelley's 'To suffer woes which hope thinks infinite . . . to defy power which seems omnipotent . . . neither to change, nor falter, nor repent . . . this . . . is to be joyous, beautiful and free, this is alone life, joy, empire and victory.'

(minor) 1. 'Rushing up again', we have a repetition of the opening theme, now firmly in F minor, as a simple 1–2–3; this time the 'rushing down' consists of the same figure, again in foreign keys (Ex. 91b). The repetition is initiated by two barked-out brass chords having the minor 2–1 in the bass and the minor 1–2 in the upper part: this emphasizes the *minor second* and leaves it in the air (Ex. 91b). Soon, against the semiquaver turmoil (the composer calls it 'fussy semiquavers'!), brass chords, *fortissimo*, in jagged rhythms, gradually crystallize into the minor 3–1 in different keys (Ex. 91c). With the turmoil still going on, a second theme (transitional) enters in C *minor*—3–2–2 (minor)– 1, switching straight to G *minor* for 3–1–3–2–2 (minor)–1 (with the implication of the *minor seventh* on the tonic (Ex. 91c)). (The minor seventh is to play a part in the work's unity.)

When the turmoil eventually dies down, there is no relief, for a grotesquely galumphing 6/8 rhythm of the 'oom-pah' kind is set up, featuring the lewd tenor saxophone, with a crude 'popular' tap of the side-drum on the off-beats; it supports a new main theme (second subject) in cross-rhythm on the trumpets, which is still concerned with the minor 3–2–1, 3–2–1 (Ex. 91d). The key is the melancholy one of G *minor*, here the key on the *minor third*, and the new subject is a strange concatenation of elements: an accompaniment recalling at once 'The Teddy-Bear's Picnic' and the cynical magician Uranus in Holst's *The Planets*, and over it a 'medium-tempo' blues-type tune, played in 'close harmony' by trumpets, with the *minor seventh* of English folk-music. The emotional connotations of 'blues' procedures and the 'English' seventh, superimposed on a grotesque stylization of 'pop' music accompaniment, are obvious. At last, over the restlessly galumphing rhythm, the final main theme of the movement enters (Ex. 91e) in a broad, relaxed, flowing 6/4; deriving from the pure strain of English folk-song, it establishes the traditional, 'strong' dominant key (B *minor*), and seems to evoke, amid all the welter, a vision of a vanished world. But even this expansive theme, rising an octave from the lower dominant to the higher, takes in the minor 1–3–(2)–1, as can be seen; falls from the higher dominant, *via* the *augmented fourth*, to the tonic, to repeat the same phrase; and ends with alternations of major and minor 1–3–(2)–1, the *minor* one having the last word.

In the development, there is a long struggle between this noble theme and the restless elements: at one point it is stamped out on the brass, triumphing over the galumphing rhythm, but it eventually falls down again by means of *augmented fourths*; and the 4/4 turmoil returns, holding the field for some time as a recapitulation (a return to the basic situation which does not, however, re-state either the first subject or the transitional theme). It dies away, and the 'folk-music' theme suddenly comes out in all its essential beauty, in the tonic key of E *major*, 6/4, *tranquillo, piano, cantabile*, in sonorous unison on violins, violas, and cellos, against harp chords whose alternations consist of the *major* 6–5. This is the only bit of peaceful *major* music in the whole symphony (though the theme still reiterates the minor 1–3–(2)–1). Its context is, of course, entirely subsidiary, despite the tonic major key of E: the only true affirmation of that key, it vanishes for ever, and the rest of the symphony, before it and after, is made up of persistent *minor* triads, in every conceivable key-juxtaposition. The theme finally lifts itself up to the high tonic, E, only to go straight over into the F minor 1–2–3 of the opening, *fortissimo*, which again falls as 3 (major)–3 (minor)–1, in E, with the major-minor third opposition drawn out over a tonic E minor triad, the minor third winning the day, and falling to the tonic.[1]

There is no need to 'translate' all this into words: the terms of musical language speak for themselves. But a warning should be given to anyone attempting to explain the emotional impact of the work by reference to these terms: the titanic power of the rhythms must be taken into consideration, and it must be remembered that this is even less subjective music than that of Mozart. The implications are obviously widely human, not individual, though expressed by an individual through his own personality.

The symphony is continuous. The tonic E remains in the bass as a pedal, and an octave of B flat on trumpets switches the key to B flat *minor* (a switch of an *augmented fourth*) for the second movement. This is still dominated by the minor 1–3–1 and the minor 2–1; the major-minor third opposition is still there, and the augmented fourth comes to the fore a little.

---

[1] Compare the 'elemental', 'non-human' ending of the *Sinfonia Antartica*, for a slow and clinching use of the same phrase.

Once again we have the powerful 4/4 rhythm, *moderato* this
time (a rather slow *moderato*); the volume is *pianissimo*. The
strings, low down in octaves, mutter the restless main theme
(Ex. 92a). It restates the first three notes of the symphony in
contracted melodic form, as 1–2 (minor)–2 (major), and takes
in the rhythm of the triplet figure from the symphony's first bar

as a 'dead' three-note rhythm with the accent on the first note. The theme moves in narrow intervals, and the effect is that of an even more restricted version of the minor 1–2–3–2–1. It makes much use of the *minor second* alternating with the major, which of course loses its normal expressive power in the minor context. The three-note rhythmic figure is to become obsessive (the word is used in its purely technical sense, though it is hard to ignore the emotional implication), and it is worth examining. It is clearly derived from drum-taps, and will in fact be played a good deal on drums: its effect cannot be called anything but ominous and disquieting. It has been used at least once before in music—by Elgar for the brooding opening of his Piano Quintet, which was written in 1918, during the closing stages of the First World War; a curious coincidence, to say the least.

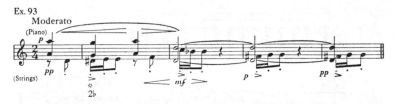

Ex. 93

The theme is repeated over and over, growing louder (with the rhythm on trumpets and drums *pianissimo* in the background); it takes in a falling phrase made out of the *minor 6–5* and *2–1*, which recurs just before the first climax in falling *augmented fourths*, *fortissimo*, the rhythmic figure suddenly hammering out *forte* in conjunction with it (Ex. 92b); this passage directly anticipates the Scherzo. A stern fanfare on brass reminds us of the E–F opposition of the symphony's opening; the tempo changes to a flowing 3/4, and the volume to *pianissimo*, for a new theme—the middle section (Ex. 92c). There is still no relief, however: this theme, again on the strings low down in octaves, opens with the minor 1–2–3–2–1, with *minor second*, in the symphony's tonic key of E (an *augmented fourth* away from B flat minor); it switches to A to re-state the tonal tensions of the triplet figure of the symphony's opening—3 (major)–3 (minor)–1; and with the D natural, there is again the implication of the *minor seventh* of the tonic; and finally the theme falls by means of an *augmented fourth* back to F. The fanfare and the new theme alternate, and the fanfare goes on to divided strings, *pianissimo*, awesomely spanning the extreme heights and depths of pitch, and taking in the 3–2–2 (minor)–1 (Ex. 92d). There is much play with alternating major and minor chords, until the major-minor opposition at the basis of the opening of the symphony takes on a new melodic form, the simple minor 3–1 (Ex. 92d; cf. Ex. 91c). As it proceeds, the obsessive rhythmic figure is tapped out on trumpets and drums at (cross-rhythmic) intervals, *pianissimo*; it persists for over forty bars, swelling out remorselessly to *fortissimo* and back again four times while the main theme returns; it persists each time the other music leaves off, and always keeps on when one hopes it is going to stop. The effect is of something from which one wishes to escape but cannot; and it is difficult not to feel a strong resemblance to the 'destructive forces' in Carl Nielsen's Fifth Symphony. Eventually the major-minor opposition of Ex. 92d reaches a ferocious climax and dies away, and the rhythm stops. Quiet references to the major-minor opposition, a soft cor anglais version of the central theme, and three final *pianissimo* mutters of the obsessive rhythm, end the movement; the Scherzo follows without a break.

The Scherzo is given over entirely to *diabolus in musica*, the augmented fourth (alias diminished fifth), which as usual destroys all sense of ordered tonality. The minor 1–3–1 and minor 2–1 are still present, however, in the Trio.

As regards the augmented fourth, we have seen from *Job* and *The Pilgrim's Progress* that there is no reason to suppose that Vaughan Williams does not agree with other composers as to its precise significance (see Ex. 41n).[1] We still have the powerful duple rhythm, this time 2/4, *allegro vivace*; the volume is *forte*, the tone-colour chiefly the 'fierce' brass, the texture most dissonantly fugal. The opening consists of what the composer calls 'bad shots' at the main theme—rising augmented fourths falling away, each part entering a fifth above, producing a string of rising augmented fourths leading off from one another by the interval of a *minor second*. The entries proceed by diminution, the effect being one of acceleration; coupled with the rising

---

[1] Compare also the use of the interval in slow tempo for the glaciers of the *Landscape* of the *Sinfonia Antartica*: as said in Chapter 2, the augmented fourth is the 'inimical' interval.

Ex. 94 *(a)*

pitch, this gives a strong feeling of 'outburst' to the music (first part of Ex. 94a). Note that the opening moves from the initial note of B flat towards the symphony's tonic key of E, both melodically (in the very first interval), and tonally (in the modulatory scheme of the first four bars). The ascent actually culminates in E major with (to quote the composer) a 'trivial little tune, chiefly on the woodwind'; trivial it is indeed, most calculatedly so, with its segments separated by the pervasive interval of the augmented fourth—it seems to be laughing at the attempt to establish the key of E, by switching the music back to B flat all the time (Ex. 94b). The main theme eventually 'settles down' (takes the form of the composite top line of the fugal opening, to be precise) as a string of rising augmented fourths (second part of Ex. 94a), and the two themes are combined into a free double fugue; with the main theme using triplets of quavers, crotchets, and finally minims, the result is a masterly organization of chaotic uproar.

The Trio, in C *minor*, is like all the other subsidiary contexts of the Symphony except the first movement's 'folk-tune', in that it brings no relief. The 'smarmy' tenor saxophone, accompanied by another 'oom-pah' bass without the 'oom' (the cheapest of jazz-rhythms, emphasized by off-beat side-drum taps), drools a kind of doodling 'improvized swing-music', which is nevertheless firmly attached to the basic minor 1–3–1, 1–3–2 (minor)–1, and to the augmented fourth (Ex. 94c). One has the clear impression of a critical stylization of the most depressingly moronic dance-hall music. The Scherzo eventually returns *via* a sequence of falling augmented fourths on the saxophone, beneath an augmented fourth *tremolando* on violins (Ex. 94d), a passage which links with the slow movement (Ex. 92b); it also recalls that humorously sinister opening movement of the *Five Tudor Portraits*—'The Tunning of Elinor Rumming', where the same phrase appears in a sturdy rhythm, more genially attached to the same sordid aspects of popular pleasure-seeking. Scherzo and Trio are both repeated with increased emphasis: the uproar of the Scherzo is intensified by a combination of the normal and inverted forms of the main theme, and the saxophone theme of the Trio is eventually blared out with deliberate vulgarity by the full brass. A repetition of Ex. 94d and a bass clarinet reference to the saxophone theme, and the finale is at hand.

Before continuing, we may notice the extraordinary similarity of conception between this Scherzo and that of Mahler's Ninth Symphony. Vaughan Williams thought Mahler 'a tolerable imitation of a composer', and may never have heard his Ninth Symphony, for all one knows, but that is neither here nor there: great minds think alike. The Scherzo of the Mahler, entitled 'Rondo: Burleske', and marked 'very defiantly', is also an uproar, a fiendish piece of dissonant counterpoint in the same powerful duple rhythm (2/2 *allegro assai*) making much use of brass; it is incredible to think that it was written by a forty-nine-year-old romantic in 1909. The themes are not the same, but they have the same 'inimical' character, and there are some strange 'coincidences'.

The opening (Ex. 95a) is quite different—Mahler's Scherzo is not in any way fugal, for he had his own conception of counterpoint; but the augmented fourth is there, on the brass, and the rising chords give an equal sense of 'outburst'. Later in the movement a theme appears (the bass of Ex. 95b), which takes on almost the same shape as Vaughan Williams's 'bad shots' a his main theme (Ex. 95c; cf. Ex. 94a). Also in Ex. 95c, we can see a studied triviality akin to Ex. 94b. The Trio (Ex. 95d) brings no more relief than Vaughan Williams's: *l'istesso tempo*, like this, it begins in exactly the same way by floating in quietly a similar type of theme with a 'popular' connotation (Viennese band-music here), which is intentionally and grotesquely banal. Mahler also eventually brings back his Scherzo proper with a passage on soft strings, high up, *tremolando*, involving augmented fourths (second half of Ex. 95d). The differences are of course enormous, but the conception is practically the same: driving duple rhythm (with triplets in chaotic cross-accent); 'ugly' linear counterpoint on brass (not quoted); 'fussy' quaver movement of insistent 'triviality'; tonal disruption by means of the augmented fourth; grotesque stylization of banal popular music. The chief difference is that Mahler eventually introduces a D major (tonic) vision of peaceful happiness, which is finally swept away, whereas Vaughan Williams offers no relief at all, having already done so in his E major (also tonic) 'folk-tune' in the first movement.

The 'coincidence' continues to the extent of both composers having followed with a slow finale, but there it stops: Mahler's is a romantic swan-song, at once affirming his love of the essential beauty and joy of life, and looking back at it with infinitely sorrowful regret (he was a dying man, and a 'subjective' composer), but Vaughan Williams's is evidently nothing of this kind.

To quote his programme-note: 'It is difficult to describe this movement analytically. It is directed to be played very soft throughout [*sempre pp e senza crescendo*]. The music drifts about contrapuntally with occasional whiffs of theme . . . and one or two short episodes. . . .'

The movement is entitled 'Epilogue', and it is indeed just that. Faced with the implications of the frenzied turbulence of the first three movements, one might well ask, with T. S. Eliot, 'After such knowledge, what forgiveness?' The finale of a symphony is the place for a summing-up, a resolution of the problems posed by what has gone before. But Vaughan Williams gives no answer at all (except perhaps one by implication); he merely adds an 'epilogue' which is void of all human feeling (as far as music can be), with one important exception, to be mentioned later. (Actually Mahler also achieves this feat in certain passages of his finale—bare, *pianissimo*, 'drifting about contrapuntally'—but the implication there is 'all passion spent', whereas here it is. . . ?).

Vaughan Williams's description is not entirely accurate: Ex. 96a is the theme of this practically monothematic movement. It will be seen that the rhythm remains duple, though the virile power is drained from it by the (slow) *moderato* tempo. We are in F *minor*, as at the opening of the symphony, and the theme begins with the same three notes, 1–2–3 in F minor: we are apparently going to pick up the thread of the whole work. This possibility seems to be confirmed by the fact that the theme is a miraculous conflation (surely unconscious) of all the significant elements of the first three movements:

(1) Minor 1–2–3 in the key on the minor second, as at the beginning of the symphony.

(2) The augmented fourth of the Scherzo: the second segment of the theme begins on B natural, an augmented fourth away from F.

(3) An inversion of the triplet figure from the symphony's opening bar: 3(major)–3(minor)–1 becomes 1–2(minor)–3(major), if we regard B as the subsidiary tonic, and the E flat as D sharp.

(4) If we treat C as the subsidiary tonic, we have the unifying minor 1–3–1 of the symphony in its basic form (cf. Ex. 94c). It becomes obsessive in this movement.[1]

---

[1] Compare the 'elemental', 'non-human' opening and closing bars of the *Landscape* of the *Sinfonia Antartica*: the words appended here are 'Ye ice-falls! . . . Motionless torrents! Silent cataracts!'

(5) The E flat is the implied minor seventh of the fundamental tonic F, recalling the same procedure in the first movement's transition theme (Ex. 91c) and the slow movement's central theme (Ex. 92c).

(6) The fall by augmented fourths from the Scherzo (C–B–F–E, see Ex. 94d).

(7) The basic key-conflict as to whether E or F is the tonic of the symphony, with the corresponding play on the interval of the minor second: the theme ends with the ambiguity of being either in E as 1–2(minor)–3(major) or in F as 1–3–1.

So that all the vital elements of the first three movements are here gathered together into one theme—*which is empty of vitality*. The whole movement is a slow wandering of this theme, 'drifting about contrapuntally', with occasional references to the once-ferocious two-chord brass figure from the first movement (Ex. 96a; cf. Ex. 91b). This figure, trying to establish the tonic of E minor in the bass, but pushing up from the tonic to the minor second in the upper part, leaving it unresolved (and keeping the E–F opposition), is also devitalized (*pp*, slow, *legato*).

The chief point about this movement is that *nothing happens*: there is no change to anything else. Slight modifications of the theme make no difference to the basic melodic obsession with 1–3–1, until, about the middle, the second of the two brass chords is left hanging on, and the oboe enters with a 'new' theme. This theme is in fact just as obsessed with 1–3–1 as the other, but it does manage to move out of that figure's constricted and constricting orbit by taking on a dying fall, extending the drop of a third in the triplet of the symphony's opening: for the first time, a scrap of human feeling intrudes against the de-humanized background. It is a slightly modified version of this theme which makes the final comment before the main material ends the movement in the basic mood, and it is worth examining in this form (Ex. 96b).

First of all we may notice that it is once more 1–2–3–2–1: the harmonic implication when it begins is G sharp minor (1–2–3), but it treats the higher G sharp as an A flat in F minor and returns 3–2–1 in that key. Taking the first three notes as being in E major (there is the characteristic ambiguity), we have yet another reference to the E–F key-conflict (the opposite way round to the symphony's opening). But the theme itself contains wide leaps (picking up that of the first movement's transitional theme, Ex. 91c), in direct opposition to the main theme's wandering in close intervals. The truth is, *it is a romantic theme.*

The first phrase of four notes derives from one of the most intensely yearning and aspiring of romantic melodic procedures, as exemplified by the mighty choral appeal to the 'Creator Spiritus' in Mahler's Eighth Symphony—'Illuminate our senses, *fill our hearts with love*':

(Compare also Vaughan Williams's own use of this melodic procedure, in a more 'homely' way, in the *Sinfonia Antartica*: it pervades the main (oboe) theme of the *Intermezzo*, to which are appended the words of John Donne 'Love, all alike, no season knows, nor clime . . .'). As for the falling phrases with which the oboe-theme continues, they derive from a style of tenderly romantic love-melody which Wagner made practically his own property. It occurs most movingly, for example, in Brünnhilde's encomium on the dead Siegfried in the closing scene of *Götterdämmerung*, at the point where she sings 'no other man loved more truly than he':

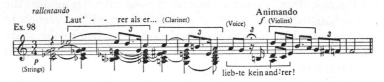

But the theme in Vaughan Williams's Sixth Symphony is in the minor, is dead slow, *pp*, played by the plangent oboe, with dissonant intervals; it emerges from faint and ambiguous harmonies, continues unaccompanied, falls down a nine-note (minor) *chromatic scale*, and then down a further four-note one, on to the tonic E; its last two notes are the minor 2–1, played with the rhythm of an *appoggiatura*, leading to the last bars of the symphony, which return to the minor 1–3–1 and the major-minor opposition. It is in fact the broken-hearted ghost of the warm passionate yearning of the romantics, as phantasmal as the two lovers in Debussy's 'Colloque Sentimentale'. This can be felt as a devastating human comment on what is happening in the rest of the music, from which all sense of humanity is absent.

As it fades out, the violins and violas pick up the major-minor opposition of the opening of the symphony, but it is now slow and *pianissimo*, and has moved down a semitone: the context is one of final darkness and depression. The original loud impetuous question, 'Is A flat the minor third of F minor or the major third of E major?' (with a turbulent struggle to lift the music to F, the higher of the two) has given way to the final quiet lifeless question, 'Is G the minor third of E minor or the major third of E flat?' (with a hardly audible alternation of the two possibilities, and a stalking bass insisting on the lower of the two, E flat, while reminding us that the question was once pitched in a higher key). (See Ex. 96c.) So that instead of, as at first, lifting fiercely up a semitone to join battle, we are apparently going to fall peacefully and contentedly (E flat *major*) down a semitone, and give up the struggle. It seems as if we are going to be glad to accept peace as the final escape—and in a symphony by Mahler we might well do so (his violent Ninth Symphony in D ends in the peace of D flat), but here we are denied even that consolation.

Vaughan Williams puts it this way: 'At the end, the strings cannot make up their minds whether to finish in E flat major or E minor. They finally decide on E minor, which is, after all, the home key.' It is obvious that a modern composer need not be concerned about ending in the 'home key', after the 'progressive tonality' of Mahler, Nielsen, and others: the symphony clearly must end in a minor key to fulfil the logic of its basic obsession with minor triads, and the minor triad in this final passage is E minor, balancing the equivalent passage at the opening of the symphony. What in fact happens is that E flat is emphasized like a tonic (by being placed on the strong beat); and after the bass has disappeared, the strings eventually sustain the triad of E flat major, giving the impression that the symphony is going to end on that key (see the tied minims in Ex. 96c), but after all change back to E minor at the last moment, and fade out on that chord.

The effect of a final soft minor triad, third uppermost, is what it always is, and needs no 'translation'. Strife and struggle (F minor) have proved fruitless; the warmth and passion of life are dead (the 'ghost' of romantic melody); and peace (E flat major) has been rejected: we are left with inactivity, emptiness, in a basic minor context, fading into nothingness (*niente*). The implications, after the fierce turmoil of the first three movements, are obvious and inescapable, and the emotional impact on the hearer entirely unambiguous.

This broad, general analysis of Vaughan Williams's Sixth Symphony (as much a miracle of formal-and-expressive unity, in its way, as Mozart's Fortieth) brings us to the end of our investigation of the language of music.

But one question remains to be answered: is ·music *only* a language of the emotions, and nothing more? In an age which views emotion with suspicion, some readers may well react strongly against the idea that music is concerned entirely with that dubious element in the human make-up. After all, man has an intellect, a moral sense, and a metaphysical faculty which we call a spirit or a soul. Can music express nothing of these?

The question of intellect has already been answered. Although music is self-evidently incapable of expressing intellectual ideas (an ability possessed exclusively by literature, science, and mathematics), it goes without saying that a vast amount of intellectual labour goes into producing any large-scale work, and that miniatures are not the work of morons. To be a master of the musical art, on any scale, a man has to do a great deal of thinking as well as feeling, and the value of any first-rate work is at least half due to the technique which has realized the expressive intention with such mastery.

With regard to the moral sense, our question is half-answered. We have seen that, by vitalizing various basic terms expressing different emotions, and juxtaposing them in an ordered pattern, making some of them fundamental, persistent, and finally victorious, and others subsidiary, intermittent, and finally vanquished, a composer can express an unambiguous moral attitude towards life. The tremendously affirmative and inspiriting impact of Beethoven's music arises from the fact that the positive emotions win through in the end, and that there is never any doubt that they are going to; the depressing effect of a work like Tchaikovsky's *Pathétique* Symphony is due to the final establishing and emphasizing of the emotion of despair. We need not feel ashamed that music should have a moral effect only by placing emotional moods in a significant order: psychology has shown that our whole life is propelled by these instinctive urges, and that it is by balancing and ordering them that we achieve a valuable, creative attitude to life.

Of course, rhythm and form play a large part in moral expression. We have seen that the painful emotions of Mozart's Fortieth Symphony are controlled and to some extent counterbalanced by rhythmic vitality and formal perfection. Needless to say, a lack of driving rhythm need not mean moral weakness at all, but only quiet meditation and serenity of mind; and sometimes it may mean that active, assertive life has been renounced in favour of other experiences felt to be of more value—transfiguration in death, for example, as at the end of *Tristan*, or longing for the unattainable, as in much of the music of Delius. In such cases, the listener's own evaluation of the experience concerned (arising from his own attitude to life) will inevitably condition his moral reaction to the music.

But what of a case like Vaughan Williams's Sixth Symphony, where a composer well known for his firm moral fibre, in life as in art, ended an undoubted masterpiece with what seems to be an objective statement of utter nihilism? One answer is that a single work only contains one of a composer's basic life-attitudes; but the uncomfortable suspicion remains that he never expressed himself so powerfully and clinchingly as in this symphony, which seems to negate the aspirations of such works as the Fifth Symphony and *The Pilgrim's Progress* entirely. Is it a case of that other kind of moral strength which insists, with Thomas Hardy, that 'if a way to the Better there be, it exacts a full look at the Worst'? Or could it be that we have missed the point, and that the Sixth Symphony has a metaphysical implication which we have not grasped?—for, as we know, Vaughan Williams was deeply concerned with spiritual values.

Whether music can express spiritual or mystical intuitions is a question that cannot at present be answered, since we have no generally established and acknowledged body of knowledge of these matters; a lack largely responsible for what Hans Keller has so rightly called 'the supreme (if unpremeditated) critical cowardice of our age . . . the refusal to face the metaphysical problem'.[1] Many people have derived experiences of this kind from music—the present writer has from the symphonies of Bruckner and Mahler—but in what way it exists in the notes is still a dark and unsolved problem. It may be that the contradiction between our knowledge of Vaughan Williams and the impact of his Sixth Symphony could be resolved only on the metaphysical plane.

What seems certain is that if music does express spiritual or mystical intuitions, it must do so through the emotional terms of musical language, just as the writings of, say, St. John of the Cross express his mystical experience in the emotional terms of spoken language. But with a metaphysical insight into music, we should undoubtedly experience these terms with a different kind of feeling: they would be revealed as the same but also something other, just like the sexual symbolism of some mystical writings.

We may say then that, whatever else the mysterious art known as music may eventually be found to express, it is primarily and basically a language of the emotions, through which we directly experience the fundamental urges that move mankind, without the need of falsifying ideas and images—words or pictures. A dangerous art, in fact, as was realized by Plato, the fathers of the medieval church, and Tolstoy, all of whom wished to control and confine the use of it. But under the guidance of the intellect and the enlightened moral sense, it is surely as safe as anything human can be—as safe at least, shall we say, as religion or science.

One last point. I am only too well aware that, by using the simple everyday words for human emotion to make my classification of the terms of musical language, I have only scratched the surface of a problem of well-nigh infinite depth; but the intention was merely to make a start on this too-long-neglected subject, to try and establish certain simple laws of musical

[1] Hans Keller: 'Schoenberg and *Moses and Aaron*', *The Score*, October 1957.

expression as clearly as possible, as a basis for further and more detailed examination. Perhaps one day, after intensive research into the various aspects of the art—acoustical, physiological, psychological, and simply musical—it may be possible, by correlating many findings, to discover *exactly* what it is that music expresses, and *exactly* how it expresses it; but if the attempt is made, it will have to be guided by the most meticulous regard for absolute truth, especially in the psychological field, where the final answer is likely to be found. Music is, after all, as Schoenberg said, 'the language in which a musician unconsciously gives himself away. . . . One day the children's children of our psychologists will have deciphered the language of music. Woe, then, to the incautious who thought his innermost secrets carefully hidden and who must now allow tactless men to besmirch his most personal possessions with their own impurities. Woe, then, to Beethoven, Brahms, and Schumann— those men who used their human right of free speech in order to conceal their true thoughts—when they fall into such hands! Is the right to keep silent not worthy of protection?' [1]

These are wise, if cryptic words. The composer, expressing unconscious emotions in the inexplicit language of music, and often not fully realizing himself exactly what he is saying, does indeed 'give himself away': being certain that whatever he has said can only be felt by the musically sensitive, and not clearly identified, explained and discussed, he can let out all that he obscurely feels in the depths of his being, while still remaining 'silent' (i.e., inexplicit). Wherefore it seems likely that the fundamental (i.e. psychological) 'content' of some musical masterpieces may be quite appalling and even horrifying; and when the language of music is finally deciphered, some terrible secrets may be revealed, not only about the particular composer, but about humanity at large. Any superficial approach here will be fatal: we all mistrust those so-called 'psychological analyses' which reduce a work of art narrowly to some supposed and only half-proven complex or neurosis of the artist, existing mainly in the psychologist's own imagination. A psychologist of deep insight and great understanding will be called for; perhaps psychology will have to link hands again with philosophy and metaphysics before the language of music yields up its

[1] Schoenberg: 'Human Rights', in *Style and Idea.*

innermost secrets. However it may be, these must eventually be yielded up, and we should not shrink from them; for man's besetting virtue is curiosity, and his ultimate quest is to discover the truth about himself.

INDEX OF SUBJECTS

Index

INDEX OF NAMES AND WORKS REFERRED TO IN THE TEXT WITHOUT ADJACENT QUOTATION

(For references to works in close connection with musical quotations, see Index of Music Examples)

INDEX OF MUSIC EXAMPLES